Rethinking Metaphysics

Rethinking Metaphysics

AMIE L. THOMASSON

Oxford University Press is a department of the University of Oxford.
It furthers the University's objective of excellence in research, scholarship,
and education by publishing worldwide. Oxford is a registered trade mark of
Oxford University Press in the UK and in certain other countries.

Published in the United States of America by Oxford University Press
198 Madison Avenue, New York, NY 10016, United States of America.

© Oxford University Press 2025

All rights reserved. No part of this publication may be reproduced, stored in a retrieval system, transmitted, used for text and data mining, or used for training artificial intelligence, in any form or by any means, without the prior permission in writing of Oxford University Press, or as expressly permitted by law, by license or under terms agreed with the appropriate reprographics rights organization. Inquiries concerning reproduction outside the scope of the above should be sent to the Rights Department, Oxford University Press, at the address above.

You must not circulate this work in any other form
and you must impose this same condition on any acquirer

CIP data is on file at the Library of Congress

ISBN 9780197787809

DOI: 10.1093/9780197787830.001.0001

The manufacturer's authorised representative in the EU for product safety is
Oxford University Press España S.A. of El Parque Empresarial San Fernando
de Henares, Avenida de Castilla, 2 – 28830 Madrid (www.oup.es/en or
product.safety@oup.com). OUP España S.A. also acts as importer into Spain
of products made by the manufacturer.

*In loving memory of my father,
Walter Neill Thomasson
(1940–2024)*

Contents

Preface   xi
Acknowledgments   xvii

PART I. WHY WE SHOULD RETHINK METAPHYSICS

1. The Traditional Conception of Metaphysics   3
   - 1.1 Problems for the Traditional Conception   4
   - 1.2 A Very Brief History   11
   - 1.3 A Diagnosis and Cure   14

2. The Explanatory Conception of Metaphysics   20
   - 2.1 Problems for the Explanatory Conception   24
   - 2.2 Why Some Terms Don't Add Explanatory Power   30
   - 2.3 Other Functional Roles   39
   - 2.4 Diagnosing the Underlying Mistake   45

3. The Structural Conception of Metaphysics   49
   - 3.1 Problems for the Structural Conception   53
   - 3.2 The Underlying Problem: Functional Monism   56

4. The Truthmaker Conception of Metaphysics   60
   - 4.1 Truthmakers as a Guide to What's Fundamental   62
   - 4.2 Truthmakers as a Constraint   65

5. Fundamentality and Grounding Projects   73
   - 5.1 Grounding: The Basic Idea   75
   - 5.2 Troubles for the Fundamentality Project   80
   - 5.3 Troubles for the Layered Picture   82
   - 5.4 Looking for Local Grounding Relations   85
     - 5.4.1 Clarifying the Epistemology   89
     - 5.4.2 The Problem of Generality   92
   - 5.5 Conclusions   97

PART II. HOW WE SHOULD RETHINK METAPHYSICS

6. Metaphysics as Conceptual Engineering — 103
   - 6.1 What Can Philosophy Do? — 104
   - 6.2 A Brief History of Philosophy as Conceptual Engineering — 107
   - 6.3 What Is Conceptual Engineering? — 112
   - 6.4 Avoiding the Problems of the Traditional Conception — 118
     - 6.4.1 Rivalry with the Sciences — 118
     - 6.4.2 Proliferation and Skepticism — 120
     - 6.4.3 Epistemological Mystery — 121
   - 6.5 Should We Engineer Concepts or Language? — 123
   - 6.6 The Work to Be Done — 130

7. Identifying Linguistic Functions — 132
   - 7.1 How (Not) to Think About Function — 134
   - 7.2 Systemic Functional Linguistics — 139
     - 7.2.1 Functions in Developmentally Early Language — 141
     - 7.2.2 Functions in Mature Language — 144
   - 7.3 Ideational Functions — 149
   - 7.4 Interpersonal Functions — 151
   - 7.5 Grammatical Metaphors — 153
   - 7.6 Conclusions — 159

8. Reverse Engineering: Unraveling Metaphysical Problems — 163
   - 8.1 Reassessing Metaphysical Criteria — 166
   - 8.2 Re-Evaluating Metaphysical Debates About Abstracta — 168
   - 8.3 Re-Evaluating Metaphysical Debates About Modality — 175
     - 8.3.1 Are There Modal Properties, Facts, or Possible Worlds? — 186
     - 8.3.2 How Are Modal Properties Related to Non-Modal Properties? — 189
     - 8.3.3 How Could We Come to Know About Modality? — 190
   - 8.4 Re-Evaluating Other Metaphysical Debates — 193
   - 8.5 Redirecting Metaphysics to More Fruitful Pursuits — 198

9. Pragmatic Conceptual Engineering — 202
   - 9.1 Reverse Engineering via Assessing Functions — 203
   - 9.2 Making Decisions in Pragmatic Conceptual Engineering — 209

	9.2.1 Revisions When We Reject the Functions	210
	9.2.2 Revisions Prompted by Technological or Social Change	213
	9.2.3 Revisions as Concerns Evolve	216
9.3	The Role of Site Constraints and Human Factors	217
9.4	Conclusions	220
10.	The Perennial Philosophical Project	222
	10.1 Should We Still Call It "Metaphysics"?	223
	10.2 What Should We Do?	227
	10.3 The Perennial Project	232
	10.4 Conclusion	234

Bibliography 237
Index 251

Preface

My recent work has aimed both to demystify metaphysics and (where needed) to redirect it to more tractable and fruitful pursuits. This book is the third of a trilogy aimed at that goal, preceded by *Ontology Made Easy* (2015) and *Norms and Necessity* (2020a). However, it is also designed to be readable on its own. Those interested primarily in questions about where (or whether) metaphysics has gone wrong, and how we can rethink it as conceptual engineering, may just start with Chapter 1 of this volume. Nonetheless, it may be helpful for some to see the ways in which the work here forms part of a larger project.[1] In this preface, I aim to make that clear.

Much of recent metaphysics has focused on two sorts of debates: ontological debates (debates about what exists) and modal debates (debates about what is metaphysically necessary or possible, or about the identity and persistence conditions of various sorts of things). In *Ontology Made Easy* I address existence questions, arguing that existence questions that are well formed and answerable can be answered by nothing more mysterious than a combination of conceptual and empirical work. Often, hotly contested debates about whether there are such things as properties, numbers, events, states of affairs, and even possible worlds, can be answered by "trivial" or "redundant" inferences from premises that no participants in the debate would deny. So, for example, questions about whether there are properties may be addressed by starting from the uncontested premise: The barn is red. From there, we can (redundantly) infer that if the barn is red, then the barn has the property of redness, and so that there is a property.[2] If ontological existence questions can be answered "easily"

---

[1] For further discussion of how the various parts of my work fit together, see my (2023a).
[2] For further details, historical background, and replies to objections, see my (2015a). The thought that the relevant inferences are "pleonastic" or redundant comes from Schiffer (1994, 1996, 2003), though the general approach reaches back (at least) to Frege.

in this way, then something is wrong with engaging in the protracted and epistemologically obscure metaphysical debates of "serious" metaphysics about what "really exists" or what we should "accept into our ontology."

This work inevitably raises the question: If existence questions become "easy" to answer in this way, does this just make metaphysics trivial and uninteresting? What (if anything) is left for metaphysics to do?[3] As I acknowledge in *Ontology Made Easy* (2015, 11), one thing that clearly remains open to metaphysics, even if we think that *existence* questions may be easily answered, is to address *modal* questions—including questions about the "natures" of things of various kinds, their identity conditions, persistence conditions, etc.

Norms and Necessity (2020a) addresses these metaphysical modal questions. There I aim to show that metaphysical modal questions, too, can be addressed by means of nothing more obscure than conceptual and (often) empirical work. The key to dissolving the old metaphysical and epistemological problems of modality, I argue, is to note that basic metaphysical modal discourse does not even *aim to* track and report on some special modal features of the world, still less of other possible worlds. Instead (I argue) modal talk functions to mandate, convey, or renegotiate rules or norms in advantageous ways (2020a, 15). For *metaphysical* modal talk, the relevant norms are semantic norms.[4] One lesson again is that the work of metaphysics can be understood as requiring nothing more obscure than empirical and conceptual work—with the philosopher's share of the work typically lying on the conceptual side. In this way, *Norms and Necessity* contributes another step to the project of demystifying the work of metaphysics.

But *Norms and Necessity* also does more than this. For it brings to the surface two ideas that are central to the approach to metaphysics I have been working to develop.[5] The first is the neo-pragmatist idea

---

[3] I begin to address this latter question in the conclusion of my (2015a), in ways consonant with the ideas further developed here.

[4] The relevant norms may vary in other cases—for example, nomological necessities may instead convey norms of reasoning given empirical evidence (see my 2020a, 121).

[5] These ideas were to some extent beneath the surface in the work of *Ontology Made Easy*, but were made far more explicit in *Norms and Necessity*. (They were also developed in several earlier articles. For an overview of the development of these ideas, see my 2023a.)

that different areas of discourse may serve many different functions,[6] and that we can diagnose and dissolve many old philosophical problems (including those of modality) by identifying those diverse functions and the rules the terms follow that enable them to fulfill those functions.[7] The second is the idea that the relevant conceptual work that remains for philosophers includes not just analyzing how our concepts or terms *do* work (what functions they serve and what rules they follow) but also renegotiating what concepts or terms we *should* use and what rules they *should* follow—and that is a matter of engaging in conceptual engineering. Both of these ideas are far more fully developed and defended in this volume.

The central goal of this book is to answer the remaining question: If both existence questions and modal questions can be deflated, what remains for metaphysics to do? In response, I aim here to motivate, develop, and defend the constructive idea that the work of metaphysics should be rethought as broadly *conceptual* work, including both *descriptive* and *normative* conceptual work: as work in conceptual engineering.

In Part I I aim to show *why* we need to rethink metaphysics, by showing how and why the traditional conception of metaphysics leads into problems. In Chapter 1 I aim to articulate these difficulties in broad terms. In Chapters 2–5, I examine several recent attempts to revive metaphysics, by thinking of its work as engaging in quasi-scientific *explanation* and theory construction, as a search for *truthmakers*, or as concerned with questions about *structure, fundamentality*, or *grounding*. In each case, I aim to *diagnose* why these models of metaphysics go wrong. I argue that the underlying mistake arises from trying to address *all topics of discourse* while tacitly assuming a kind of "functional monist" view that all the areas of discourse of interest to metaphysics function in the same way.

In Part II I aim to show *how* we should rethink metaphysics—and those who are interested primarily in the positive story are invited to start or focus their reading here. I aim to develop a new positive

---

[6] I am hugely indebted to the work of Huw Price (e.g., 2011) for bringing me to more explicit recognition of this idea.
[7] I develop that line of diagnostic work further here in Chapter 8.

picture of metaphysics as engaged in *conceptual engineering,* where this includes both the *reverse-engineering* work of understanding how our language functions, and the *constructive* work of determining whether and how we *should* aim to revise the language we use and how we use it. I argue in Chapter 6 that this approach enables us to develop a view of what metaphysics can do that avoids the problems of the traditional conception. For on this approach, the work to be done is epistemically transparent, requiring nothing more than empirical and conceptual work, and is clearly not a rival to the empirical work of the natural sciences. It can also avoid the kind of skepticism about the work of metaphysics that can arise by noticing the wide proliferation of metaphysical views. Nonetheless, I also argue that it is closely enough related to much work in traditional metaphysics to retain the name. For much of the most lasting and interesting work in metaphysics has always involved work in understanding and renegotiating our concepts or language.

The approach to conceptual engineering I recommend begins with reverse engineering that aims to identify the functions various terms serve, and the ways they are introduced to our language. But how can we identify linguistic functions? I address that question in Chapter 7, making use of work in systemic functional linguistics to shed new light on the functions various areas of discourse serve. The work done here on linguistic functions in turn provides further support for my prior work in both *Ontology Made Easy* and in *Norms and Necessity.* For the easy ontological inferences I identify in *Ontology Made Easy* (2015) are intuitively *redundant*—as it is redundant to say "The barn is red *and* the barn has the property of redness," leaving us with the question: Why we would want a language with so much capacity for redundancy? The functional assessment here makes it clear what functions it serves to have a language that entitles us to make redundant (easy) inferences like these. The work on functions also provides support for the work on modality in *Norms and Necessity* (2020)—for it shows how we can justify claims that a certain area of discourse has a certain (range of) functions—including claims that modal discourse serves fundamentally *normative* functions.[8] The work on linguistic functions

---

[8] I had not yet discovered work on systemic functional linguistics at the time when I wrote *Norms and Necessity* (2020a). I give a more thorough reconsideration of the functions of modal discourse in light of that work in linguistics in my (2023b).

also enables us to better defend the diagnoses of prior approaches given in Part 1—for we can more clearly see why it is a mistake to assume that all discourse serves the same functions.

In Chapter 8 I show how the work on linguistic functions enables us to engage in reverse-engineering work, in ways that enable us to unravel many old problems of metaphysics, to distinguish genuine problems from pseudo-problems, and to make better evaluations in conceptual engineering about what to do with our old terms or concepts. In Chapter 9 I show how this work on function enables us to develop a pragmatic approach to questions in conceptual engineering—in a way that does not require a basis in "serious metaphysics" but can nonetheless provide us with reasoned and non-arbitrary decisions in conceptual engineering. In closing in Chapter 10, I aim to make clear what difference it makes to rethink metaphysics in this way. I argue that doing so enables us not only to see how to dissolve old puzzles and pseudo-problems, but to avoid old problems of rivalry with science and epistemological obscurity. It also enables us to see the worldly relevance and importance that our work in metaphysics, and in other areas of philosophy, may have. For changes in our language and concepts can lead to changes in the world by shaping the way we think, investigate the world, and structure our laws and our lives.

In short, reconceiving metaphysics in this way does more than give us a view of metaphysics that is defensible and non-mysterious. It also shows ways in which metaphysics can be centrally and enduringly important to human life—not as a search for eternal truths, but as part of the perennial human project of rethinking how we should think, talk, and live.

Acknowledgments

I am extremely grateful to the Guggenheim Foundation for the fellowship (in Academic Year 2022–2023) that allowed me a year's break from teaching and administrative duties to write this book. It would not have been possible otherwise.

I also wish to express my thanks to Harvard University for inviting me to present the Whitehead Lectures in 2021. Although it was in pandemic days and had to be on Zoom, that nonetheless provided the occasion for beginning to work out these ideas and for a rich discussion. I am also grateful for the opportunity to present fuller, more developed versions of these ideas in person as the Anna Tumarkin Lectures at the University of Bern, Switzerland (2022) and the Pufendorf Lectures at Lund University, Sweden (2022). The discussions in each case were extremely insightful and valuable in enabling me to develop these ideas and present them better, and I am very grateful to my hosts and to all those who attended.

I have also been able to present portions of this material in many other conferences and colloquia, including at the University of Connecticut, Wake Forest University, Columbia University, the University of New Hampshire, the University of California–Irvine, the University of St Andrews, the Principia conference in Florianopolis, Brazil, and other conferences in Bonn and Günzburg and at MIT.

I am especially thankful to those people who kindly read the entire manuscript and provided valuable feedback, including Simon Blackburn, Jerzy Brzozowski, Gabriel Andersen Eugênio, Joshua Gert, Cristian Santiago Kraemer, Italo Lins Lemos, Huw Price, Matthieu Queloz, and Twan Stiekel. I would also like to thank my outstanding research assistant, George Gerber, who worked through the whole manuscript with helpful suggestions and assisted with compiling the bibliography.

For reading large parts of the manuscript and providing insightful comments and/or discussion, I would also like to give my sincere gratitude to Michelle Moody Adams, Georg Brun, Justin Garson, Charlotte Gauvry, Kathrin Koslicki, Peter Lewis, Ted Locke, Ryan Nefdt, Mark Povich, Katherine Ritchie, Jonathan Schaffer, David Woodruff Smith, and Naomi Thompson. In addition, I am thankful for the selfless help of linguists with the portions on linguistics— for this, my thanks go to Emma Collier, Gerard O'Grady, and Mary Schleppegrell.

Earlier versions of parts of this material originally appeared in article form. Chapter 1 draws on material from my "Philosophy as Conceptual Engineering," *The Philosopher* 109, no. 3 (Summer 2021): 7–14, as well as from my "Metaphysics and Conceptual Negotiation," *Philosophical Issues* 27 (2017): 364–82, and my "What Can Philosophy Do?," *Philosopher's Magazine*, no. 17 (4th Quarter 2015). Chapter 4 includes material from my 2020 paper "Truthmakers and Easy Ontology," in Karen Bennett and Dean W. Zimmerman, eds., *Oxford Studies in Metaphysics* (Oxford: Oxford University Press), 3–34. Chapter 7 makes use of material from my paper "How Should We Think About Linguistic Function?," *Inquiry* (2022), https://doi.org/10.1080/0020174X.2022.2074886. Chapter 8 includes work in my "A Neo-Pragmatist Approach to Modality," from Joshua Gert, ed., *Neo-Pragmatism in Practice* (New York: Oxford University Press). Finally, some material from my "Philosophy as Conceptual Engineering," *The Philosopher* 109, no. 3 (Summer 2021): 7–14 also appears in Chapter 10.

I also want to express my gratitude to the Estate of Roy Lichtenstein for permitting me to use his art for the covers of this book and my two prior books (*Ontology Made Easy* and *Norms and Necessity*). I have been an enormous fan of his work since I was a kid, and am honored to have his works as my cover art. The current cover art image, *Brushstroke Still Life with Lamp* (1997) is especially apt for this book, and I was thrilled to find it, for it demonstrates the central point I aim to make here. The brushstrokes of the work serve many different functions: Some depict worldly objects (such as a lamp and a book); others are simply expressive; still others *depict* expressive brushstrokes. The functional pluralism visible in these brushstrokes is analogous to the functional pluralism I wish to identify in language. Ignoring those functional differences has led metaphysics astray, just as it would lead art history (and art) astray to think that all brushstrokes must represent or "imitate" parts of the world.

My greatest thanks go to my family, Peter, Natalie, and May, for being the best companions, and for their endless love, and confidence in me and in each other. Also for putting up with me rambling on about systemic functional linguistics at all hours—and even listening. I'm so lucky to spend my life with you all.

PART I
WHY WE SHOULD RETHINK METAPHYSICS

1
The Traditional Conception of Metaphysics

It is time to change how we think about metaphysics.[1]

Metaphysics is typically presented as an area of philosophy that aims to discover highly general, basic, or fundamental facts about the world. This conception of metaphysics shows up in just about any introductory text on metaphysics. For example, Jonathan Lowe writes that the "central concern [of metaphysics] is with *the fundamental structure of reality as a whole*" (2002, 2–3). Peter van Inwagen concurs: "When I was introduced to metaphysics as an undergraduate, I was given the following definition: metaphysics is the study of ultimate reality. This still seems to me to be the best definition of metaphysics I have seen" (2009, 1).[2]

This way of thinking of metaphysics originated long before the inquiries of philosophy and the natural sciences were separated at all—in fact, long before natural science, as we now know it, began to be systematically developed and practiced. In that context, it was perhaps natural to think of metaphysics as a basic inquiry into the structure of reality, as part of a general "love of wisdom." But by now this traditional way of thinking of metaphysics has come to seem outdated and has proven to be undeniably problematic.

---

[1] Portions of this chapter draw on work from my (2021), (2017a), and (2015b).
[2] Similar characterizations can be found, for example, in Kim et al., who write, "Metaphysics is a philosophical inquiry into the most basic and general features of reality and our place in it" (2012, xii); and in Geirsson and Losonsky, who say: "*metaphysics is a sustained and rational study of what there is and the ultimate nature of what there is*" (1998, 1).

1.1 Problems for the Traditional Conception

For if metaphysics really thinks of itself as discovering deep facts about reality, it seems to be caught in a rivalry with the sciences—a rivalry it seems bound to lose. Stephen Hawking expressed this skepticism, writing (with Leonard Mlodinow in *The Grand Design*) that

> people have always asked a multitude of questions: How can we understand the world in which we find ourselves? How does the universe behave? What is the nature of reality? Where did all this come from? . . . Traditionally these are questions for philosophy, but philosophy is dead. Philosophy has not kept up with modern developments in science, particularly physics. Scientists have become the bearers of the torch of discovery in our quest for knowledge. (2012, 5)

This is a familiar challenge for philosophy that has been around ever since, in the 17th century, the natural sciences began to separate themselves from what was once called "natural philosophy." As physics, chemistry, biology, and other sciences became explicit about their own goals, methods, and criteria for success, the question remained: What (if anything) is left for philosophy?

A common response to the threat of a rivalry with the sciences is to say that the work of metaphysics is *more general* than that of the sciences. As Robin LePoidevin puts it, "One way of distinguishing metaphysics from science is by pointing to the level of generality in metaphysical discussion" (2009, xviii).[3] That is to say, metaphysics is *general* in the sense that it is concerned with *all sorts of topics*—we can ask about the metaphysical structure of the physical world or about numbers or properties or freedom.[4] We can ask metaphysical

---

[3] Geirsson and Losonsky say much the same: "Scientists in their work as scientists studying particular subjects do not step outside of their domain and take a bird's eye view of what all the sciences study, and try to understand how these subjects relate and depend on each other. Doing that is left for the philosopher and metaphysician" (1998, 7).

[4] This echoes points made in Bennett (2017, 230–35) and Barnes (2014) about the need to allow that metaphysics is, and should be, about more than "the fundamental."

questions about the social world, race, gender, or social structures, or about the metaphysics of geographic objects, art, or artifacts. We can even ask questions about the metaphysics of modality—about the existence of modal facts or possible worlds—or dive into metaethics and ask metaphysical questions about moral properties, norms, and moral rules. It is this claim to *generality* that lends metaphysics much of its interest, as well as its apparent difference from the work of the natural sciences. As Karen Bennett puts it, at least one central project of metaphysics can be seen as "investigating the nature of certain particularly puzzling phenomena that seem somehow recalcitrant to purely empirical investigation: consciousness, freedom, time, laws of nature, modality" (2017, 234).

But even if we understand the task of metaphysics broadly in this way, this still doesn't relieve it of an apparent rivalry with the sciences where the sciences (physical or social) *do* speak to the relevant issues. Where there are conflicts between the claims of metaphysics and the sciences, the sciences deserve priority. For as the natural sciences have gradually come to converge in their results and provide the basis for impressive technological and medical achievements, their credentials for claiming to tell us about the world have gotten pretty good. By contrast, the "theories" of philosophers on any given issue, far from converging, have only proliferated as time goes on, with ever new proposals for ever more radical and counterintuitive metaphysical views—for example, that there are no composite inanimate objects (van Inwagen 1990), or no people (Unger 1979), or that there are many concrete possible worlds just like this one, but spatially and causally isolated from it (Lewis 1986). In short, in metaphysics, unlike the empirical sciences, we have nothing like convergence on the truth to reassure us that we are making progress in discovering the relevant "facts" about the world. Instead, we are embarrassed by an ever-increasing proliferation of views. If we think of philosophy as aiming to tell us "how the world is," it seems to be caught in a rivalry with the sciences. This is a rivalry that it is bound to lose.

The proliferation of metaphysical views also leads some—both within and outside of philosophy—to a despairing skepticism. For (as undergraduate students often lament) it seems that we can never know the answers to these metaphysical questions—and if not, it seems like we might do better to just give up and put our efforts somewhere more useful. In fact, the proliferation of philosophical views and failures of convergence alone might lead to skepticism about the ability of philosophy to "discover" truths about the world. Here's a way of quantifying it. The first Philosophical Survey was conducted in 2000. It was a poll of 3,226 philosophers—the vast majority of whom were philosophy professors, PhDs, or grad students—asking their opinions on 30 core philosophical questions (questions about whether we have free will, about the existence of God, the objectivity of aesthetic value, what counts as knowledge), with generally two options (plus "other") for reply. Bryan Frances (himself a philosopher) did a statistical analysis of the results.[5] Based on the diversity of answers given, Frances argues that (assuming we think there are correct answers to these philosophical questions), where definite answers are given, the average philosopher can be thought to get 47%–67% right. Hardly an impressive score! Indeed, it is not clearly different from what one would expect from random guessing. And these should be the experts. (I'm sure we all hope to get more accuracy from our medical experts.) As a result, he argued that the vast majority of those who think they have knowledge about these controversial issues do not. The radical disagreement in philosophy might even lead us to a skeptical torpor—thinking that, undiscoverable as such facts are, we may as well give up trying and turn our attention elsewhere.

It has become increasingly common for philosophers themselves to express doubt that the answers to metaphysical questions can ever be known. Robert Nozick (2001) argues that we should be skeptical that we have any knowledge about what is metaphysically necessary or possible. Karen Bennett (2009) argues for the "epistemicist" position that, for many metaphysical disputes about what exists, there is little justification for believing either side. Edouard Machery (2017) expresses skepticism about many traditional philosophical questions, arguing that many of these require a form of modal knowledge that we can't have. For saying what, in general, is required for knowledge, or for an act to be morally permissible, or for an agent to be free requires

---

[5] "The Epistemically Troubling Philosophical Survey," presented at the GAP.9 conference in Osnabrück, Germany, September 14, 2015.

knowing what would be the case *in all possible worlds*. But (he argues) we can't get that kind of modal knowledge: "While there may be such facts, I will argue that we cannot know many of the metaphysical possibilities and necessities of philosophical interest" (2017, 2), and so these issues can't be resolved. He suggests that we would do better to suspend judgment and "abandon the hope of resolving modally immodest philosophical issues" (2017, 8).

Such skepticism hardly seems out of place given the formidable epistemological mysteries about *how* we could come to know the facts metaphysics purportedly aims to discover. Most mainstream metaphysicians agree that no empirical facts could settle who is right about central questions of metaphysics. Yet they almost uniformly deny that their questions can be answered merely by "conceptual analysis." For (they insist) these are questions *about the world*, not questions about our language or concepts. This leaves us with the question: What *is* the epistemology for metaphysics, then?[6] How can we hope to gain knowledge in metaphysics?

Even those who retain hope that we *can* come to know which views are right, tend to acknowledge the epistemological difficulties that arise in determining which, among the contending views, is "correct." Theodore Sider writes, "A sensible attitude is that metaphysics, like much of philosophy, is just hard. Its epistemology is hard, too" (2011, 82). And Ross Cameron writes, "Ontology is not just not easy, it is very, very hard" (2021, 242). While we can admire the honesty here, to say that it's "hard" goes no way toward showing that knowledge of this sort *is* possible, or saying how we could hope to acquire it. (Compare: Q: "How can you build a timber-framed structure on the open sea?" A: "It's just very, very hard.")

Nearly all of the serious metaphysicians who have addressed the epistemological problem, and aimed to show how we can acquire knowledge in metaphysics, have (usually in a quick paragraph or two) simply appealed to the idea that our ways of acquiring knowledge in metaphysics are *parallel to* those in the empirical sciences—so that metaphysics encounters no special epistemological

---

[6] For discussion of these problems, see my (2017a, 364–82).

problems.[7,8] As L. A. Paul puts it, "we can understand the methods employed by metaphysicians to be very similar, *modulo* the change in subject matter, to the methods employed by scientists" (2012, 9).

Broadly, the idea—popularized by David Lewis's (1986) argument for possible worlds—is that metaphysical theories are confirmed *in the same sorts of ways* that scientific theories are: by appeal to their theoretic virtues. Paul develop a version of this approach, arguing that "We use theoretical desiderata as guides to truth in metaphysics just as we use such desiderata as guides to truth in science" (2012, 21). Thus, one regularly sees metaphysical theories defended by appeal to their having greater simplicity, unity, or explanatory power than their rivals, or as serving as part of an inference to the best explanation. Metaphysicians often take these virtues to give us reason to think that our theories are true. Again, Paul describes a version of this view, thinking of metaphysics as engaged in "modeling," and arguing that "Once the [metaphysical] models are developed, just as in science, theories are compared with respect to the elegance, simplicity, and explanatory virtues of their models, and theories are chosen over their competitors by inference to the best explanation" (2012, 12).

But despite its central influence on the way metaphysics has been conducted in recent years, increasing doubts have been raised recently about the viability of inference to the best explanation, or reliance on theoretic virtues including explanatory power, in metaphysics. A first concern is that competing metaphysical theories are, as their defenders acknowledge, typically empirically equivalent. As metaphysicians will insist, for example, one cannot establish whether or not there are Platonistic or Aristotelian universals, or merely property tropes, by pointing to any empirical differences among these theories. Nor can one refute eliminativists about ordinary objects by citing any experiment or observation (if you say: "But I see a table over there", they

---

[7] Another common suggestion is that our metaphysical views are confirmed *along with* (as part and parcel of) our scientific theories. I will return to this suggestion in Chapters 2 and 3, since it is part of the neo-Quinean approach seen in explanatory approaches to metaphysics (discussed in Chapter 2) and broadened in Theodore Sider's structural conception (discussed in Chapter 3).

[8] The remainder of this section draws on work in my (2017a).

will simply reply that what you see is *particles arranged tablewise*). By contrast, in science "even approximate empirical equivalence is very rare" (Paul 2012, 12). If it is only theoretic virtues other than empirical adequacy at issue in debates between distinctively metaphysical rival theories, it is unclear why we should think that these differences—in the simplicity of the theory or its ontology, in its explanatory power, etc.—are really apt to track truth rather than just marking the usefulness of the theory for limited creatures like ourselves (see Bricker 2020, ch. 2). A related worry, as Karen Bennett (2009) and Uriah Kriegel (2013) have argued at length, is that, quite typically, competing metaphysical theories involve simply trading off one theoretic virtue for another, leaving us at sea in aiming to determine which metaphysical theory to choose. Paul accepts that there is a difference of degree between the indeterminacy in scientific versus metaphysical theorizing but insists that this difference in degree doesn't undermine the truth-conduciveness of appeals to the theoretic virtues in metaphysics: "If such theoretical desiderata are truth conducive in science, they are also truth conducive in metaphysics" (2012, 21).[9]

But even if one is prepared to accept that the theoretic virtues (other than empirical adequacy) are truth-conducive in the sciences, and one is willing to live with relative indeterminateness and uncertainty for metaphysics, deeper worries can be raised. For there are grounds for thinking that there may be a difference not just in degree, but in kind, between metaphysical theories and scientific theories—differences that prevent us from thinking that any truth-conduciveness the theoretic virtues bring to scientific theories carries over to metaphysical theories. Michael Huemer (2009) works through four different accounts of the evidential value of parsimony in empirical theorizing and argues that none applies to the philosophical cases, suggesting that in typical philosophical contexts ontological simplicity has no evidential value. Scott Shalkowski (2010) argues that inference to the best explanation can be empirically shown to be a reliable mode of inference where it concerns observables (so that there is the

---

[9] Like Paul, Sider accepts that there are differences in degree between using the theoretic virtues in science and metaphysics; see his (2011, 12) and discussion in Chapter 3.

possibility of independent access to confirm its results), but not where its conclusions concern unobservable facts (2010, 177). Shalkowski concludes that, while inference to the best explanation may be perfectly good in the ordinary empirical cases that motivate it, "there is little hope to be found in the use of [inference to the best explanation] to settle metaphysical questions" (2010, 184). Juha Saatsi (2017) argues that there are differences in kind for the use of inference to the best explanation in science (whether one deals with claims about observable or unobservable entities) versus in metaphysics. These differences, he argues, suggest that its reliability in science doesn't carry over to metaphysics, in part since it is hard "to conceive of a naturalistically acceptable account of the truth-conduciveness of explanationism in metaphysics" (2017, 176) given the absence of empirical feedback to guide our explanatory practices in metaphysics. By contrast, we may have such an account available for using inference to the best explanation in inferences about both observables and unobservables in science.

I do not aim to settle this issue here, but only note that relying on parallels between metaphysical and scientific appeals to theoretic virtues brings in much wider issues about whether those parallels hold—and about whether, even if we assume the theoretic virtues other than empirical adequacy are truth-conducive (rather than merely pragmatic) in the sciences, we have reasons to think that carries over in metaphysics. The metaphysician's usual replies are insufficient to address the problem of epistemological mystery.

Without good responses to these threats of rivalry with science, proliferation of views, and epistemological mystery, metaphysics threatens to make itself suspect, obscure, and irrelevant. And indeed, that is how it has come to seem to many, both within and outside of philosophy. If we want a conception of metaphysics that avoids rivalry with the natural sciences, makes it epistemologically clear, and avoids a despairing skepticism, we have reason to rethink metaphysics. I aim to do that in this volume, in ways that condemn some recent work as misguided, while showing the enduring value and importance of the work metaphysics is capable of doing and often has done.

1.2 A Very Brief History

Of course, in some ways these difficulties, including rivalry with the sciences, proliferation of views, and epistemological mystery about how we could answer our questions or resolve our debates, are all too familiar. They arise for any conception of metaphysics, or more generally of philosophy, that sees its work as a matter of making discoveries about what exists or what the world is like. They have arisen at least for as long as the natural sciences have separated themselves from philosophy—since around the seventeenth century[10]—and various responses have been tried out before.

One early attempt to distinguish the work of philosophy from that of the sciences (and to preserve a role for philosophy), popular in the nineteenth century, was to say that philosophy involved the study of *internal*, mental phenomena, while the sciences studied *external*, physical phenomena. This led to the view that became known as psychologism: that logic and epistemology are parts of psychology—studies of the laws of thought. But psychology, too, would separate itself from philosophy around the end of the 19th century. Moreover, the doctrine of psychologism fell on hard times, in part due to devastating criticisms raised by Gottlob Frege and Edmund Husserl.[11] A central problem, emphasized by Husserl, is that psychological studies of how we actually think or reason cannot tell us how we *ought to* reason. But logic, as Husserl argued, is a "practical-normative" discipline, about how we *ought* to reason, and so logical truths cannot be identified with empirical generalizations about how people actually think.

Questions about the proper role of philosophy were an obsessive concern for philosophers in the early 20th century. As Gilbert Ryle put it in his "Autobiographical" reflections, "We philosophers were in for a near-lifetime of enquiry into our own title to be enquirers" (1970). In this stage of the discussion, a broad consensus emerged

---

[10] Prior to this, the work of philosophers and scientists was not distinguished. As Quine puts it, "All these luminaries [Aristotle, Plato, Descartes, Leibniz, Locke, Berkeley, Hume, and Kant] and others whom we revere as great philosophers were scientists in search of an organized conception of reality" (1981, 191).

[11] Frege raises these criticisms in his (1884) *Grundlagen der Arithmetik*; Husserl's critique is developed in the Prolegomena to his (1900) *Logical Investigations*.

about the answer. Early 20th-century philosophers as diverse as Ryle, Wittgenstein, Husserl, and Carnap—despite their many differences—embraced a relatively cohesive view of the relation between philosophical and scientific work. Philosophy, on this view, is *conceptual* work, while the sciences are engaged in *empirical* work. This seemed, at least, to provide a clear division of labor for philosophy and the sciences, and a distinctive (if limited) role for the former—whether in distinguishing sense from nonsense and dissolving pseudo-problems that way, in examining the concepts used in the sciences, or analyzing the concepts of ordinary language.

The idea that philosophy can legitimately do conceptual rather than empirical work had its heyday in the first half of the 20th century, with positivism, phenomenology, and ordinary language philosophy. Philosophers in all of these movements rejected traditional metaphysics—thought of as discovering facts about what exists or what the world is like. In this era, the very term "metaphysics" was used mostly as a term of abuse by positivists, who considered metaphysical statements to be "nonsense." Ordinary language philosophers and phenomenologists steadfastly avoided metaphysical questions, and focused instead on questions about *meaning*, whether these were understood in terms of doing conceptual analysis, exposing the linguistic nonsense behind alleged philosophical problems, or analyzing the types of meaning-giving acts that could enable us to be presented with a world of objects, artifacts, and persons.

Philosophers working in all of these traditions seemed to reach something of a consensus: that, broadly speaking, philosophy is properly concerned with conceptual or linguistic work.

But it didn't last.

Why not? First, to many it seemed—and still seems—disappointing to think that philosophy can do no more than investigate our ordinary language or concepts, abandoning its traditional grander ambitions. As Ted Sider puts it in *Writing the Book of the World*: "Who would prefer exploring our perhaps parochial conceptual scheme to exploring the fundamental features of reality?" (2011, xxiv). Philosophers working in other areas raised similar worries: Many ethicists, for example, would say that they aren't just interested in our *concepts* of right and wrong; they care about working out what's *really* right and wrong. The conceptualist move provoked an inevitable backlash from those who hoped to preserve the idea that philosophy could do something more.

Second, Quine (1951/1953) famously rejected the analytic/synthetic distinction that seemed to be needed to distinguish the work of philosophy, as involved in conceptual analysis, from the empirical work of the sciences.[12] Quine famously concluded that

> if there is no proper distinction between analytic and synthetic, then no basis at all remains for the contrast which Carnap urges between ontological statements and empirical statements of existence. Ontological questions then end up on a par with the questions of natural science. (1951/1976, 211)

These were widely, though prematurely, taken on board as reasons for rejecting the division-of-labor view.

Around the same time, a well-known debate arose between Quine and Carnap, which many (mistakenly, in my view) took to leave Quine as the winner, and (even more mistakenly) took to lay out a path for a neo-Quinean approach to metaphysics: one on which metaphysical work, centrally including "ontological" questions about what exists, was perfectly legitimate and "on a par with," or (as some thought) *continuous with* or *part of* the explanatory enterprise of natural science. This in turn led to a great revival of metaphysics in the decades after that debate—a revival that went largely unquestioned for a half century thereafter.[13] (I will have more to say about developments out of Quine's views in Chapter 2.)

But the explanatory approach to metaphysics inspired by Quine was not the only approach to take root in the metaphysical revival.

---

[12] I critically discuss these Quinean arguments in Chapter 2 of my (2007).

[13] For the Carnap/Quine debate see, especially, Quine (1948/1953 and 1951/1976), and Carnap (1950/1956). For discussion and re-evaluation of this debate, see Price (2009) and my (2015, ch. 1). Questions about the standing of the revived version of metaphysics did not really become prominent again until around the end of the 20th century, after which a renewed interest in "metametaphysics" set in. Some early landmarks of this renewed questioning include Hirsch (2002a, 2002b), and the conference "Metametaphysics" held at the Australian National University in 2005, and another held at Boise State University in March 2007. Many of the papers from both conferences are reprinted in Chalmers et al. (2009).

14 RETHINKING METAPHYSICS

The alternative conceptions of metaphysics have all arisen out of forms of dissatisfaction with the neo-Quinean approach to metaphysics—dissatisfaction which began to surface in the early years of the 21st century, along with an emerging interest in metametaphysics. Several other prominent ways of reconceiving the work of metaphysics have been developed since then, including at least the following: seeing metaphysics as concerned with *structure of reality*, as engaged in the search for *truthmakers*, as addressing questions about *fundamentality*, or *grounding*, as concerned with a special kind of "metaphysical explanation," or with the study of *essences*, and so on.[14]

1.3 A Diagnosis and Cure

In the current context, rethinking metaphysics requires re-evaluating those ways of thinking about and practicing metaphysics. So, I will begin in Part I by discussing several of these views in turn. Doing so will enable us to move beyond the generic problems for metaphysics described above, to develop a more general *diagnosis* of *why* these views go wrong. Space constraints, and concern to avoid redundancy, have led me to focus just on a few prominent contenders. In any case, new ways of thinking of metaphysics, like the creatures in a game of Whack-a-Mole, will continue to pop up, so I cannot aim to treat them all here. I will have to hope that those I do discuss cover enough territory to make for a plausible general diagnosis of the ways metaphysics

---

[14] Another important approach, which I won't discuss here (given space constraints and given that this has been done elsewhere) is the "Canberra Plan" inspired by David Lewis and developed by Frank Jackson (1998). Jonathan O'Leary Hawthorne and Huw Price criticize the Canberra Plan in terms very much relevant to the criticisms I will raise of other approaches here. The Canberra Plan was the plan of replacing metaphysically puzzling terms with "existentially quantified bound variables and [taking] the folk to be talking about whatever makes the resulting Ramsey sentence true" (O'Leary-Hawthorne and Price 1996, 291). This was then supposed to provide a general way of making "problematic" entities (e.g., the mental, moral, or modal) reducible to something more naturalistically respectable. O'Leary-Hawthorne and Price, however, argue that undertaking the Canberra Plan relies on assuming "that the reduced theory is doing the same linguistic job as the reducing theory. Unless this assumption is valid in the case in question, the proposed reduction involves a kind of category mistake" (1996, 291).

at least *tends to* go wrong, and I will leave detailed analyses of other actual or possible views as an exercise for the reader.

To prefigure, the diagnosis I will reach of the views discussed here is this: Despite their many important differences, all of these common ways of thinking of the work of metaphysics implicitly rely on what we might call a "functional monist" assumption—a generally unreflective and unarticulated assumption that all the indicatives metaphysics takes interest in serve to *represent, track,* or *describe features of* the world.[15] Children who make this kind of assumption, and treat language as if its only use is to state facts, are often sent to speech therapy for "pragmatics" lessons. But in metaphysics you can make a living out of it. Call this the "metaphysical malady."[16]

The troubles are aggravated by combining this assumption of functional monism with the ambition of metaphysics to be "completely general"—and to apply to topics from material objects to modality to morality to causation and time. For it forces very different areas of discourse, with very different functional roles, into a single (often inappropriate) mold. The lesson of this diagnostic work is that, before launching into metaphysical questions and debates, or laying down general "metaphysical criteria," we should take a step back to ask questions about the *functions* of the forms of discourse in question, and the *rules* they follow—including how they come to be introduced into language. Taking this step back requires us to say more about how we can identify and understand the functions served by different parts of language.

---

[15] R. M. Hare notes that "one kind of indicative sentences, that which expresses value-judgments, behaves logically in a quite different way from the ordinary indicative sentence" (1952, 4).

[16] Speech act theorists have recently made vivid the problems that arise in defenses of "freedom of speech" that "depend on the assumption that the function of speech is to express beliefs and share information" (Harris et al. 2018, 28)—and have worked to show the ways that speech is often used to incite violence (see Tirrell 2017), derogate, silence, or subordinate (see, e.g., MacKinnon 1993; Langton 1993). Here I will aim to show some of the problems that arise for *metaphysics* when we assume that all indicatives (or at least all of those we care about in metaphysics) should be understood as *informing, representing,* or *describing* in ways that involve tracking features of the surrounding world.

In both the diagnosis and the cure, the approach I develop here can be seen as inspired by and aiming to contribute to work in the neo-pragmatist tradition. What I take to be the central core of a neo-pragmatist approach is the idea that we should begin our philosophical inquiries (whether into morality, modality, causation, time, the mind, etc.) by asking first about the relevant forms of discourse, how they work, and what functions they serve.[17] As Joshua Gert puts it, the overarching advice of the neo-pragmatist is "look at how the words that are central to that topic are used, and try to provide a naturalistic explanation of a practice in which words are used in that way" (2023, 5). In doing so, as Price and Macarthur emphasize, the "guiding intuition is that if we can explain how natural creatures in our circumstances naturally come to speak in these ways, there is no further puzzle about the place of the topics concerned, in the kind of world described by science" (2007, 95).

Work in the neo-pragmatist tradition, of course, harkens back to the classical pragmatism of Dewey, James, and Peirce. As Cheryl Misak (2016) makes clear, this early pragmatist work was an influence on both Frank Ramsey[18] and Ludwig Wittgenstein;[19] and later on ordinary language philosophers such as Gilbert Ryle and J. L. Austin. There is also a largely forgotten core of women philosophers

---

[17] For excellent overviews of the neo-pragmatist approach, see MacArthur and Price (2007) and Gert (2023). For a history of pragmatism from Cambridge, Massachusetts through Cambridge, England, see Misak (2016).

[18] Ramsey's contributions and connections to pragmatism have recently been brought to attention by Cheryl Misak (2020).

[19] No doubt it is associated most strongly in the minds of many with the work of Wittgenstein (who tended to not cite his sources). The work here will indeed have affinities with later Wittgenstein in some respects—including an emphasis on understanding differences in different forms of language (or "language games"), and on engaging in a kind of therapy with respect to certain traditional metaphysical problems. There are two large differences in what I aim to do, however, as will become clear in Part II. First, I aim (drawing on work in systemic functional linguistics) to take a more *systematic* approach to understanding linguistic functions than Wittgenstein did. Second, I aim to give not just a therapeutic but also a constructive approach to philosophy—in seeing its work as including constructive conceptual engineering. (Here an important predecessor is Wittgenstein's student Alice Ambrose—see Chapter 6 below.) Interestingly, the anthropologist Bronislaw Malinowski was an influence on both Wittgenstein and the linguist J. R. Firth, who would become the teacher of Michael Halliday and the intellectual grandfather of work in systemic functional linguistics—so those two traditions share some common roots. Though they have long diverged since then, I aim to bring them back together here.

of the mid-20th century who developed the approach in new ways—including Margaret MacDonald (whose (1937) work, as Cheryl Misak (2024) argues, was a central inspiration for Ryle's), Mary Midgley (1992), and Alice Ambrose (1952).[20] In the world of contemporary analytic philosophy, neo-pragmatism is just coalescing to become visible as a movement and theoretical option.[21] Similar approaches applied to particular topics (sometimes under the heading of "expressivism") are familiar from work by Simon Blackburn and Allan Gibbard in metaethics, Paul Horwich on truth, Dorit Bar-On (2004) for areas of mental discourse, Perez-Carballo (2016) for mathematical discourse, and many others.[22] The general ideas of the more recent neo-pragmatist tradition will be most familiar through the work of such figures as Richard Rorty, Robert Brandom, and Huw Price.

In the work developed here, I am particularly indebted to Huw Price (2011), who develops a diagnosis of the reductionist program in metaphysics as relying illicitly on "a substantial semantic thesis, namely that the various bits of language in question have a common purpose—that of describing the world, saying how things are, or some such" (2011, 78), and urges that we begin by "standing back from the concepts in question and asking how they arise, and what functions they serve in the lives of the creatures who employ them" (2011, 79)—where these are fundamentally *empirical* questions to be addressed by linguistics or anthropology.

This book aims to develop and broaden that project—both the negative project, in aiming to show that several prominent conceptions of metaphysics make the functional monist assumption; and the positive project, in aiming to make use of work in linguistics to address the naturalistic questions about the functions various areas of discourse

---

[20] Ambrose began to take the turn from neo-pragmatist assessments of problems to work in what would now be called "conceptual engineering"—for further discussion, see Chapter 6 below. I am grateful to Matthew Shields for tuning me into Ambrose's work, to Cheryl Misak for showing me the MacDonald-Ryle connection, and to Clotilde Torregrossa for suggesting Mary Midgley's work to me.

[21] As witnessed by the recent collection entitled *Neopragmatism* (2023) edited by Joshua Gert, and by recent conferences organized by Huw Price, and works by Price, Blackburn, Brandom, Horwich, and Williams in Price (2013).

[22] See also the essays applying neo-pragmatism to various topics in Gert (2023).

serve in our lives—and to show why this makes a philosophical difference. Price argues that we must begin from a "subject naturalist" approach, that "philosophy needs to begin with what science tells us *about ourselves*" (2011, 186).[23] Following this idea, I will argue that work in linguistics—more particularly, work in systemic functional linguistics, focused on questions about how language is structured to serve various functions in human life—can aid us in the positive project. For it addresses just these questions and provides a framework from which we can more clearly see why various "completely general" conceptions of metaphysics lead us astray. I will argue that these functional analyses also enable us to re-evaluate many old (alleged) "metaphysical problems." The work on linguistic functions also will play a central role in developing and defending the positive vision for how we can rethink the work of metaphysics.

The view I develop and defend in Part II is that we should reconceive the work of metaphysics as work in conceptual engineering, understanding "conceptual engineering" broadly, to include both work in *reverse* engineering that aims to understand how our linguistic or conceptual scheme works, and work in *constructive* engineering that aims to evaluate and improve our conceptual scheme. As I will argue, thinking of the work of metaphysics in this way enables us to avoid an apparent rivalry with science. Descriptive questions of reverse conceptual engineering are answerable *empirically*, in ways that work with (not in rivalry with) the work of linguistics, psychology, and cognitive science. (I aim to illustrate how profitable this working-with can be in the use I make of work in systemic functional linguistics.) Questions in constructive conceptual engineering are fundamentally *normative* or *practical* questions—questions about *what we ought to do* with (parts of) our language or conceptual scheme. Such *normative* questions are not addressed by empirical scientific enquiry—though that can be relevant to determining *how well* various proposed changes *would fulfill* the desired functions. In fact, I will suggest, we can think of a central

---

[23] Price argues that this should come prior to evaluating "object naturalist" metaphysical views holding that "in some important sense, all there *is* is the world studied by science" (2011, 185).

province for philosophical work more generally as addressing *normative* questions, whether these concern how we should live, how we should arrange our laws and government, how we should reason, or what concepts we should use.

Thinking of the work of metaphysics as work in conceptual engineering enables us to avoid the epistemological mysteries and skepticism that have plagued metaphysics.[24] For some of the questions are answerable empirically. Others are not matters for *discovery* where there seem to be "deep facts" that we can't know, but rather are matters that require difficult practical *decisions*.[25] On this model, a proliferation of metaphysical views also ceases to be an embarrassment that might lead us to skepticism. For engineering questions (such as how to build a bridge over a particular river) do not seek to find a single "true" answer that corresponds to deep "facts" of the world. Instead, we answer such constructive engineering questions by developing various practical *proposals*, which give us different options we might choose from, depending on our needs, constraints, and goals. In this way, I will argue, rethinking metaphysics as work in conceptual engineering can enable us to overcome the problems of rivalry with science, epistemological mystery, and skepticism that have plagued traditional approaches to metaphysics. At the same time, as I shall argue, it makes clear the ongoing relevance that work in metaphysics can have for human life. For our language and concepts have an enormous impact on how we develop our government, laws, and institutions, on how we conduct our scientific investigations, and most broadly, on how we live.

---

[24] I have already aimed to avoid some of the epistemological problems of metaphysics in my prior work—by showing how existence questions may be answered "easily" (in my 2015a), and by developing a clear approach to how we can answer metaphysical *modal* questions (an approach that relies on nothing more than conceptual competence, reasoning abilities, and empirical knowledge) (in Chapter 7 of my 2020a).
[25] As some readers will have noticed, there are constraints on what metaethical views may be joined with this approach if we hope to retain this epistemological benefit. That is, we must not think of moral facts or truths as mysterious deep facts awaiting discovery if we hope to avoid the same sort of epistemological difficulties and skepticism arising again. The approach here, of course, in any case fits more naturally with a broadly pragmatic understanding of moral discourse (not a hyper-realist metaphysical approach). While I have now begun working on metaethical issues (see Warren and Thomasson 2023 and my in progress), these metaethical debts will have to be paid later.

2
The Explanatory Conception of Metaphysics

Quine is usually given credit for reviving metaphysics out of the ashes of positivism. Though Quine declared himself "no champion of traditional metaphysics" (1951/1976, 204), his work inspired an approach to metaphysics that was dominant at least through the end of the twentieth century, and which is still going strong in many quarters.[1] As Putnam put it, "It was Quine who single-handedly made Ontology a respectable subject" (2004, 78–79).

Quine's approach was broadly scientific, seeing ontology as continuous with science, and sharing an epistemology:

> Our acceptance of an ontology is, I think, similar in principle to our acceptance of a scientific theory, say a system of physics: we adopt, at least insofar as we are reasonable, the simplest conceptual scheme into which the disordered fragments of raw experience can be fitted and arranged. Our ontology is determined once we have fixed upon the over-all conceptual scheme which is to accommodate science in the broadest sense. (1948/1953, 16–17)

This inspired the view that metaphysics and the natural sciences are "in the same boat," both aiming to develop a best total explanatory theory.

There are good reasons for doubting that Quine himself would have endorsed the metaphysical glory days that followed, under the reign of what was often called a "neo-Quinean" approach to metaphysics; those who sought inspiration in Quine's work for reviving

---

[1] One articulation of this approach is in van Inwagen (2009), where he explicitly lays out a meta-ontology that he claims is "essentially Quine's" (2009, 475).

metaphysics seem to have forgotten Quine's pragmatism. As Huw Price puts it, "a metaphysician who takes this as a vindication of his position—who announces triumphantly that Quine has shown us that metaphysics is in the same boat as natural science, that 'ontological questions [are] on a par with the questions of natural science'—is someone who has not been told the terrible news. Quine himself has sunk the metaphysicians' traditional boat, and left all of us, scientists and ontologists, clinging to Neurath's raft" (2009, 326-27)—and left us with a "thoroughgoing post-positivist pragmatism" (Price 2009, 327).[2]

I will leave aside these historical/interpretive questions here, however.[3] Here I am instead interested in isolating and examining the explanatory conception as a view of metaphysics that many metaphysicians (aptly or not) *trace to* Quine, and that has been enormously influential. It was the dominant view behind the revival of metaphysics in the second half of the twentieth century, and it persists today.

The task of ontology, on this model, is to answer the question "What exists?" or "What is there?" The way of answering it, as Quine made famous, is to begin by determining what overall explanatory theory to accept and expressing it in first-order logic. Then we can see that we are "ontologically committed" to accepting the existence of all and only those entities over which our quantifiers must range to make the statements of our accepted theory true (Quine 1948/1953, 13). This has developed into what is sometimes labeled the "neo-Quinean" approach to ontology; here I will more neutrally call it the "explanatory" conception of metaphysics. For on this view, metaphysics (or at least ontology) is considered (part of) an explanatory enterprise, concerned with offering a best total explanatory theory. That is what gives this approach the right to claim that the work of metaphysics is *like* or even *is continuous with* the work of the natural sciences. This form of scientism is supposed to both make ontology respectable and ensure that there are no distinctive problems with its epistemology.

---

[2] Jonathan Schaffer also notes and aims to correct the common mistake of forgetting Quine's pragmatism (2009, 349).

[3] I undertake some of this historical work in Chapter 1 of my (2015); see also Price (2009).

While "explanation" is a term used in many ways, in the context of this scientistic "explanatory" conception of ontology, the appeal to "explanation" is generally meant in the sense of scientific/causal explanation—since the idea is that metaphysics is in the same explanatory business as the theories of the natural sciences. And it is in the context of scientific and everyday empirical explanations that explanatory arguments *for the existence of something* seem compelling.[4]

The explanatory conception has been developed in both broad and narrow forms. The narrow form involves treating *whether or not the alleged entities add explanatory power* to our theories as a central criterion in determining whether to accept that they exist.[5] That is, we ask whether Ks would contribute any "explanatory power" to our theory as (at least partial) grounds for answering the ontological question about whether *there are* Ks. Sometimes metaphysical "posits" are alleged to explain certain facts or observations (such as why the red barn and the red house have something in common, or why it is true that grass is green). In other places, they are taken to explain *norms*, such as why we *should* act in certain ways (because this is dictated by the moral facts), or why we *should* theorize using some concepts rather than others (because these concepts pick out the *natural* properties and relations).

In the broad (holistic) form of the explanatory approach (which is clearly closer to the settled version of Quine's view), we are to determine what our best total explanatory theory is, and regiment it by

---

[4] More recently, the idea has been popularized that metaphysics is concerned with its own sort of "bottom-up," or "grounding," explanations. Such purported "grounding explanations," however, aren't commonly thought to give us reason to think that the explainers exist—and so they aren't the relevant sort of "explanation" at work in this conception of ontology. For example, while some will say that Socrates explains the existence of the singleton set {Socrates}, no one thinks that we have reason to *posit* the existence of Socrates because that would provide the best explanation of the existence of the set. I discuss grounding views in Chapter 5.

[5] This, of course, isn't Quine's full and settled position about how to address existence questions (which famously involves regimenting our best "total" theory and determining what entities we *must* quantify over to render its statements true). The point here is that these remarks have been very influential in promoting attention to "explanatory power" as a central criterion for whether or not we "posit" certain metaphysically contested entities. On Quine's more considered approach, as I will argue, we still have something of a functional monist view in narrowing our gaze, considering only our best total *scientific* theory—failing to notice the many different roles that vocabulary may play within a scientific theory, as well as to notice the many purposes we have beyond those of scientific theorizing.

expressing it in (first-order) logical notation. On this version of the view, to answer questions about what exists, we first ask what total explanatory theory we should accept, and then determine what entities that theory (properly regimented) must quantify over if the statements of the theory are to be true.

These two versions of an explanatory view of metaphysics have been popular for decades in metaphysics. They play a role not only in arguments explicitly about explanatory power, but also in arguments about "causal redundancy"—for those who allege that some entities (such as minds, ordinary objects, etc.) are "causally redundant" with respect to "more basic" physical entities are alleging that the former play no essential causal/explanatory role in our theories. The explanatory view also lies behind the use of "Alexander's dictum" that *to be real is to have causal powers*, and "eleatic arguments" that insist that we should only accept entities with causal powers—for those entities that can't be said to have causal powers are often presumed to be explanatorily impotent.[6] Arguments along these lines have been employed in arguments for or against an enormous range of (purported) objects, including meanings and properties (Quine 1948/1953), mental states (Kim 1993, 336–57), numbers (Quine 1976; Field 1980/2016), ordinary objects (Merricks 2001), and social groups (see discussion in Ritchie 2015).

I will argue in section 2.1, however, that the explanatory approach to metaphysics is no improvement over the traditional conception—for it leaves us with the familiar difficulties of rivalry with science and epistemological mystery. But the central aim here is not to refute the explanatory approach, but rather to *diagnose* where the explanatory conception has gone wrong, and to suggest a different way of looking at many of the central "ontological problems" that have attracted so much work in metaphysics.

---

[6] The explanatory conception also plays a role in "(in)dispensability" arguments in philosophy of mathematics—which center on questions about whether numbers (which seem to figure usefully in our explanatory scientific theories) are dispensable to our scientific explanations. I return to discuss these issues below.

2.1 Problems for the Explanatory Conception

Many have found an explanatory conception of the project of ontology tempting, since it seems to lend a sort of scientific respectability to metaphysics—making ontology "of a piece" with science. Of course, in doing so, it raises again the problem of a rivalry with the sciences. If ontologists offer different answers to existence questions from scientists (as they often do: as many deny the existence not only of artifacts or meanings studied in archaeology and linguistics, but even deny the existence of organisms or other composite material objects studied by biologists, geographers, astronomers, etc.), then they seem threatened to lose in the rivalry with the sciences. If they do not offer different answers to existence questions than the sciences, it's hard to see how metaphysicians have any role at all, except in "just repeating what science says" (Price 2009, 338).

The neo-Quinean conception of metaphysics has also led to a notorious proliferation of ontological views—as more and more diverging views have been defended about "what exists," with some who claim to use this approach accepting, and others denying, the existence of numbers, properties, ordinary objects, fictional characters, social groups, and pretty much any other kind of thing you care to name.

One reason many have found this characterization of metaphysics appealing, however, is that it has been thought to ease the epistemological problems of ontology. For (the thought goes) *just as we can have reasons to accept (or reject) the existence of a new planet, fundamental particle, or microbe* given the explanatory power it brings (or fails to bring) to a relevant scientific theory, so can we have reason to accept (or reject) metaphysical "posits" such as universals or natural properties, based on the explanatory power they add (or fail to add).[7] Broadly, the thought is that our metaphysical views are confirmed along with (and as part of) our best total explanatory theory—via

---

[7] Along these lines, Stathis Psillos treats as "the only workable criterion of reality" that "something is real if its positing plays an indispensable role in the explanation of well-founded phenomena" (2005, 398).

inference to the best explanation.[8] Theodore Sider gives a clear statement of this form of the view:

> Quine's advice for forming *ontological* beliefs is familiar: believe the ontology of your best theory. Theories are good insofar as they are simple, explanatorily powerful, integrate with other good theories, and so on. We should believe generally what good theories say; so if a good theory makes an ontological claim, we should believe it. The ontological claim took part in a theoretical success, and therefore inherits a borrowed luster; it merits our belief. (2011, 12)

On this model, the *ontological content* of a theory is supposed to be confirmed with the rest of the theory (which includes empirical content allowing for confirmation)—giving us an inference to the best explanation argument that its ontological content (too) is true.[9]

So, can we use inference to the best explanation to infer that the ontological content of our best total theories is true?[10] Appealing to inference to the best explanation is a popular move for metaphysicians, defended not only by Sider but also by L. A. Paul, who writes, "just as in science . . . [metaphysical] theories are chosen over their competitors using inference to the best explanation" (2012, 12). Let us begin with the claim that we can make inferences to the best explanation that the ontological content of our most successful theories is true. Those working to defend a form of realism in philosophy of science against pessimistic induction arguments[11] have found it important to draw a distinction between what parts of a scientific theory *are* and *are not* confirmed with a theory's successful predictions. As far as I know, this move was introduced with Philip Kitcher's distinction

---

[8] "One attractive strategy for answering these questions emphasizes the continuity of metaphysics with science. On this conception, metaphysics is primarily or exclusively concerned with developing generalizations from our best-confirmed scientific theories" (van Inwagen and Sullivan 2021, sec. 4).

[9] Sider also takes this to confirm that the theory's ideology "carves nature at its joints"—I will return to this claim in Chapter 3.

[10] This section draws on work from my (2017a).

[11] The pessimistic induction argument (famously developed by Larry Laudan [1981]) argues (roughly) that since most of our past well-confirmed scientific theories have turned out to be false, our current well-confirmed theories are likely to be false, too.

between the "working posits" of a theory ("the putative referents of terms that occur in problem-solving schemata" [1993, 149]) and the "presuppositional posits" ("those entities that apparently have to exist if the instances of the schemata are to be true" [1993, 149]).[12] Kitcher argued that if Laudan's story in the pessimistic induction argument "has an anti-realist moral, it is that the *presuppositional* posits of contemporary science may not exist" (1993, 149). As a result, we have independent reason to distinguish what is and is not confirmed with a scientific theory—and to deny that a theory's presupposed *ontological* content is confirmed in the way that the "working posits" of the theory are. Those who fail to make this distinction (in aiming to defend metaphysics) may unwittingly block an important route to defending scientific realism.

Stathis Psillos (1999) builds on this work, drawing out a similar distinction between claims that "fuel" a theory's predictive success and those that are "idle" (1999, 110). I don't like the term "idle." For there still may be work done, though not the same *kind of* work. (The foresters who calculate where the trees should be cut to make the most effective firebreaks aren't cutting any trees, but they aren't *idle*.) So, I will use terminology that distinguishes those components that *fuel* an explanation from those that merely (otherwise) *figure in it*.[13] "Figure in" I understand quite loosely here: as *appearing in* an explanation without fueling the theory's predictive success. To say that a component merely *figures in* a theory without *fueling* it is *not*, however, to suggest that it is eliminable—certain mathematical claims may be

---

[12] Kitcher aims then to argue that ether was a presuppositional posit, not a working posit, and so to undermine one of Laudan's prime cases in the pessimistic induction argument (Laudan 1981).

[13] Note that this kind of distinction between what figures in versus what fuels an explanation relies on a broadly epistemic conception of explanation: on which, in the words of Wright and van Eck, "explanations are complexes of representations of entities in the physical world" (2018, 998)—rather than thinking of explanations (as those holding "ontic conceptions" of explanation do) as the mere *things* in the world that are appealed to (by those offering explanations) as causally responsible for the observed phenomenon. The thought behind the various ways of distinguishing what "fuels" and what "figures in" an explanation is based on thinking of explanations as a particular kind of representation that can contribute to our knowledge—and part of the point I wish to make here is that such explanations may include different parts or aspects with different functional roles. For arguments against the ontic conception of "explanation," see Wright and van Eck (2018).

ineliminable from a theory without their *fueling* the theory's success in the sense given below.

Which theoretical constituents then "fuel" the theory's success? Katherine Hawley provides a helpful and succinct way of elucidating the distinction: "If a claim H is to be involved in generating a prediction in a way that entitles it to share in the confirmation which successful prediction brings [and so to 'fuel' its success] . . . H must satisfy two conditions with respect to the generation of the prediction. First, it must be the case that the theory minus H cannot generate the prediction alone. Second, it must also be the case that there is no available, sensible alternative to H which could have done the work just as well" (2006, 462).[14]

As I have argued elsewhere (2017a), we can understand the idea of a "theory minus H" in terms of Stephen Yablo's (2009) method of "subtracting" presuppositions from the content of a theory. The assertive content of a theory is the analytic implications that remain when we subtract a presupposition. So, for example, we can (in Yablo's terms) "subtract" the presupposition that numbers exist from the claim "The number of planets is eight," in the sense that the assertive content of that claim (which we can also state as "There are eight planets") remains true even if that presupposition "fails" (Yablo 2009, 520). As Yablo thinks of it, the presupposition that our number terms refer is "fail-safe," in that it *doesn't matter* whether it is true or false, as that has no effect on "what is claimed and on whether the sentence counts as true, false or gappy" (2009, 520). In such cases, then, we have reason to deny that the subtracted content is confirmed with the theory. By contrast, in other cases, such as "The planet beyond Uranus is the densest giant planet in our solar system," the relevant presupposition (that there is such a planet) cannot be subtracted without "wrecking" the whole assertive enterprise—here we can't identify an assertive content that remains true even if it turns out that there is no appropriate heavenly body beyond Uranus, and so we have reason to think that the

---

[14] Where that alternative, as Psillos also insists, must be independently motivated, non–ad hoc, and potentially explanatory in the sense that it not have the prediction "written into" it.

existence of the planet Neptune *does* share in the confirmation of the relevant astronomical theory.

I have also argued (2014) that if one is inclined to accept Yablo's approach at all, it should be generalized: that by his lights all specifically *ontological* claims—those that comprise the differences among rival ontological theories—are *fail-safe*, whereas empirical claims are not.[15] Even if we reject an ontology of composite material objects, speaking instead by using a feature-placing language or talk of particles arranged planet-wise, the assertive content of "There is a planet beyond Uranus" remains true—and could be stated using an "ontologically alternative" language, for example, one that appealed to "particles arranged planet-wise." And even in such a language, Leverrier's inference to the best explanation argument would have the same power to explain the aberrations in the orbit of Uranus—we must simply now express it as an argument that there are *particles arranged planet-wise* beyond the *particles arranged Uranus-wise*. In general, specifically *ontological* claims (those that distinguish one ontological view from its rivals, where all are (according to their defenders) empirically equivalent) are *fail-safe*. What is not fail-safe is the *empirical* claim, which would lead to various predictions about what we would see if we had powerful enough telescopes, etc. But such fail-safe claims can be "subtracted" from a theory, and so do not share in confirmation.

If this is correct, then inference to the best explanation arguments may give us reason for accepting various empirical claims. But they cannot be used to support an *ontological* claim over its mere *ontological* rivals, or one total theory over another which varies only *ontologically* from it. This gives us reason to think that ontological "theories" cannot be defended over their (empirically equivalent) ontological rivals by appeal to inference to the best explanation—at least not in anything like the same sense in which it is used in the sciences.

---

[15] See my (2014). Now it may be that there are problems with thinking the ontological content of a claim can be "subtracted out" if we adopt the easy ontological approach. As I have argued elsewhere (2014 and 2017c) it is hard to articulate a sense of *what more it would take* for the original claim to be true than for the remainder to be true. Nonetheless, this section examines what options are open for those who would *deny* easy ontology and think that it *does* take something more for the "controversial" ontological claim to be true.

Another reason to doubt that the ontological content of a theory is confirmed with the theory comes from taking a contrastive approach to confirmation. On Elliott Sober's (1993) contrastive view of confirmation, a theory is never confirmed in isolation, but rather *relative to alternative theories:* "the evidence we have for the theories we accept is evidence that favors those theories *over others*" (1993, 39). As a result, Sober argues, mathematics is not confirmed with scientific theories—however well confirmed the scientific theories that employ mathematics may be—as long as the competing theories employ the same mathematical assumptions. For "if the mathematical statements M are part of *every* competing hypothesis, then, no matter which hypothesis comes out best in the light of the observations, M will be part of that best hypothesis. M is not tested by this exercise, but is simply a background assumption common to the hypotheses under test" (1993, 45). "If the mathematical statements M are part of each hypothesis under test, then the observational outcome does not favor M *over any of its competitors*" (1993, 45).[16]

What Sober says about mathematics can be applied equally well to the purely ontological aspects of a theory. Suppose we have two competing scientific theories, for example, both of which employ terms apparently referring to material objects. The ontological assumption that there are material objects, however, is not confirmed with those theories since it is common to both theories. One could "confirm" the ontological presuppositions only if one could compare two theories that *differ* in these respects, where the change in ontology confers "different probabilities on some set O of statements that can be checked by observation" (1993, 45). And so, by this principle, a theory's ontology could be confirmed only if the differences in ontology between two theories led to different probabilities on certain predictions of each—there is no default confirmation of the purely ontological aspects of a theory. But theories that are merely *ontological rivals*—those that are not empirically distinct but do accept a different ontology—will

---

[16] Is something different going on in distinctively mathematical explanations? For discussion, and to see a take on how a modal normativist approach can be used to undermine the idea that indispensability in distinctively mathematical explanations gives us reasons to adopt mathematical Platonism, see Mark Povich (2024).

have no such predictive differences. Indeed, in typical ontological debates, all participants agree that there are *no* differences in empirical predictions that arise based on whether we accept, say, an ontology of ordinary material objects, or only particles in certain arrangements, or only features.[17] Without such differences attributable to the two competing ontologies,[18] we cannot hold that the specifically *ontological content* of the theory (whatever it may be) is confirmed with the theory itself, instead of being a common presupposition of the ways in which the competing theories are articulated.

The contrastive method and the assertive content method both seem like good ways to start to clarify what it means for a part of a theory to be "involved in generating a prediction in a way that shares the confirmation." But both of these methods cast doubt on the idea that the specifically *ontological content* of a theory shares in the theory's confirmation. As a result, it's not clear that we can resolve the epistemological difficulties for metaphysics by appealing to the idea that our metaphysical views are confirmed with our best total explanatory theories—and so this central attraction of scientific "explanatory" views of metaphysics comes into doubt.

2.2 Why Some Terms Don't Add Explanatory Power

The central question I aim to address here, however, is not whether the explanatory conception can give us an adequate epistemology for metaphysics. Instead, it's this: Is addition of explanatory power a legitimate criterion for accepting or rejecting entities in ontology (assuming it is in empirical matters)? More broadly, is it legitimate to think of the project of ontology as an *explanatory* project in which we aim to say what there is by determining what we must "posit" in our best explanatory theories?

---

[17] Of course, matters are different for *empirical* existence questions, as contrasted with merely *ontological* differences. See my (2014).

[18] Even if two languages differed in expressive power, so that one could *express* predictions the other could not, that would not be enough to meet Sober's criterion. For the criterion is that the ideological differences must lead the theories to confer *different probabilities on the same predictions*.

THE EXPLANATORY CONCEPTION OF METAPHYSICS

I will argue that the answer to both questions is no.

The simplest version of an explanatory approach to metaphysics is one that holds that we should "posit" entities only if they add "explanatory power" to our "theory." Quine's official view, of course, is that we are ontologically committed to all and only those entities over which we must quantify in our best total explanatory theories. And this, of course, is not *quite* the same as requiring that any given putative (kind of) entity itself contribute explanatory power in order for us to posit it (or things of its kind). Perhaps if some total explanatory theory that quantified over Ks were sufficiently better—in terms of possessing theoretic virtues *other than* explanatory power—we would have reason to accept it over a rival that didn't quantify over Ks. Nonetheless, it is not unreasonable to move from this to a prima facie case for accepting entities (and reducing parsimony) in a theory only if it enables us to increase other theoretic virtues (such as explanatory power) in a way that more than compensates for the loss in parsimony.

In any case, Quine himself certainly does make use of the idea that we should appeal to the *explanatory power* to be gained as a crucial criterion for whether or not we should accept that entities of a given kind exist. His use of the idea initiated an extensive tradition in metaphysics of arguing for/against certain entities on grounds of their allegedly contributing/failing to contribute explanatory power.

In "On What There Is," Quine appeals to failures to contribute to explanatory power in his argument against his imagined opponent McX, who holds that "Ontological statements follow immediately from all manner of casual statements of commonplace fact," so that, for example, "There is an attribute" follows from "There are red houses, red roses, red sunsets" (1948/1953, 10). In response, Quine writes: "That the houses and roses and sunsets are all of them red may be taken as ultimate and irreducible, and it may be held that *McX is no better off, in point of real explanatory power*, for all the occult entities which he posits under such names as 'redness'" (1948/1953, 10, italics mine). Similarly, in addressing the question of whether there are *meanings*, Quine writes that while we may speak of utterances as significant or insignificant, synonymous or heteronomous, "the explanatory value of special and irreducible intermediary entities called meanings is surely illusory" (1948/1953, 12).

Since Quine, this form of argument has become ubiquitous in metaphysics—both among those who accept and those who reject the existence of contested entities. So, while Quine rejects "positing" attributes or meanings, at least in part on grounds that they would not add any explanatory power,[19] others have argued that we must accept the existence of universal attributes to "explain" why certain predicates apply to certain individuals (see Katz 1998). This form of argument plays a crucial role among those who reject (or accept) entities as disparate as numbers, properties, meanings, fictional characters, composite objects, social groups, and minds. This criterion is also closely related to the "Eleatic" criterion of existence championed by David Armstrong (1997, 41–43) and Jaegwon Kim (1993), among many others. For the addition of explanatory power that warrants positing something's existence is presumably that it is capable of serving as a *causal explainer* of certain facts or observations.

Quine doesn't say why he thinks that accepting properties or meanings would not give McX any (additional) explanatory power. So why might one, with Quine, think that such entities don't add explanatory power to McX's "theory"?

Let us begin by considering ordinary empirical cases in which we think we *are* justified in positing an entity, or a kind of entity, because it would explain certain facts or observations. The paradigmatic cases for good inference to the best explanation arguments in ordinary empirical and scientific reasoning go like this: if we notice ragged holes in our packets of food and tiny feces on the floor, and hear scuffling in the night, we might make an inference to the best explanation and hypothesize that there are mice in the pantry, which are the cause of all of these observed effects. Doctors often hypothesize about the presence of microbes in the body as the best explanation of various observed

---

[19] Quine (1960) is also motivated to reject entities and properties on grounds of their lacking clear criteria of identity; indeed in *Word and Object* (ch. 2; also pp. 183–84 and 225), this is visible as his main reason for rejecting propositions. (Thanks to Jorge Ferreira for pointing this out). Nonetheless, the failure of such entities to add explanatory power also plays a visible role, which has been very influential on later work in metaphysics. It is the lingering emphasis on that criterion that is being examined here. I shall have to leave for elsewhere discussion of the idea that (alleged) entities should be rejected if they would lack clear criteria of identity (but see my (2020a, ch. 8) for discussion of how to understand and address such metaphysical modal indeterminacies).

symptoms. And Leverrier and Adams (independently) famously inferred the existence of a planet beyond Uranus as the best explanation of unexpected deviations in the orbit of Uranus. These are classic arguments for positing the existence of something in order to explain a phenomenon. And I think Quine is right in suspecting that—even if they are good in their home empirical contexts—arguments of this form can't be used to justify "positing" attributes or meanings.

Since Quine doesn't say why accepting attributes or meanings wouldn't add explanatory power to McX's "theory," let me suggest some reasons to doubt that it would. McX says that statements, say, about the existence of properties "follow immediately from all manner of casual statements of commonplace fact" (1953/2001, 10). That is, we can apparently derive nominative property talk or meaning talk, or come to quantify over properties and meanings (in the way that Quine treats as bringing "ontological commitment" to "new entities"), by means of trivial inferences from sentences that don't refer to any such entities. So, from "The house is red and the barn is red" we can apparently infer "The house has the property of redness and the barn has a property of redness" and "There is a property of redness that the barn and house have in common." Similarly: From the claim that the English word "dog" means the same as the German word "Hund," we can infer that "dog" has the same meaning as "Hund," and so that there is a meaning the words have in common.[20]

But if we are (as McX assumes) entitled to introduce new referring terms for these entities by hypostatizations from these simpler sentences, then the entities cannot be used to *explain* why the original sentences are true. I would rather not get caught up in debates about how to understand explanation in scientific cases, so let me start from a simple and (I hope) uncontroversial observation: Whatever an explanation is, dormitive virtue "explanations" are *not* genuine explanations. As Molière's old joke has it, the doctor offers only the illusion of explanation if you ask, "Why do poppies make us sleepy?"

---

[20] Of course, Quine would also reject the idea that there are such conceptual truths or analyticities underlying these inferences—but that is not the central point at issue here. Rather, it's that, if we accept McX's view, we do (as Quine insists) have reason to doubt that the relevant entities could add explanatory power.

and the doctor replies, "Because they have the dormitive virtue." You don't need a full-blown theory of explanation to recognize that, whatever explanation may be, dormitive virtue explanations are not explanatory.[21] Yet the following claims all have the pattern of dormitive virtue explanations: "The fact that barn is red is *explained by the fact that there is a property of redness possessed by the barn*," "The fact that the predicate 'red' applies to the barn *is explained by the fact* that there is a property of redness possessed by the barn," and the fact that "'dog' means the same as 'Hund'" *is explained by* "dog" and "Hund" having the same meaning."[22] In each case, we introduce a fancier, nominative form of speech (apparently referring to a property or meaning), but that cannot provide anything analogous to a scientific, causal explanation that might justify us in *positing* the explainer.[23] *Whatever* explanation may be, to restate a fact in fancier terms (or in different grammatical form) is not to explain it.[24]

Quine's McX thought that existence claims followed immediately—perhaps trivially—from all manner of commonplace fact. In my terms (2015a), McX was a defender of easy ontology. And I have aimed to flesh out Quine's intuition that *if we are thinking along McX's lines*, it seems that accepting the existence of properties and meanings will fail to add any real explanatory power to our theories.

---

[21] Some are inclined to respond: Well, maybe there *is* a real explanation in the wings here, at least—because a "dormitive virtue" is a certain chemical kind that can explain the effects of the flowers on drowsiness! But they have missed the joke: "dormitive virtue" here is just a nominalization out of "can make us sleepy"; that is why the doctor is being both pretentious and uninformative. A helpful and not funny reply would be to refer to some chemical kind(s) that could figure in a causal-explanatory story.

[22] Or: The fact that glass tends to break when struck is explained by the fact that the glass has the disposition of fragility.

[23] As will become clear later, I don't mean to suggest that the introduction of these nominal terms, and shift to a different grammatical form, serves *merely* to make the talk (or speaker) sound "fancier." There are various functions served by the change in grammatical form. I will return to this point in Chapter 7.

[24] Serious metaphysicians typically resist the idea that these are just restatements in alternative grammatical forms. But the fact that such trivial inferences are readily permitted in ordinary speech suggests that this *does* capture the introduction rules for the terms in ordinary English, and that those who think more is required are implicitly changing the rules. As I have argued elsewhere (2015), pressure may then be put on the serious metaphysician to clarify *what more is required* for the nominative statement to be true, beyond the truth of the uncontroversial statement with which we began. As I shall argue in Chapters 7 and 8, we can also get evidence from linguistics that the inferences are trivial.

The lesson to draw so far is that, if we do take claims that there *are* properties or meanings to follow by simple hypostatizations from claims like "The house is red and the barn is red" or "'dog' can be translated as 'Hund,'" then the relevant entities cannot aid in *explaining* the original facts. Thus far, Quine was right.[25]

Nonetheless, as we will see, a deeper understanding of easy arguments will also give us reason to think that contribution of novel explanatory power was a misguided criterion to begin with.

But should we accept easy inferences to existence? I have argued extensively elsewhere (2015a) that we should accept "easy" ontological arguments for the existence of things of various kinds—and that, as a result, we should not waste our time on protracted debates about whether meanings, numbers, properties, or tables "really exist."[26] The discussion here makes clear an important consequence of accepting easy arguments: that if you think the existence of certain metaphysically controversial entities follows trivially from other (noncontroversial) claims, you should not think of them as *explaining* the truth of those claims (or the facts stated in those claims).[27]

It is of course controversial whether we should accept that there are such valid "easy" arguments for the existence of properties, meanings,

---

[25] Not all claims to get "explanations" by "positing" certain metaphysical entities are as flat-footed as that—not all involve simply "positing" the entities to explain the observation (out of which the referring terms might be derived by hypostatization). Other sorts of explanatory claims would have to be addressed separately. Nor, as I have argued elsewhere (2015a, ch. 3), should one say in general that where we derive a noun term via a trivial inference, its referent can't explain *anything*. If Smith has high blood pressure, we can go on to make the trivial inference that Smith has the property of having high blood pressure. And that may figure in explaining, for example, why he suffers a heart attack. But it does not offer any "additional" explanatory power beyond the original claim, and certainly does not "explain" the truth of the original claim. The point here is that (provided that we accept that there are these trivial inferences), if an existence claim is derived by trivial inferences from an uncontroversial claim, it cannot contribute any *more* explanatory power than we got from the uncontroversial claim itself (Thomasson 2015a, 156).

[26] The original development of the idea behind easy ontology can be traced to Frege's (1884) view that a noun term, say, for "direction" can be introduced by simple inferences from, "Lines A and B are parallel" to "A and B have the same *direction*." For more recent developments and defenses of the idea, see, e.g., Hale and Wright (2001), Schiffer (2003) and my (2015a). These developments of the idea differ in significant ways, too. For comparison among them, see my (2015a, ch. 3).

[27] Cf. my (2015a, ch. 3).

and other contested entities.[28] Metaphysicians typically reject the trivial arguments. Instead, they think it is a highly *nontrivial* matter whether there are properties, and a nontrivial question whether the best "total metaphysical theory" will "posit" Platonic properties, Aristotelian *in rebus* universals, tropes, or some other variant. Some (following Quine 1953/2001 or, more recently, Williamson 2007) reject altogether the idea that there are the analytic entailments needed to get easy arguments off the ground.[29] Others think it would take something like "magic" for there to be analytic entailments that lead to conclusions that something (not mentioned in the original claim) *exists*.[30] Still others appeal to long-standing "bad company" objections that allege that the supposedly analytic inferences can lead us to contradiction or conflict with known fact.[31] There is not space here to review or respond to all of the reasons given against accepting easy arguments. For that I must refer readers to the lengthier discussions in my (2015a) and (2019).

Nonetheless, it may be worth reminding ourselves of the sorts of evidence we can appeal to *in favor* of the idea that there are such trivial entailments. What sort of evidence can we give that a conditional of ordinary English is analytic? One way to go is to appeal to our common responses and linguistic intuitions: We can (with Schiffer 1994, 1996, 2003) appeal to the felt redundancy of "The house is red *and* the house has the property of redness." We can appeal to our standard epistemic norms, which don't require further investigation to move from "The house is red" to "The house has the property of redness," whereas they do require further investigation to move from "The house is red" to "The house has a door." We can (with Strawson and Grice 1956) appeal to the different reactions we might have to someone who said, "The house is red and it's not the case that the house has a door" (doubt or disbelief), versus to someone who said, "The house is red and it's not the case that the house has the property of redness" (bewilderment, not knowing what to make of it). Or we can appeal to our different

---

[28] For criticisms of easy arguments see, e.g., Yablo (2000), Hofweber (2005), Bennett (2009), Eklund (2009), and Evnine (2016).
[29] I respond to these arguments in my (2007, ch. 2) and (2015a, ch. 7), respectively.
[30] For discussion and response see my (2015a, ch. 6).
[31] For discussion and response, see my (2015a, ch. 8).

reactions to someone who says, "The house is red, *so* the house has the property of redness," versus "The house is red, *so* the house has a door" (acceptance versus puzzlement at the non sequitur). We could appeal to the way in which we would correct those who violated or denied this rule—by aiming to understand what they might be trying to say, or by attempting to teach them the rule, rather than questioning their evidence. We could appeal to the inappropriateness of inserting "probably" in "The house is red so the house *probably* has the property of redness," although such insertions are normally appropriate where mere evidential support is in question ("The house is in Vermont so it *probably* has a pitched roof"). And we can note that these are precisely the kinds of clue we use to identify analyticities in other cases—cases metaphysicians have not made contentious. And in any case, we can either do this in the first person, by reflection on our own linguistic intuitions (and on the assumption, for each of us, that we are reasonably typical competent speakers), or we can engage in empirical analysis or experimental work to see how broadly shared these reactions and intuitions are across the linguistic community. We can also press the opponents (who insist that it isn't that easy, that something more is required) to give a clear and non-problematic view of *what more is needed*.[32]

Another point in favor of accepting that property terms, number terms, etc., are introduced by these sorts of rules—rules that take us from a non-referring use of a term ("red" in an attributive use or "two" in a determiner use) to the relevant noun terms—is that it gives us the basis for a plausible account of how these terms could be introduced to language and how the relevant entities could be known. That is, it makes clear how we can begin from the "core language" we use in describing the perceptible world around us to make inferences that enable us to acquire terms (on what Friederike Moltmann (2022) calls the "periphery") for abstract entities. If there are easy inferences licensed by introduction rules for the relevant terms, we can account for our ability to acquire the terms by appealing to how terms for properties, numbers, and the like are introduced to the language by

---

[32] See my (2013).

way of inferences from "core" parts of language (speaking of two red apples) to introduce derivative terms via these rules. But if we deny that there are such rules, then it is hard to see how terms for such abstract entities could be *learned*—for clearly nothing like worldly observation, tracking, or ostension will work here. Such an account also gives hope of helping with the notorious problem of how we could come to know about abstracta, given that we are not in causal contact with them. For (as neo-Fregeans in the philosophy of mathematics have aimed to show [e.g., Hale and Wright 2001]), if we can derive truths about abstract entities via an analytic route from other forms of talk and other truths, we can see how we could come to know truths about numbers, properties, or other abstracta. In short, there is hope for getting an account of how we could learn the relevant forms of language and come to know truths about the relevant kinds of objects, if there are trivial inferences. But those who deny that there are the relevant rules owe us an account of both how we could learn the terminology and how we could come to know about the relevant entities.

If we do take seriously the linguistic evidence that it is redundant to say (for example), "The house is red *and* the house has the property of redness," then we have reason to reject the idea that whether there *really are* such things as properties, meanings, and numbers is a deep, theoretic question warranting extensive ontological debate. But if we take this route, a new question arises: *Why would we have, or want, a language with such redundancies built in?*[33] Some might even think: Surely our language can't be so redundant; so there must be *more* required for the metaphysical criteria to be met!

To answer questions about why we would want a language with such redundancies, we should turn to work in linguistics—as I will, in Chapters 7 and 8 below. As I will argue there, work in systemic functional linguistics gives us some new reasons to think that the trivial inferences are perfectly acceptable. For it gives us a deep and plausible account of why we would *want* a language that enables us to make such redundant grammatical transformations—given that it enables us to fulfill crucial new linguistic *functions*, enabling us to do things with

---

[33] This is a question I did not address in my (2015a) and have only recently found an answer to, in systemic functional linguistics.

language that we couldn't otherwise do, or do so easily. This work in functional linguistics will also help show why it was misguided to ever expect terms like "property," "meaning," and the like to play a similar role to terms for mice, planets, or microbes—in referring to "posits" that could add "explanatory power" to our theories. For, as we will see, their roles in our theories are functionally very different.

2.3 Other Functional Roles

But even before coming to that work in linguistics, we can note that recent philosophical work already points to the ways nominalizations of various kinds (including terms for numbers, properties, propositions, and other abstracta) can figure in and aid in our scientific-explanatory theories in *other* ways than serving to name observed or unobserved "explainers." For example, they can lend expressive power to the language, simplify our statements of theory or law, enable us to give a unified articulation of what is to be explained, and so on. Laws are involved in explanations, and Stephen Yablo (2005) argues that reference to numbers enables us to finitely state physical laws that it would otherwise take an infinitely long series of infinitely long sentences to state—thereby simplifying and improving our explanations. Alejandro Perez Carballo (2016) argues that mathematics gives us a picture of logical space "rich in structural propositions," which can help us get propositions with "high explanatory value" and systematize data and make predictions without getting lost in irrelevant detail (2016, 475). Agustin Rayo (2009, 25) argues that learning logical truths is useful because it increases one's ability to distinguish between intelligible and unintelligible scenarios, and to use old information in new ways. For example, one can move from the information that there are 7 apples and 12 pears to the information that there are 19 pieces of fruit (Rayo 2009, 26). This isn't a matter of acquiring new information, but of using old information in new ways, enabling us to answer new questions like "how many pieces of fruit?" (Rayo 2009, 27). And I have argued elsewhere (2015a, 157 n. 23) that introducing new noun terms might pragmatically enhance our ability to formulate explanations. For example, medical researchers might do better to have a noun term "heart attack" to enable them to demand, and perhaps ultimately give (in general terms), an explanation of why heart attacks occur, rather than having to put things in terms of explaining why Smith's heart stopped beating, and why Lopez's heart stopped beating, and why ... Similarly, while we may not have much use for explaining what a red house and a red barn have in common, we might have far more use for property talk in explaining *what properties all or most of the severe Covid-19 patients have in common* (is it the property of *being of a certain age*, of *having a certain blood type*, or of *having certain preexisting conditions*, or *having a certain level of exposure*, or ... ?). Using property terms can help us in *formulating* explanations, as it may (for example) enable us to *express* certain kinds of question, such as, "What do severe Covid-19 patients have in common?" Similarly, as Sally Haslanger's (2012) work suggests, some important *questions* (*Why is it that African Americans have a higher rate of police stops?*) cannot even be formulated as demands for explanation without having something like race terms in our vocabulary.

In short, we need not deny that terms for entities like properties, events, numbers, and propositions may *figure in* and play important roles in enabling, enhancing, and simplifying our explanations. But this emphatically does *not* mean that the entities are "posited" as metaphysical "explainers" in the way that mice or microbes are. As we have seen above, we have reason to deny that typical entities contested in metaphysical debates, such as meanings, properties, and numbers, "fuel" a theory's success (even though the relevant terms may usefully *figure* in our theories). For, as we have seen, claims about their existence can be "subtracted out" from the relevant predictive theories and thus can't be thought to be confirmed with the theory. The terms may be centrally useful (or even ineliminable) in formulating explanatory theories (and the terms may be introduced in a way that guarantees that they refer), without the *entities* serving as "posited explainers" that fuel the empirical success of the theory.

This brings us to an important point often overlooked by serious metaphysicians: that our terms may serve many different *functions*. It is an idea clearly visible in work by Wittgenstein, Ryle, Austin, and Sellars, and more recently in work in the neo-pragmatist tradition by people like Huw Price, Michael Williams, and Robert Brandom.[34] There are some terms (perhaps: "wolf," "river") that are observationally introduced, whose job is to co-vary with (and enable us to communicate about, track, and learn more about) some external factor or environmental condition. Other terms are *theoretically* introduced to refer to (as yet unobserved) theoretic entities that would fuel an *explanation* of our observations (perhaps: "electron," "black hole"). Still others play entirely different roles—and many of those terms that refer (if at all) to entities contested in specifically ontological debates appear to serve functions *other than* tracking entities or fueling explanations. Perhaps nominative number terms function to enable us to state laws in finite form that couldn't be otherwise stated, and/or to systematize data in ways that enable us to see patterns and get explanations we wouldn't otherwise get. Perhaps talk of properties or events enables us (inter alia) to state in briefer and more unified terms what it is that needs explaining, or to unify and/or simplify the explanations given. I don't want to commit to any specific functional theses here—I will return to these issues later. I aim only to point to the idea that *alternative functional stories* come naturally once we see these terms not as aiming to refer to entities that would *fuel* our explanations, but as terms that nonetheless may *figure* usefully in them.

If the proper role of terms for properties is not to fuel explanations, but rather to enable us (for example) to even simply ask *questions* about what various patients had in common, then the failure of "posited" properties to "fuel our explanations" should be no mark against introducing and making full use of property vocabulary. If the functional role of nominative number terms includes enabling us to simplify our statements of laws or to structure logical space in a way that is epistemically useful (Perez Carballo 2016, 461), then the fact that numbers don't themselves serve as causal explainers is no knock against them. On this view, in short, where Quine (and many who followed him) went wrong is not in *denying* that such entities can be *explainers* (carefully stated, there is a sense in which this is exactly right). Instead, we go astray if we assume that contribution of explanatory power *is*

---

[34] The idea also plays a key role in expressivist work on moral discourse, for example by Simon Blackburn (1993) and Allan Gibbard (1990).

a relevant criterion for accepting forms of language that enable us to quantify over meanings, properties, or numbers.

A common response at this stage is to insist that my opponents, too, could accept that certain terms may (also) play these roles in explanation or elsewhere. There is, it is true, nothing to stop them from accepting these assessments. Welcome aboard. But if (in acknowledging these other roles) they accept that the role of the relevant terms is *not* to refer to a posited entity to fuel explanations, then *why should the ability to contribute explanatory power be a relevant criterion for accepting the entities*? Alternative functional stories should be equally plausible for everyone, but the point here is that they undermine the across-the-board use of an explanatory power criterion and undermine the explanatory view of the project of metaphysics. They also, fully understood, support the easy ontological view that *there are* such entities—rendering deep metaphysical inquiries about whether there "really" are numbers, properties, etc. out of place.

Could one, however, simply retreat to the holistic version of an explanatory criterion—not requiring that each posited entity serve to fuel our explanations, but holding that we should accept the existence of all and only those entities over which we must quantify in our best total explanatory theory? This has not been ruled out yet—it is consistent with the idea that reference to numbers or properties may play other roles in our explanations, and that (given that), we should therefore "posit" them even if they aren't themselves playing the role of causal explainers.

Yet it looks acceptable only as long as we keep blinders on that prevent us from noticing the many, diverse functions language serves. Quine had such blinders on—caring only about the work and discourse of natural science. What he said may be fine in the area of his attention, but we should be cautious about generalizing it.

What we have seen so far about the diverse functional roles of different forms of vocabulary should give us pause even in accepting this holistic version of an explanatory approach to metaphysics. As has become clear from the discussion so far, those who take contribution of explanatory power to be an important criterion for whether or not we accept that there are entities of any kind fail to acknowledge an important point: *that there may be different functional roles* for different forms of language. When we are theorizing, we may sometimes introduce terms to track things we observe, and we may sometimes introduce terms for (as yet) unobserved entities that are "posited" to explain various observed phenomena. But we are not *always* doing that. In fact, *we are not always theorizing at all.*

Consider debates about whether there are chances, moral properties, and natural properties. Such debates often have centered around questions about whether such entities could *explain* why our credences should be guided in certain ways, why we should act in certain ways, or why we should theorize in certain terms (see Sider 2011). But there are familiar problems with these attempted "explanations." Shamik Dasgupta (2018) argues that, even if we accept such metaphysical posits, they can't do the work of explaining *why* our credences, theorizing, or actions *should* be guided by them. As he puts it (roughly): Posit whatever whatnots you like, they can't explain why we *ought to* believe, theorize, or act this way. This is what Dasgupta calls the "problem of missing value." As Dasgupta nicely emphasizes, the problem of missing value arises in questions about why moral facts should be action-guiding, why chances should be credence-guiding, and (the case he newly presses) why natural facts or properties *should* guide our theorizing. In each case, the metaphysician "posits" some feature of the world that is supposed to have normative import: for how we should act, believe, or theorize. In each case, the problem of missing value arises with the demand to *explain why* our action, beliefs, or theorizing should be guided by this worldly feature (Dasgupta 2018, 287). And in each case, there seems to be no adequate explanation available, since the entities "posited" are (in Dasgupta's words) "normatively inert" (2018, 289).

Here again, the metaphysical "posit" seems unable to *explain* why we *should* act, believe, or theorize in certain ways. And here again, we might be able to see why we can't get genuine explanation, if we take talk of moral facts and properties (say) to arise from hypostatizations that take us from, for example, from "You shouldn't kill"[35] to "Killing

---

[35] Plausibly, this inference is only valid when the first ("You shouldn't kill") is uttered as a *categorical imperative*, not a mere recommendation or imperative of prudence. For more on the role understanding this series of grammatical shifts plays in metaethics, see Warren and Thomasson (2023) and my (in progress).

has the property of being morally wrong" and "It is a moral fact that killing is wrong." For as we have seen, such hypostatized claims cannot *explain* the original "should" claims from which they are derived.

The problem of missing value gives us good reason to deny that "positing" such things can "explain" our norms. It is also unlikely that we will have to quantify over moral properties or requirements anywhere in our best scientific, explanatory theories—so moving to the more holistic version of an explanatory requirement won't show that they aid in theories that explain anything else. Does that mean that we shouldn't accept that there are moral properties? I think that's a good conclusion to draw *only if* these terms have *an explanatory function*, and indeed only if all we ever (should) aim to do with language is to build explanatory theories. But we have good reason to deny this.

I have argued above that many nominalized terms may play useful roles in explanation and theory construction, *even when they do not function to refer to posited "explainers."*[36] But now we can go beyond this. For attending (for example) to moral discourse makes it clear that the functions of an area of discourse *needn't have anything to do with explaining at all.* For it is plausible that moral discourse fundamentally serves some kinds of *prescriptive, regulative, expressive*, or (broadly) *normative* function. As Ryle put it, "We are ready to discuss the truth of ethical statements . . . but the point of making such statements is to regulate parts of people's conduct" (1949, 128).[37] Of course, many proposals have been developed in this vicinity, from the early forms of prescriptivism developed by Stevenson (1937) and Hare (1952) to the expressivisms of Blackburn (1993) and Gibbard (1990). More recently one can see suggestions that moral discourse acts as a kind of "chaperone for human behavior" (Warren 2015) or provides a kind of "social glue, bonding individuals together in a shared justificatory structure and providing a tool for solving many group coordination problems" (Joyce 2006, 117). We needn't settle these disputes here. The point for now is simply that it is at least highly plausible that moral

---

[36] I will be able to give more detail of and justification for this view when we get to the discussion of "grammatical metaphors" in systemic functional linguistics in Chapter 7.

[37] For further development of these ideas about the distinctive functional roles of various forms of moral discourse, see Warren and Thomasson (2023) and Thomasson (in progress).

terms (to choose but one example) serve useful functions in our lives together that may *not* be best characterized as serving in an explanatory scientific theory—and the Quinean is not entitled to assume that that is the only legitimate function of any terms.

In short, even assuming that adding reference to moral properties doesn't add explanatory power to a theory, the move to say, "Such entities wouldn't add explanatory power" so "we shouldn't say there are such things" is a complete wrong turn, a non sequitur. And even if we needn't quantify over such things in our best explanatory theories, that doesn't give us any reason to reject them. If I am right that such terms were never *supposed to function* in an *explanatory* way (whether as fueling explanations or as contributors to an explanatory theory), then the failure of their (alleged) referents to *explain* is no knock against them.[38]

We should reject the explanatory power *criterion*, not the entities.[39]

2.4 Diagnosing the Underlying Mistake

I have argued that the explanatory approach to metaphysics, which has directed a great deal of metaphysical work over the past three-quarters of a century, falls prey to the familiar difficulties of a rivalry with science and epistemological mystery. More important for present purposes, I have argued that it relies on an unargued presupposition: that the

---

[38] Of course, this is not to deny that some forms of "explanation" may be relevant in moral philosophy: We may, of course, look to general moral principles in explaining how to resolve concrete moral dilemmas or problems of applied ethics, for example. But these senses of "explanation," which involve an appeal to general normative principles to derive applications and the like, are very different from the *causal* explanations we seek in our scientific explanations and "best total explanatory theories." It is the latter, taken as a scientistic approach to metaphysics, that I am arguing against.

[39] Another consequence that's interesting and important from my point of view is this: I have argued elsewhere (2015a, 156ff) that the "easy approach to ontology" can get us a form of "simple realism" about many kinds of entity—saying that there are numbers, properties, events, modal facts, etc. *in the only sense that has sense.* What it can't get us is a form of *explanatory realism* that would take these entities to explain certain observations, or to "explain what makes the relevant discourse true." But now we can see that this is no loss. For the tendency to think such explanations should be forthcoming is the product of an unreflective assumption that the function of these forms of discourse is explanatory.

noun terms at issue in metaphysical debates (including terms for animals, artifacts, numbers, obligations, rights, properties, possibilities, etc.) all serve an *explanatory* function.

The crucial lesson here is that controversial metaphysical "posits" do not typically add "explanatory power" that "fuels" a theory's explanation. And appeals to metaphysical whatnots typically can't explain why we *ought to* do anything either. But the underlying problem is not with saying there are such entities. Instead, the mistake arises from a scientistic conception of metaphysics that presents metaphysics as in the business of positing entities to fuel our explanations.[40]

If the above is correct, it has several important consequences. One is that we should give up using "explanatory power" as a criterion for whether or not we accept that there are certain entities. Whether we formulate this as a demand that, to accept the existence of Ks, Ks themselves must fuel our explanations, or as the looser demand that we should accept the existence of Ks only if we must quantify over them in our best explanatory theories, the demand can only look suitable if we are blind to the other roles terms serve in explanation (for the first formulation), and (for the second) if we are blind to the many functions areas of language serve, other than to formulate explanatory theories.

Along these lines, we should also give up using quasi-scientific terminology to characterize what we're doing and give up talking in terms of metaphysical "theories" and "posits." Some readers may have noticed my use of scare quotes whenever I have used the terms "posit" and "theory" above. I can now clarify why I distance myself in this way.[41] To treat entities such as properties, meanings, numbers, and other entities contested in metaphysics as "posits" of certain metaphysical "theories" is to suggest that the existence of these entities is something like an empirical hypothesis, to be confirmed or disconfirmed by further evidence. Some people are undoubtedly attracted to this—perhaps in hopes that it will lend metaphysics the respectability of the sciences.

---

[40] As Price puts it, "this kind of functional pluralism challenges a kind of monofunctional conception of language that seems implicit in Quine's own view—for Quine, *the* significant task of the statement-making part of language is that of recording the conclusions of an activity that is ultimately continuous with natural science" (2011, 13).

[41] I have similar reservations about speaking of metaphysical "explanations," as it is prone to encourage an inappropriate model of what metaphysics can do.

But it leads us down the wrong path, encouraging us to ask the wrong questions ("What facts can these entities enable us to explain?") and to employ inappropriate standards in answering questions about what there is (insisting that entities we accept should contribute explanatory power to our "theories").

The misleading terminology is symptomatic of the underlying problems that come from assuming that metaphysics gives, or should give, theories that are *like scientific theories*, and that the criteria for accepting or rejecting the existence of any entities should be thought of as a matter of asking *whether we should posit them as explainers.*

The underlying trouble with thinking of metaphysics on a scientific model is this. As I noted at the start, metaphysics has traditionally been concerned with all kinds of topics in life or—put in the linguistic mode—all kinds of areas of discourse. This breadth is part of what gives it claim to do something different from the sciences. Metaphysics inquires about moral properties, modal facts, objects and properties, persons and actions, causes and events, mental states, and (increasingly) interesting social phenomena such as genders, races, classes, and the like.

In adopting an explanatory power criterion, serious metaphysics imposes standards suitable for scientific theories onto ontological questions. This is a mistake. Science may aim to causally explain and predict. But not all discourse does. Subjecting it all to the same standards is like evaluating all artifacts—from knives to hairdryers to coffee mugs—according to how well they cut steak. Even *within* science, as we have seen, terms may fulfill many different functions—not just serving to quantify over entities that are meant to fuel our explanations. *Beyond* science we have a far wider range of functions our language serves to fulfill—in regulating our conduct, conveying rules of use for our terms, assigning praise and blame, guiding our methods of reasoning, etc.

If the job of metaphysics includes assessing all these traditional and contemporary topics, then we need to begin by assessing how each of these forms of discourse works and what functions it serves—without just forcing them all into a quasi-scientific mold and assessing them by criteria suitable for a scientific-explanatory theory.

The crucial lesson here is that we should give up thinking of metaphysics as analogous to or continuous with science. Nor should we even think of the job of metaphysics as aiming to discover what "really exists." We might do better to start a step back. Before asking traditional metaphysical questions about the putative referents of our terms—their explanatory power, their causal efficacy, their relation to "natural" objects—we should stop to ask why we have such terms in our vocabulary, what functions they serve, and by what rules they come to enter language. Then we might find we can really make progress. We should question the underlying functional monist assumption, taking seriously the idea that language may serve many functions.

I will next turn to make the case that a similar functional monist mistake underlies other popular ways of thinking of the work of metaphysics—whether we think of it as engaged in addressing questions of structure, truthmakers, fundamentality, grounding, or metaphysical explanation. This enables me to show how thoroughly the "metaphysical malady" permeates various approaches to metaphysics which, despite their differences, all rely on the false assumption that all of the many forms of discourse considered in metaphysics serve the same function.

But what can we mean by "function" here? How can we make good on the idea that language may serve many functions—and come to know what functions various parts of language serve? What difference would acknowledging and developing a kind of functional pluralist approach make to our philosophical work? I will return to these questions in Part II, where I aim to develop the positive approach to understanding linguistic functions, to show how doing so can enable us to unravel a variety of old metaphysical problems, and to develop a plausible and powerful way of rethinking metaphysics as conceptual engineering.[42]

---

[42] Thanks go to Peter Lewis, Ted Locke, Michelle Moody Adams, Mark Povich, Katherine Ritchie, and audiences at Columbia University and the University of New Hampshire for very helpful input and comments on prior versions of some of this material.

3
The Structural Conception of Metaphysics

As we have seen, the neo-Quinean conception of metaphysics was thought to have revived metaphysics. For decades, it set metaphysicians on the project of addressing the question "What exists?", employing broadly explanatory criteria. But in the 21st century, increasing doubts have been raised about this conception of metaphysics, and alternative ways of looking at metaphysics have been developed. The explanatory conception of metaphysics inspired by Quine's work has played such a central role in the revival of metaphysics that all the other approaches since then have been developed explicitly out of dissatisfactions of various sorts with the neo-Quinean approach.

One recent and influential development is Theodore Sider's view that metaphysics is (or should be) about *structure*.[1] As Sider boldly puts it:

> Metaphysics, at bottom, is about the fundamental structure of reality. Not about what's necessarily true. Not about what properties are essential. Not about conceptual analysis. Not about what there is. Structure. (2011, 1)

Sider's project, like the neo-Quinean project, involves adopting a scientific view of metaphysics: that metaphysics is involved in discovering the "fundamental structure of the world" (a project one

---

[1] For interesting criticisms of Sider's approach, along entirely different lines than those developed here, see Donaldson (2015), who argues that there is no good reason to think that the existential quantifier is more "natural" than predicate functors, and Dasgupta (2018), who argues that even if we accept that there are some "natural" properties in the world, we cannot bridge the is/ought gap to say that we *should* theorize in those terms.

might have thought of as a scientific project), and is confirmed as part of a best total (scientific) theory. Yet Sider also explicitly broadens the conception of metaphysics beyond the neo-Quinean focus on questions about what there is. He adopts a strong realism about structure, taken as the view that "the world has a distinguished structure, a privileged description" (2011, vii). The task of metaphysics, on Sider's view, is not to answer questions about what exists, but rather to discover this *structure*—and thereby also determine what *concepts* we should use:

> For a representation to be fully successful, truth is not enough; the representation must also use the right concepts, so that its conceptual structure matches reality's structure. (2011, vii)

Thus, on this approach, the project of metaphysics comes to include questions not just of what exists—of ontology—but also of "ideology": of what concepts we should use to "write the book of the world."

Sider introduces a crucial innovation to make this project work—to enable us to link questions about the *concepts* we should use with questions about the *metaphysical* structure of the world. That innovation is to generalize the idea from David Armstrong (1978) and David Lewis (1983/1999) that some predicates stand for *natural* features of the world, while others do not. On the Armstrong/Lewis view, while some predicates (say, "is grue" or "is a cow or an electron") are clearly gerrymandered, others (say, "is an electron") more plausibly reflect genuine similarities and differences in the world. Lewis (1983/1999), following a suggestion by Gary Merrill (1980), had introduced the idea of "naturalness" in part to respond to Hilary Putnam's concerns about the indeterminacy of reference, by insisting that *the world* can help relieve the indeterminacy—as reference consists "in part" in "the eligibility of the referent. And this eligibility to be referred to is a matter of natural properties" (1983/1999, 47).[2] Correct interpretations of a language, on Lewis's view, must do more than make the right sentences come out as true and false. They must also, "as much as possible, assign

---

[2] Armstrong (1978) introduced a similar idea of "sparse" predicates as the only ones that pick out universals.

natural properties and relations... to predicates" (Sider 2011, 26). On this view, some properties are more "natural" than others, and those act as (what later came to be called) "reference magnets" to attract the reference of predicates and thereby help relieve us of the indeterminacy of reference. Those predicates that are "attracted" to refer to the (perfectly) natural properties, in Sider's terms, "carve the world (perfectly) at the joints."

Sider's innovation is to broaden this idea of "joint-carving" to evaluate *all kinds of* terms, not just predicates: "Just as Lewis and Armstrong ask which predicates get at the world's structure, we can also ask which function symbols, predicate modifiers, sentence operators, variable binders, and so on, get at the world's structure" (2011, 85). In this way, "the question of joint-carving can be raised for predicate modifiers, sentential connectives, and expressions of other grammatical categories" (2011, vii).

Sider then uses this generalized notion of structure as a standard in terms of which *any* concept (not just those expressed by predicates) can be evaluated. So, regardless of whether metaphysical disputes are presented in terms of predicates, quantifiers, tense operators, modal operators, or whatever (2011, 86), we can ask whether the disputes are "cast in joint-carving terms" (2011, 67). For example, Sider argues that modal concepts and tensed concepts fail to "carve at the joints" but that logical concepts do. Those concepts we should use (Sider insists) are those that "carve nature at the joints."

For Sider, one goal of broadening the notion of "structure" in this way was to respond to accusations that many disputes of metaphysics are not substantive but are merely verbal disputes. Sider uses the idea of joint-carvingness as a way to evaluate whether various metaphysical (or other) disputes are substantive: Whether or to what extent a dispute is substantive "depends on how well its crucial expressions carve at the joints" (2011, 86).[3] He applies this understanding of "substantivity," for example, to respond to arguments (pioneered by Eli Hirsch) that many metaphysical debates about *what there is* are merely "verbal disputes,"

---

[3] More precisely, questions are non-substantive if their answers "turn on which of a range of equally good meanings we choose for the words in those questions" (Sider 2011, 46). For a still more precise formulation and discussion, see Sider (2011, 46–54).

in which participants talk past each other. For Hirsch argued (2002a, 2002b) that there are many different possible meanings of "there is" and of the quantifier, with no special "privileged" meaning. As a result, when we have two disputants (one of whom asserts, say, that there are tables, while the other denies it), if we interpret them charitably, we may take them to each be uttering truths in their own language, with their own use of the quantifier.[4]

In response, Sider uses his notion of "joint-carving" terms to argue that there is one *distinguished, joint-carving* meaning of the quantifier. Metaphysicians (Sider suggests) can agree to introduce a new language, "Ontologese" with a quantifier that is *stipulated* to "carve at the joints" (2011, 172):

> Ontological questions in Ontologese are substantive, even if those in ordinary language are not. Moreover, Ontologese is a better language, since its structure better matches reality's structure. (2011, 172)

If metaphysicians can introduce an Ontologese quantifier, Sider argues, they can thereby guarantee that their debates about what there is (phrased in terms of that quantifier) are substantive.

Some of the problems that immediately arise for Sider's structural approach to metaphysics are by now familiar. One is that (taken as a sole or central project for metaphysics) it is overly narrow—in a way that invites rivalry with the sciences and threatens to neglect or devalue many interesting projects in metaphysics. Another is that (like the explanatory conception, and for much the same reasons), it leaves us with an epistemological mystery about how we could come to know the answers to the relevant questions of metaphysics.[5] But the underlying problem, as we will see, is again that it assumes a kind of functional monism that prevents us from seeing the many different functions different forms of language have, and the different sorts of

---

[4] If we interpret them as speaking English literally, however, Hirsch suggests that it will often be the case that at least one of the disputants is saying something plainly false.

[5] See Jared Warren (2016) for an argument that beliefs about structure would be a matter of luck, if structural facts are supposed to be objective, mind independent, and acausal.

criteria by which they are appropriately evaluated. I will treat these three sorts of problem in turn.

3.1 Problems for the Structural Conception

Sider clearly develops a scientistic picture in taking the work of metaphysics to be about "the fundamental structure of reality," aiming at "insight into what the world is like, at the most fundamental level" (2011, 1)—a task many would have thought belongs to physics. Elizabeth Barnes (2014) and Mari Mikkola (2017) criticize Sider's reconception of metaphysics for failing to leave room for other topics in metaphysics—particularly feminist metaphysics. For "feminist metaphysics is *not* about fundamentality and it does not consider gender or sex to be fundamental—the nature of gender is not carved in reality's joints" (Mikkola 2017, 2440). According to all disputants, such phenomena as gender and social structures are not *fundamental*, and none of the competing candidate meanings for such terms are thought to be (very) joint-carving. As Barnes puts it:

> In response to criticisms that metaphysics is somehow confused or illegitimate, proponents of the discipline have tried to characterize *what metaphysics is* in a way that avoids such scepticism. Many attempts to do this have focused extensively—in various ways—on the idea of fundamentality. And such attempts have made the discipline increasingly hostile to the prospect of feminist metaphysics. (2014, 347–48)

The same could be said for many other topics of interest in metaphysics—work in social ontology, the ontology of art, and many other areas. All of these are left behind if we merely seek to understand the fundamental structure of reality.

To his credit, Sider has admitted this difficulty and has sought to correct it. He acknowledges that he suggested that the central goal of metaphysics is to inquire into the fundamental nature of reality ("The truly central question of metaphysics is that of what is *most* fundamental" (Sider 2011, 5)) and that this portrays feminist metaphysics as less important. He writes in conciliatory mode:

> I suggested that *the* central goal of metaphysics is to inquire into the fundamental nature of reality. Not only does this have the vice of inaccuracy, it also has a moral vice in contexts where metaphysics is esteemed: feminist metaphysics is not counted as central metaphysics and hence portrayed as less important. Metaphysics certainly includes many questions other than those about fundamental reality, questions about the nature of race and gender among them, and I wish I hadn't suggested otherwise. (2017, 2468)

He goes on to argue that his approach *is*, however, compatible with taking some questions of feminist metaphysics to be substantive (for being phrased in fundamental terms is [roughly] a sufficient condition for being substantive, but not a necessary condition [2017, 2470]). We needn't enter into those disputes here.

The point here is to note how narrow such fundamentality conceptions of metaphysics are. Thinking of metaphysics in this way abandons much of the interesting work in metaphysics and lands us squarely back in the problems of rivalry with science. For if the task is to "inquire into the fundamental nature of reality," then isn't that what physics does, and with better epistemological credentials?

Sider might reply that he can still treat the task of metaphysics as *more general*, as we can address questions that physicists don't: questions about whether modality, tense, quantifiers, and the like are joint-carving terms. But this brings us to a further, equally familiar problem: epistemological mystery. For how could we hope to come to know these facts about structure? Sider is sensitive to this problem and discusses it up front, admitting:

> The epistemology of metaphysics is far from clear; this any metaphysician should concede. For what it's worth, I prefer the vague, vaguely Quinean, thought that metaphysics is continuous with science. We employ many of the same criteria—whatever those are— for theory choice within metaphysics that we employ outside of metaphysics. Admittedly, those criteria give less clear guidance in

metaphysics than elsewhere; but there's no harm in following this argument where it leads: metaphysical inquiry is by its nature comparatively speculative and uncertain. (2011, 12)

We have already seen Sider's response to the epistemological puzzle in Chapter 2: it is to suggest (roughly following Quine) that our metaphysical views are confirmed *along with some best total (broadly scientific) theory of which they are a part*. (We have also already seen there [in section 2.1] the problems with thinking that the specifically *ontological* content of a theory is confirmed with it.) Sider takes the same approach for understanding the epistemology of structure, arguing that both the *ontology* of a theory and claims that its *ideology* is joint-carving can be confirmed along with the broader scientific theories they are in:

> A good theory isn't merely likely to be *true*. Its ideology is also likely to carve at the joints. For the conceptual decisions made in adopting that theory—and not just the theory's ontology—were vindicated; those conceptual decisions also took part in a theoretical success, and also inherit a borrowed luster. So we can add to the Quinean advice: regard the ideology of your best theory as carving at the joints. We have defeasible reason to believe that the conceptual decisions of successful theories correspond to something real: reality's structure. (2011, 12)

As a result, Sider argues, "we can *support* claims about joint-carving by showing that the ideology in question is part of a good theory" (2011, 14).

At least a large part of what makes a theory "good" is that it is *well confirmed*, which comes with success at prediction and explanation. In some cases that might have to do with a predicate's "carving the world at the joints"—or, less metaphorically and more neutrally, serving in a wide range of law-like generalizations. Plausibly, some biological terms do this better than others (think of the improvements in moving to a concept of "fish" that excluded aquatic mammals).[6]

---

[6] See Carnap (1950/1962), 5–6. But also see current debates about whether we need to replace the "fish" concept altogether: https://medium.com/illumination/there-is-no-such-thing-as-a-fish-eca048dd6163.

But to think that this is the *only* virtue that elements of our ideology could have is to exhibit a kind of blindness to the *many* different, important roles that different concepts can play in our successful theories.[7] We have already seen in Chapter 2 some suggestions about other important roles played by number talk, in enabling us to simplify statements of law (Yablo 2005) or systematize data (Perez Carballo 2016); and by property talk in enabling us to formulate explanatory demands. To show that a concept figures in a successful theory does not, on its own, give us reason to think that it "carves nature at the joints"—only to think that it is doing *something* useful for us in formulating and using those theories. But (as we will see most clearly with work on systemic functional linguistics discussed in Chapter 7) there are *many* ways in which parts of our conceptual scheme and language can prove useful in developing scientific theories—for example, in enabling us to generalize and to qualify and quantify processes and events, and enabling us to form ordered chains of generalized explanations.

3.2 The Underlying Problem: Functional Monism

But Sider's proposed project for metaphysics suffers from a deeper problem. Like other attempts to take metaphysics to be more purely *general* than the sciences, his generalizing move threatens to obscure crucial *functional* differences between discourse that does in some sense aim to track structure (say, natural kind structure) and discourse (including logical, moral, and modal discourse) that has very different functional roles.

Like the explanatory conception, Sider's vision for metaphysics is based on focusing on one sort of human activity: scientific inquiry. And he sees that as having one point: "the point of human inquiry—or a large chunk of it anyway, a chunk that includes physics—is to *conform*

---

[7] To say nothing of the many roles terms can play *outside* of our theories. For after all (as mentioned in Chapter 2) theorizing is only *one* among many important and worthwhile human activities.

itself to the world. . . . The world is 'out there,' and our job is to wrap our minds around it" (2011, 18). He also seeks to model metaphysical knowledge on scientific knowledge: "metaphysical knowledge is continuous with science. We employ many of the same criteria—whatever those are—for theory choice within metaphysics that we employ outside of metaphysics . . . [though] metaphysical inquiry is by its nature comparatively speculative and uncertain" (2011, 12). And he considers only one role for terms to play in our theories: to "carve nature at the joints."

Since Sider thinks of metaphysics as concerned with "structure," seeking "insight into what the world is like, at the most fundamental level" (2011, 1), he proposes thinking of classic metaphysical questions in these terms, asking questions such as whether mentality, mathematical entities, or nomic notions have a place "in a fundamental description of the world" (2011, 6), or whether modal concepts, tensed concepts, etc. "carve at the joints" (2011, 7).

Of course, metaphysics has long been concerned with all kinds of topics (material objects, consciousness, numbers, causation, modality, morality, etc.). So, thinking of metaphysics in this way requires broadening the conception of "structure" and of "joint-carving" beyond its original home in evaluating predicates for naturalness. And as we have seen, Sider's central innovation is to *generalize* the conception of structure. On his generalization, we can aptly ask of terms in *any grammatical category, concerned with any topic*, if they "carve nature at the joints" and evaluate them accordingly. This conception of structure "must allow us to ask, of expressions of any grammatical category [and concerned with any topic], whether they carve at the joints" (Sider 2011, 8).

But this is exactly where the mistake comes in. Generalizing the notion of "structure" in this way and using it to evaluate terms *of any sort* assumes that *all of* the terms of interest in metaphysics (including modal and moral terms, tense operators and quantifiers, etc.) function, or should function, as predicates used in scientific theories do: to "carve the world at its joints" or *track structure*. For only if they have the same function is it appropriate to *evaluate them* according to whether they carve nature at the joints or not (as Sider says simply: "joint-carving languages and beliefs are better" [2011, 65]). Sider's approach, in short, relies on an unquestioned functional monism that treats all terms on the model of predicates used in scientific theories—thought of as terms that are *supposed to* appear in our explanatory theories to track natural kind structure.

There are good reasons, however, for doubting this functional monist thesis. I can only fully develop these doubts (along with an alternative functional assessment) after the work on linguistic function in Chapter 7. I have argued elsewhere (2015a, ch. 10), however, that the idea that *logical* terms (quantifiers, conjunction, disjunction, etc.) "carve at the joints" arises from a mistake about the functions of logical terms—taking them to be tracking logical features of the world, when in fact we have reason to deny that they aim to *track* or *describe* features of the world at all (as our natural kind terms plausibly do) or aim to "map structure." Instead (I argue), there is reason to think that our logical terms serve useful functions of enabling us to *reason* with and from our other judgments (2015a, 315).[8] I have also argued elsewhere (2020a and 2023) that *modal* terms function not to describe possible worlds or track modal features of this world but rather to serve *normative* functions—enabling us to convey, make explicit, and reason with and from rules and permissions of various kinds (2020a, 63). Neo-pragmatists and expressivists have suggested alternative functional views of other areas of discourse, including universal generalizations (Ramsey 1929/1978, 137), statements of nomological necessities (Ryle 1949) and scientific laws (Sellars 1958), moral language (Hare 1952; Blackburn 1993; Gibbard 2003), meaning talk (Lance and O'Leary-Hawthorne 1997), number talk (Perez Carballo 2016), and much more.

The point here is not to settle any of these functional questions, but merely to *raise* them (our discussion of linguistic functions in Chapter 7 below will enable us to come closer to answering some of them). The Siderian proposal for how to conceive of metaphysics—as

---

[8] In this I also draw on McFarlane (2000). In my (2015a, secs 10.3–4), I use this point to argue that deflationists may reject Sider's attempt to introduce a "joint carving quantifier," without themselves taking a substantive metaphysical stand on what sorts of "structure" there are or aren't in the world—and so without (*pace* Sider 2011, 83) doing "just more metaphysics." It is a functional analysis of the language that gives us reason for rejecting his proposal, not a substantive view about the metaphysics of the world.

asking questions about structure that involve evaluating which out of *all of* our terms (of *all* grammatical categories) "carve at the joints"—simply *assumes* that all of these terms can be appropriately evaluated in terms of whether or not they "carve the world at its joints" and track structure. Thus, like the explanatory conception of metaphysics, the structural conception of metaphysics assumes a form of functional monism. It is a somewhat different functional monist assumption than one sees on the explanatory conception: where the explanatory conception assumes that any terms we treat as referring should pick out entities that would help fuel our explanatory theories, the structural conception assumes that all our concepts should aim to carve the world at its structural joints. This functional monism is built into the idea that it makes sense to *generalize* the idea of joint-carving beyond its original application to natural kind terms.

One crucial point is again that metaphysics has traditionally been concerned with a wide range of topics. Taking one narrow range of discourse (say, the theoretic discourse of the natural sciences)—and indeed one type of *terms* in that discourse (natural kind terms)—as the paradigm and evaluating all discourse on that model can lead to important mistakes. Rather than assume that all our terms should function in the same way, and are subject to the same standards of evaluation, we might do better to start a step back and investigate what functions the diverse areas of terminology—including natural kind terms, logical terms, mathematical terms, modal terms, moral terms, ordinary object terms, gender terms, and many more—serve in our theories and, more broadly, in our *lives*. Only with this kind of functional analysis in place can we properly examine what standards are appropriate to evaluating different areas of our discourse—and what forms of language we *should* use to theorize, govern, moralize, or do any of the many other things we do with language.

4
The Truthmaker Conception of Metaphysics

I turn now to another family of views about metaphysics.[1] One of the earliest and most influential alternatives to the explanatory approach, developed out of dissatisfaction with neo-Quineanism, has been the truthmaker approach. While the explanatory conception generally has been used in the service of answering the ontological questions "What is there?" or "What exists?" the truthmaker conception sees the task of metaphysics differently—as asking, "What makes our true sentences (or propositions) true?"

I will begin by articulating the truthmaker view of metaphysics and the ways in which it differs from the explanatory conception. I will go on to argue that, like the explanatory conception and the structural conception, it suffers from the metaphysical malady of relying on an unargued and problematic functional monist assumption. This again is not an explicit assumption, nor one that most truthmaker theorists have explicitly considered at all. But it is an assumption that must be presupposed for the truthmaker approach to be valid. And it is an assumption that leads into troubles.

The truthmaker approach has long presented an alternative to the explanatory approach to metaphysics. Truthmaker approaches were inspired by Wittgenstein's *Tractatus*, more recently popularized by Kevin Mulligan et al. (1984) and by David Armstrong (1997, 2004), and have been developed in different forms by many others, including John Heil (2003), Heather Dyke (2007), and Ross Cameron (2008, 2010). Truthmaker theorists do not hold that metaphysics is, or should be, explanatory in much the same sense as the natural

---

[1] Parts of this chapter are based on my (2020c).

sciences are. Instead, they take the project of metaphysics to be the search for *truthmakers*: "To postulate certain truthmakers for certain truths is to admit those truthmakers to one's ontology. The complete range of truthmakers admitted constitutes a metaphysics" (Armstrong 2004, 23).

The truthmaker approach was developed as a challenge and an alternative to the Quinean approach to ontological commitment. Armstrong famously accused Quine of having "stacked the ontological deck against predicates as opposed to subject terms" (2004, 23). For in taking the Quinean approach to looking for the ontological commitments, say, of "Some dogs are white," we look only to what we need to quantify over (dogs) for that statement to be true. But this, Armstrong thought, is to ignore the predicate side.[2] On this model, our ontological commitments are determined not by what we *must* quantify over to render true the statements of our best explanatory theories, but rather by *whatever* is required of the world for the truth of our statements—including both subject and predicate. This leads into its own conception of the work of metaphysics, for "The complete range of truthmakers admitted constitutes a metaphysics . . . looking for truthmakers is an illuminating and useful regimentation of the metaphysical enterprise" (Armstrong 2004, 23).

In some modes the truthmaker approach can resemble, and even make use of, the explanatory strategy—if we think of the requirement for truthmakers as a demand to *explain* what *makes* the sentences we accept true. So I don't mean to be suggesting that they are entirely separate approaches—though their defenders are keen to emphasize their differences, for example, in their criteria of ontological commitment. Nonetheless, the drive to find truthmakers for claims, even if we think of it as an explanatory enterprise, focuses on just *one sort of* explanation: the explanation *of the truth of* (some of) our sentences.

---

[2] Moreover, as Alston (1958, 13–14) pointed out, it makes irrelevant grammatical differences implausibly lead to huge differences in our ontological commitments, say, between the commitments of "Some dogs are white" and "Some dogs have the property of being white," where the first commits us only to dogs and the second (untranslated) commits us to properties as well as dogs. The virtue of the truthmaker model, as Armstrong saw it, was that "subject and predicate start as equals, and we can consider the ontological implications of both in an unbiased way" (2004, 23–24).

The truthmaker project is developed in various ways. In its ambitious form, the truthmaker project comes with a certain conception of metaphysics: not that it should be explanatory in the way the sciences aim to be, but rather that the goal of metaphysics is to *describe* the world, in the sense that it aims to give an inventory of *what the (ultimate) truthmakers are*. For example, Ross Cameron (2008, 2010)) presents it as the project of arriving at a sparse *fundamental* ontology, by determining what the *fundamental* truthmakers are for those truths we accept. Cameron aims to determine the *fundamentality commitments* of a sentence, where the fundamentality commitments of a sentence are those entities that "*must* number amongst the ontology of the world if the world is to provide an adequate grounding of the truth of the sentence" (2010, 249–50). Then, to determine what we should say is *fundamental*, we should figure out our best total theory, and what it is fundamentality committed to, and accept that those (and only those) things are *fundamental*.[3]

The goals of other truthmaker theorists are more modest: The appeal to truthmakers is often seen only as a *constraint* on ontologies—a way of "catching cheaters" by insisting that metaphysicians be ready to countenance *some* plausible truthmaker for each truth they accept.

I will begin by giving some independent reasons for thinking that the truthmaker approach—in both its ambitious and modest forms—leads us into troubles and should be rejected. Then I will diagnose where these troubles come from and suggest how we can do better.

4.1 Truthmakers as a Guide to What's Fundamental

To the extent that the truthmaker approach is supposed to enable us to defend a "sparse" ontology—or at least a sparse view of what is

---

[3] It is certainly not true, however, that all of those who appeal to truthmakers think that they can be used to get a uniquely true statement of what is fundamental. John Heil and Heather Dyke, for example, would clearly reject this goal. Jonathan Schaffer holds that the fundamentality commitments "are best viewed as constraints" (2008, 19), and so is not committed to the idea that appeal to truthmakers can get us to a unique statement of what is fundamental (see below for discussion). Ross Cameron has argued most prominently for using the appeal to truthmakers to determine one's fundamentality commitments. This section is largely directed toward his views.

fundamental—we again face difficult epistemological questions: How can we determine what the fundamental truthmakers for a given claim are? Armstrong tends to be admirably upfront in *acknowledging* the difficulty, writing: "the hunt for truthmakers is as controversial and difficult as the enterprise of metaphysics" (2004, 23), and again, "it is no easy and automatic road" to determine the truthmakers (2004, 23). But he offers little in the way of *solutions* to the epistemological problem.

If the truthmaker approach is to give us a method of determining what we are committed to saying is fundamental, it seems to need some criterion—some way of deciding, given a sentence or theory one accepts, what one is committed to saying is *fundamental*. Say that a sentence's *fundamentality commitments* are whatever entities one is committed to saying are fundamental, in virtue of accepting that sentence. Even if truthmaker theorists don't give us a recipe for determining what we *are* fundamentality committed to, to make good on their claim to defend a more "parsimonious ontology" via this method, they must at least provide a criterion that will tell us when we *aren't fundamentality committed to* entities of a kind apparently referred to in a given sentence or theory. So: Under what conditions can we say that an entity *isn't needed* as a fundamental truthmaker and thereby deny the apparent commitment?

How can a truthmaker theorist justify claims that, while a sentence (say, "The cathedral is either Gothic or rococo") may have many *apparent* ontological commitments, we needn't (in virtue of accepting that sentence) be committed to saying that all of those are *fundamental* ("Everything is Fundamental" being an even worse slogan than "Everything is Awesome")? Actual truthmaker theorists have not (to my knowledge) articulated such a criterion. Elsewhere (2020c) I have considered some possible attempts and found them wanting.

Cameron holds that the (fundamentality)[4] commitments of a sentence are those entities that "*must* number amongst the ontology of the world if the world is to provide an adequate grounding of the truth of

---

[4] In some work (e.g., 2008, 2010) Cameron speaks simply of "ontological commitments." I find speaking of "fundamentality commitments" clearer and (for consistency) will use it throughout.

the sentence" (2010, 249–50). But an underlying problem awaits the truthmaker theorist who wants to use the appeal to truthmakers to tell us what is (and is not) fundamental. That is, that language is apparently *ontologically flexible*.[5] That is, it seems that there are typically various grammatically alternative ways of stating what the truthmakers could be for any sentence—ways that would give us what the truthmaker theorist would see as a different set of ontological commitments. If we ask for the truthmakers even for a simple statement such as "The ball is red," we may look to the ball and its possession of a redness trope, or to the ball and its instantiation of a universal, or to the state of affairs of the ball being red, or to particles arranged ballwise jointly instantiating the relevant property (or possessing the relevant trope), or to its balling redly around here, or... If, with Cameron, theorists aim to use the truthmaker approach as a *way of answering metaphysical questions about what exists at the fundamental level*, it seems they must be committed to the idea that at most *one of these* gives the correct account of the fundamental truthmakers. But then we face a huge epistemological problem: How could we tell which it is? Before embracing this form of a truthmaker approach to metaphysics, we would need some response to these epistemological mysteries.

Given the ontological flexibility of language, there is typically *no* unique statement of what entities *must* be in the ontology of the world to account for its truth: The target sentence could be made true by any of a range of ontological alternatives. As a result, if we accept (with Cameron) that we are ontologically committed only to what *must* be posited to account for the truth of a sentence, then it seems we must conclude that there is nothing we are fundamentality committed to.[6]

---

[5] Later, in Chapter 7, we will see that work in systemic functional linguistics gives us good reason to accept that language is indeed ontologically flexible in this way and that there are good pragmatic *reasons* that languages are structured in ways that allow for such grammatical alternatives.

[6] The Quinean approach faces a similar problem if addressed at the level of determining what our theories commit us to, rather than of what a *particular regimentation* of a theory commits us to. For Quine insists that we can avoid an ontological commitment as long as we can paraphrase a sentence that quantifies over the suspect entities in a way that shows that the "seeming reference" was an "avoidable manner of speaking" (1953, 13). Given the ontological flexibility noted above, it seems that we can quite typically avoid apparent ontological commitments by paraphrasing a given sentence with an ontologically alternative one that shows the original to have been an "avoidable manner of speaking."

In recent work,[7] Cameron seems to accept that there is no criterion we can use to determine what is needed to make a claim true, and in response rejects the need for the truthmaker theorist to give "some general principle about what is or is not needed to make some claim true" (2021, 242). Instead, he suggests that we can discover what the unique fundamental truthmakers are only by "engaging in the highly speculative and highly fallible project of metaphysics." "We have to get our hands dirty and engage with all the arguments metaphysicians give concerning the benefits of an ontology of tropes versus an ontology of states of affairs, or of the costs and benefits ontological nihilism" (2021, 242).

But how, exactly, should we do that? In Chapter 1 I have discussed the problems with the idea that we can appeal to theoretic virtues to justify one metaphysical view over another. Moreover, the differences between theories that are couched in "ontologically alternative languages" will be precisely those aspects of a view that (as we have seen in Chapter 2) cannot be thought to be *confirmed with* the relevant theories. The appeal to truthmakers thus seems to do nothing to resolve the familiar epistemological problems with metaphysical attempts to determine what "really" exists or what is "fundamental."

4.2 Truthmakers as a Constraint

Not all truthmaker theorists embrace the goal of getting a uniquely true statement of what exists, or of what's fundamental. Early on, Armstrong acknowledged that "in metaphysics we have a certain latitude in what we assign as truthmakers for particular truths.... There can very reasonably be disagreement among metaphysicians ... about what the truthmakers for certain truths are" (2004, 33). It seems that Heil and Dyke would also reject such projects. Heil does not suggest that we can appeal to truthmakers to determine what the fundamental ontology is, saying, for example, "It is an open question

---

[7] Which was responding to an earlier version of this material, as it appeared in my (2020c).

what the ultimate truth-makers are for true descriptions of the world" (2003, 189).[8]

Jonathan Schaffer argues that an appeal to truthmaking (which he understands in terms of grounding)[9] does not provide a viable measure of ontological commitment, but holds that appealing to truthmaking can give us a *constraint* on what we say is fundamental. He explicitly notes that often a theory will only have *disjunctive* fundamentality commitments—say, to arrangements of particles, or objects, or a wave function, or . . . which simply act as *constraints* without telling us the true fundamental ontology (2008, 18). The theory that simply states, "You exist," for example,

> is fundamentality-committed to the existence of fundamental entities sufficient to ground the truth of the proposition that you exist. This does not tell us whether these fundamental entities are an arrangement of particles, or perhaps an effective wave-function abstracted from the wave-function of the whole universe, or anything else. But it does impose constraints. Supposing that particles are fundamental, it tells us that the fundamental entities include particles arranged you-wise. (2008, 18)

But (given the openness of the truthmaking constraint) this does not even purport to give us guidance in determining *which* of various ontologically alternative statements gives us a uniquely true statement of what those fundamental truthmakers are.[10]

---

[8] Instead, Heil appeals to truthmakers largely in opposing the "picture theory" and insisting that statements about ordinary objects, mental states, and the like may be made true by the world without requiring that we "posit" "higher level" entities as truthmakers (2003, 55).

[9] Truthmaking as grounding Schaffer presents as: "For all p, for all w, (if p is true at w, then p's truth at w is grounded in the fundamental features of w)" (2008, 10).

[10] Rettler (2016, sec, 5) similarly accepts that "we are not able to distinguish between whether tables or simples-arranged-tablewise are the truthmakers for sentences about tables" (2016, 1413–14). His "general truthmaker view" just maintains that we are committed to there being *something* that makes the statements we accept true, and so also seems to retain the needed ontological neutrality (2016, 1416). As Rettler puts it, on his General Truthmaker View, ontological commitments "can't be read off of sentences at all" (2016, 1422). Schaffer's own proposed answer to what the fundamental truthmakers are also remains neutral among statements that could be made in ontologically alternative languages. His proposed answer is that the one and only truthmaker (in any given world) is *the world* (2010a, 307). But what is the world? At one point he speaks of it as a

Taking the appeal to truthmakers merely as a *constraint* still captures something of what truthmaker theorists wanted: the idea that, as Heather Dyke puts it, "what reality is like dictates which of our utterances are true. Truths are true in virtue of the way reality is" (2007, 80). Jonathan Schaffer similarly lists three things we want a theory of truthmakers to do: connect "truth to being," give "a sense of correspondence," and permit "cheater detection" (2010a, 312). And it does seem to me clearly a better alternative to take truthmaker theory to have a more modest goal: simply imposing a *constraint* or *requirement* on any acceptable ontological view, that one must at least give *some* account of what the fundamental truthmakers *are* for the claims one accepts. One might, of course, accept this job for truthmakers without embracing the idea that there is a uniquely true statement of what the fundamental truthmakers are. Indeed this seems to be the more standard view among contemporary truthmaker theorists.

Truthmakers have often been invoked as a constraint in metaphysics. Both Armstrong (2004) and Heil (2003) trace the idea of truthmakers to C. B. Martin, who introduced the truthmaker principle, that "when a statement concerning the world is true, there must be something about the world that makes it true" (Heil 2003, 61). As the idea of truthmakers was popularized by Armstrong, the primary role of the appeal to truthmakers was to serve as a constraint on metaphysics. Armstrong introduces his book on truthmakers by criticizing Ryle for failing to say what the truthmakers are for dispositional truths, writing, "the truthmaker insight ... prevents the metaphysician from letting dispositions 'hang on air' as they do in Ryle's philosophy of mind. That is the ultimate sin in metaphysics, or at any rate, in a realist metaphysics" (2004, 3). Thus, the appeal to truthmakers is often thought to play a central role in "catching cheaters." Sider writes that the point of the truthmaker principle (that "for every truth T, there exists an entity—a 'truth-maker'—whose existence suffices for the truth of T") is to "rule out dubious ontologies that posit 'ungrounded'

"big concrete object," but quickly adds that this "will play no role in the discussion. It is merely grammatically impossible to speak of the truthmakers in a category-neutral way. The fan of facts may substitute a fact, namely, *the way the world is*. . . . The fan of tropes may substitute the global tropes, namely, *the ways that are the world*" (2010a, 309).

truths'" (2001, 36), and to catch "cheaters" who are "unwilling to accept an ontology robust enough to bear the weight of the truths [they feel] ... free to invoke" (2001, 41).

And so, since its inception, a popular use of truthmaker theory has been the idea that the appeal to truthmakers can enable us to *rule out* certain views: that if (some) truthmakers are *not* provided, the view is *il*legitimate. This idea is enshrined in the doctrine known as "the truthmaker principle": the view that every true proposition must be made true by something (Beebee and Dodd 2005, 1). Armstrong proposes the same idea under the name "Truthmaker Maximalism"— the idea that "every truth has a truthmaker" (2004, 5). Yet he admits that he does not "have any direct argument" for Truthmaker Maximalism, adding simply, "My hope is that philosophers of realist inclinations will be immediately attracted to the idea that a truth, any truth, should depend for its truth on something 'outside' it, in virtue of which it is true" (2004, 7). This hope has been borne out—many *have* been immediately attracted by it. But the question is whether that attraction comes from considering a too narrow diet of examples, and from insufficient appreciation of the strengths of alternative views, particularly those that begin from noting that some areas of discourse originate with functions other than to track, represent, or describe certain features of reality. Call these "non-descriptive" views.[11]

The Rylean example immediately shows the problem with the idea that appeal to truthmakers provides a suitable way of "catching cheaters" and ruling out certain views. For Ryle (1949) is not properly criticized as failing to answer the question of what the truthmakers are for dispositional truths (about the mind or anything else). The very point of Ryle's discussion in *The Concept of Mind* (which Armstrong seemed to miss) was to argue against the assumption that all forms

---

[11] Blackburn (1993, 3) uses the term "non-descriptive," and I will follow suit here (such views are sometimes also called "non-representational"). It is important to note that to say that a form of discourse is non-descriptive does not mean that it can't be said in some (deflationary) sense to "describe" or "state facts about" something. Metaphysical modal discourse, for example, as I argue in (2020a), originally serves the (non-descriptive) function of conveying semantic rules and their consequences in object-language indicatives. But these modal claims may be expressed in indicative form, and, given easy ontological inferences, there is a harmless sense in which we can say that "The statue couldn't survive being squashed" describes modal facts.

of discourse served the same functional role—of aiming to *describe* portions of reality (such that we can then aptly ask, "What way is the world in virtue of which these truths are true?"). Instead, as Ryle (1949) argues at length, dispositional talk does not even *aim to describe* covert dispositional properties, categorical properties, laws of nature, or powers. Instead, it serves a very different function: *licensing inferences* about what might happen in a variety of circumstances.

Using truthmakers, even in the limited role of "catching cheaters" by requiring metaphysicians to state the truthmakers for their claims, completely ignores the possibility of a *functional pluralism* in language: the idea that areas of discourse may have different functions, and that not all forms of discourse (not even all indicative utterances) serve the purpose of describing or tracking some portion of reality that must be a certain way to "explain what makes the statement true." Truthmaker theorists assume that all true simple indicative sentences have truthmakers (Mulligan et al. 1984, 313–14)—but this is to assume a kind of functional monism. It presupposes something like what Huw Price calls a "Representationalist" theory of language that all our "statements 'stand for,' or 'represent,' aspects of the world" (Price 2011, 5). This is an assumption that Ryle fought against, Wittgenstein warned of, and, more recently, such authors as Huw Price (2011, 14–33), Robert Brandom (1994), and Michael Williams (2011) have inveighed against in general terms. While we can find it in a variety of approaches to metaphysics (including explanatory, structural, and grounding approaches), it appears most blatantly in truthmaker approaches and in the truthmaker constraint.

If we take on board the assumption that all true indicative statements require truthmakers, taken as "some portion of reality in virtue of which that truth is true" (Armstrong 2004, 5), then we presuppose that all such indicative statements *have the function of tracking certain features of the world*—such that the relevant statements are *defective* if there fails to be some feature of the world that can *make them true*. But there are well developed, viable philosophical approaches to many areas of discourse that *deny* this (Price 2011). As an early example, one can find Ramsey's (1929/1978) view that universal generalizations (what he called "variable hypotheticals") "are not judgments but rules for judging. 'If I meet a phi, I shall regard it as a psi.'" Ramsey's reason for this is in part that "what would make [For all x, Px] true" would "force us to make it a conjunction, and to have a theory of conjunctions which we cannot express for lack of symbolic power" (1929/1978, 134). In more recent work, consider the expressivist views of moral discourse developed by Simon Blackburn (1993) and Allan Gibbard (2003); the treatments of modal discourse by Wilfred Sellars (1958), Robert Brandom (1994), and myself (2020a, 2023b); and many other cases. Such non-descriptive approaches treat an area of discourse as fundamentally serving some other function[12]—say, to express and coordinate attitudes, to endorse prescriptions, to make explicit the rules of use for our terms, or to license inferences. Fully developed,[13] alternative functional stories may also explain why we come to make the relevant statements in the indicative mood, and how they may be *true*, without that requiring that they be *made* true by some "portion of reality" (Price 2011, 8–9).[14] Tellingly, it is precisely in cases where the most plausible alternative functional stories have been told that truthmaker theorists have had the most trouble with "finding truthmakers" for the relevant truths: consider the difficulties in finding truthmakers for universal generalizations, moral statements, mathematical statements,[15] and modal claims.

If we adopt the truthmaker principle, not only do we implicitly rule out a whole range of options without argument, we also land ourselves in the middle of a host of familiar problems. For if we do seek the truthmakers for the moral, modal, or mathematical claims we accept, for example, we are stuck with the familiar range of unappealing

---

[12] The term "fundamentally" here is meant to signal that discourse that originates to serve functions like regulating behavior or expressing attitudes may come to take derivative grammatical forms that enable it to *also* serve functions of stating propositions that can be reasoned with, etc. As we will see with the work in systemic functional linguistics in Chapter 7, nearly every utterance in mature language serves several functions at once. We will also see how to put this point more precisely by noting that forms of language that enter to serve interpersonal functions (for example) may come to also serve ideational and textual functions.

[13] For example, in Simon Blackburn's (1993) "quasi-realist" program.

[14] More on this below. I also make this sort of case for metaphysical modal discourse in my (2020a).

[15] See Thomas Donaldson (2020) for an excellent discussion of Armstrong's difficulties with accounting for mathematical truth.

options.¹⁶ "Posit" moral properties to make our moral claims true (for example), and we have a range of problems about how to "place" them in the natural world,¹⁷ how these mere worldly features could be "action-guiding" (Mackie 1977, ch. 1; Dasgupta 2018, 287–88), or how they could be known—given that the standard empirical methods seem inapplicable. Or we face a range of other unappealing options—such as denying that there are truthmakers, and so denying the literal truth of the claims with which we began. In Chapter 7 I will do more to lay out the empirical case for functional pluralism and to show how we can begin to systematically identify a range of different linguistic functions for different sorts of discourse.

For now, I want only to note that truthmaker theorists *are not entitled to presuppose that all such views are false, untenable, or involve "cheating."* Accepting a "truthmaker principle" as a way of ruling out certain views does just that and blinds us to the possibilities that different areas of discourse may serve different functions, in ways that make it inappropriate to demand some account of what the "portion of reality" is, *in virtue of which* they are made true. Before demanding truthmakers for all truths, we had better step back and settle whether we have an adequate understanding of how the discourse in question functions, whether it aims to track worldly features, and if not, what functions it does serve in our lives and in our language, and how the discourse works—including by what rules it is introduced.

This gives us reason for pause in accepting even this weakest from of truthmaker theory: appealing to truthmakers as a constraint on ontologies, even if it is stated ontologically neutrally in terms that say only that all true propositions must be made true by "the world" or (with Rettler 2016) say merely that all true propositions must have "something" that makes them true.

In short, then, the truthmaker approach to metaphysics leads us into intractable epistemological problems if we aim to use it to determine what the *real* truthmakers are for our claims, in a way that

---

[16] Several empiricist approaches to modal discourse have recently been offered. For discussion of those and their limitations, see my (2020a, ch. 7).

[17] The term "placement problem" comes from Huw Price (2011, 186), following Frank Jackson's earlier discussion of "location problems" (1998, 3).

is supposed to tell us what *really exists* or *is fundamental*. Taken in a weaker form merely as a constraint, it rules out without argument a range of interesting and plausible approaches to various areas of discourse. Instead, it leaves us with a familiar range of unappealing options. As Ramsey put it, "it is a heuristic maxim that the truth lies not in one of the two disputed views but in some third possibility which has not yet been thought of, which we can only discover by rejecting something assumed as obvious by both the disputants" (1925, 404). In this case, the "obvious" assumption is that the discourse in question serves a *world-describing* function. This, of course, is a version of the functional monist assumption I have been aiming to bring to light, which arises in an especially vivid way with truthmaker approaches to metaphysics. As I shall argue in Chapter 8, freeing ourselves from that assumption can enable us to make new progress on a variety of old metaphysical problems.

5
Fundamentality and Grounding Projects

Over the past twenty years or so, it has become increasingly popular to reject the neo-Quinean focus on existence questions,[1] and to hold instead that metaphysics is concerned with questions of fundamentality or grounding.[2] Kathrin Koslicki aptly describes (without endorsing) the enthusiasm with which the topic of grounding was received:

> After many years of enduring the drought and famine of Quinean ontology and Carnapian metaontology, the notion of ground, with its distinctively philosophical favor, finally promises to give metaphysicians something they can believe in again and around which they can rally: their very own metaphysical explanatory connection. (2015, 306)

In this chapter I aim to examine the motivations for such reconceptions of metaphysics and to clarify what we should take from them, and what should be left behind. Several different projects along

---

[1] I am very grateful to Naomi Thompson, Kathrin Koslicki, and Jonathan Schaffer for helpful comments on an earlier version of this chapter.
[2] Some (Schaffer 2009 and Thompson 2023) have suggested that this conception of the work of metaphysics is compatible with the deflationary "easy" approach to ontology I have championed, and present versions of this project as one that remains even if we accept that answers to existence questions can be arrived at "easily." As Thompson puts it, "an attractive line for Thomasson to take would be to combine her simple realism with fundamentality realism" (2023, 14). One goal of this chapter will be to respond to this idea, clarifying that I do endorse certain local grounding questions (understood in a deflationary manner) as remaining areas for interesting work; but that I also want to lay down general cautions against fundamentality projects or developing a layered "picture of reality." More broadly, I want to caution us against thinking that all metaphysical questions are appropriately addressed in terms of "grounding"—as that relies on an inappropriate functional monist assumption.

these lines have been developed that to some extent must be considered separately. The most ambitious such project aims to determine what the "fundamental entities" are, and how the rest are grounded in them, as part of a "hierarchy of reality." Naomi Thompson describes this as a project of "fundamentality realism": "Fundamentality realism involves recognizing both some way to mark out or distinguish whatever is fundamental, and some kind of level connector to connect the fundamental to the derivative" (2023, 9)—where that "connector" is often identified with a "grounding" relation.

I will examine the fundamentality approach first, raising difficulties for the idea that metaphysics should aim to identify "what's (absolutely) fundamental." Then I will turn to the idea that metaphysics should aim to develop a layered or "hierarchical" picture of reality. I will argue that this is a problematic view that presupposes a form of functional monism and leads us into pseudo-problems.

Even if one leaves behind the idea that metaphysics can tell us what's *fundamental* or give a *layered picture of reality*, some might hope to develop other new projects for metaphysics along these lines, perhaps thinking of the work of metaphysics as at least capable of identifying *local* grounding relations, or various sorts of local dependence relations. I will examine that reformulation in section 5.4. While I agree that some projects of finding local dependence relations of various kinds can be worthwhile and can be a clear improvement over projects that aim to determine "what exists," I will argue that two cautions are in order. One is epistemological: How are we to discover the relevant dependence relations? The other concerns generalizability: Always thinking in terms of dependence relations and asking what dependence relations things of various kinds (numbers, possible worlds, etc.) bear to other worldly entities again presupposes a kind of functional monism. This can lead us astray and leave us unable to appropriately address some central problems of metaphysics.

The best way to avoid both of these problems, and to make the work epistemologically transparent and generalizable, is to begin by asking about *conceptual* rules and *conceptual* interrelations. Once we start to think explicitly in terms of conceptual interrelations, we can see how these relations might be knowable. We can also see that there are *many different kinds of* conceptual interrelations, which shouldn't be collapsed under a single heading such as "grounding," or even as several types of "ontological dependence relations."

The deeper point is to argue that, in each case, we need to start by taking a step back to ask about the functions and rules governing the relevant terms and concepts before we assume that any particular set of metaphysical questions is appropriate.

5.1 Grounding: The Basic Idea

The idea of grounding was introduced into recent philosophical work by Kit Fine (1995, 2001, 2012), though something along these lines has much deeper roots in philosophy. The idea is commonly traced to Socrates, as Plato reconstructs the Euthyphro argument—as Socrates asks after a kind of explanatory priority in pressing the question of whether an action is pious *because* the gods love it; or if the gods love it *because* it is pious.[3] Jonathan Schaffer also traces grounding questions to Aristotle, and Fine refers back to Husserl's notion of "foundation" from the *Logical Investigations*.

Schaffer (2009) explicitly makes use of the idea of grounding in developing a revised view of what metaphysics can and should do. He argues that metaphysics should not focus on the Quinean question, "What is there?" For such questions, he argues (largely in harmony with the work of easy ontology),[4] can be answered trivially via simple arguments from obvious premises (2009, 356–57). For example, we can argue, "There are prime numbers. . . . Therefore there are numbers," and thereby answer the question of the existence of numbers (2009, 357).

The interesting question for metaphysics, Schaffer argues, is instead, "What grounds what?" "Grounding" is typically taken as a primitive,

---

[3] Jessica Wilson (2014, 539) also shows that attention to notions of metaphysical dependence is not new, and traces the ways in which various specific metaphysical dependence relations have long played a central role in metaphysics.
[4] For a thorough development of "easy ontology" see my (2015a). There are nonetheless some notable differences, in that Schaffer does not suggest that answers to any existence questions can be arrived at via analytic conditionals—only that the answers are often *obvious* (Schaffer 2009, 360).

described as a relation of ontological dependence, foundation, or determination, that can be used in non-causal explanations, especially where we would be prone to say, for example, that something exists or is the case *in virtue of* something else (Schaffer 2009, 364–65).[5] The notion of grounding is generally introduced through examples: The holes are grounded in the Swiss cheese, {Socrates} is grounded in Socrates, moral features are grounded in natural features, etc. (Schaffer 2009, 375). Understanding "grounding" in this way, Schaffer writes:

> metaphysics is about what grounds what. Metaphysics so revived does not bother asking whether properties, meanings, and numbers exist. Of course they do! The question is whether or not they are *fundamental*. (2009, 347)

As that quotation suggests, this way of thinking of the project of metaphysics typically ties grounding questions to questions of *fundamentality*. The picture is this: some entities (or entity) are (absolutely) *fundamental* or *basic*;[6] other "derivative" entities are *grounded in* the fundamental entity or entities, and the goal of metaphysics is to discover this structure. As Schaffer puts it, someone pursuing this project

> will begin from a *hierarchical view of reality* ordered by *priority in nature*. The primary entities form the sparse structure of being, while the grounding relations generate an abundant superstructure of posterior entities. The primary is (as it were) all God would need to create. The posterior is grounded in, dependent on, and derivative from it. The task of metaphysics is to limn this structure. (Schaffer 2009, 351)

---

[5] See also Rosen (2010, 113–14). There has come to be debate about pretty much everything to do with grounding, including whether it *is* a form of (non-causal) explanation (Dasgupta 2017) or refers to some metaphysical relation that *backs* non-causal explanatory claims (as Schaffer (2009) seems to hold). See Bliss and Trogdon (2021, sec. 1.1).

[6] Sometimes "absolute" fundamentality is distinguished from "relative" fundamentality, with the latter phrase enabling us to ask, say, whether one type of entity is *more fundamental* than another, without the need for assuming that either is *absolutely* fundamental. Kathrin Koslicki (2015) and Elizabeth Barnes (2014), for example, accept talk of *relative* fundamentality without endorsing talk of *absolute* fundamentality. When I speak of "fundamentality" above, I will always have in mind *absolute* fundamentality.

The grounding conception of metaphysics is related both to the explanatory conception and to the truthmaker conception of metaphysics. While Schaffer rejects the idea that the project for metaphysics should be answering the question "What is there?" he retains the idea that metaphysics is in some way involved in the business of *explanation*. But crucially, on the grounding conception, metaphysics is distinguished from the natural sciences in that it is concerned with bottom-up "metaphysical" explanations, rather than with the *causal* explanations familiar from the sciences, where (according to many grounding theorists) grounding relations "back" metaphysical explanations, just as causal relations "back" causal explanations.[7] Since it is not concerned with *scientific* explanation, as Thompson makes clear (2023, 9), the grounding approach to metaphysics is not a target of my general arguments (in Chapter 2 above) against the scientistic explanatory conception.

Grounding is also closely related to the truthmaker conception of metaphysics—for on some popular ways of understanding truthmaking, truths are said to be *grounded in* their truthmakers (Schaffer 2008; Correa 2011).[8] Nonetheless, many friends of grounding would see their project in broader terms: In asking "what grounds what" we need not limit ourselves to asking questions about what grounds the *truth* of our *statements*, but (according to some) can ask grounding questions about entities in other categories as well.[9] As Kit Fine puts it, "From the perspective of the theory of ground, truth-maker theory has an unduly restricted conception of what is grounded" (2012, 43).

Over the past two decades, interest in and literature on grounding and fundamentality has exploded, and much is contested about how we should understand and formalize "grounding," and what roles, if

---

[7] Not all fans of metaphysical explanation think it requires "backing" in a single relation of grounding, or even that it requires any "backing" relation or relations at all. I return to this idea below.

[8] Schaffer also explicitly connects the neo-Aristotelian notion of grounding to Armstrong's idea of an "ontological free lunch" (2009, 353).

[9] There is also controversy about whether grounding relations have to hold among facts, or if they may hold among other types of entity. Schaffer takes them to be capable of holding between entities of any categories; Rosen (2010, 114) allows only grounding relations between facts.

any, it should play in metaphysics. I will leave most of those debates to one side here. For here I want to focus just on this question: Should we accept a reconception of the work of metaphysics along these lines?

One attraction of the grounding project is that it gives hope of avoiding a rivalry with the sciences. Kit Fine, for example, writes, "Ground, if you like, stands to philosophy as cause stands to science" (2012, 40). Of course, the natural sciences *do* sometimes aim to give synchronic, bottom-up explanations of observed phenomena—not just diachronic causal explanations. For example, we might get scientific explanations of the way the observable properties of fluids are determined by their chemical structure; or of the way colors (as they appear to us) arise in virtue of certain microtextural properties of surfaces, combined with wavelengths of light absorbed and reflected; or of ways in which certain of our emotional states are determined by our neurochemical state. But although the natural sciences might be thought to address some grounding-type questions, metaphysics might still be characterized as dealing with the *most general* kinds of grounding questions that are the province of no individual science— for example, with questions about how the entities studied by the social sciences are grounded in those studied by chemistry and physics. Moreover, some sorts of synchronic, "bottom-up" explanations don't seem best addressed by the empirical sciences, and might provide remaining work for metaphysics. Fine distinguishes different kinds of "in virtue of" relation and limits cases of *metaphysical* ground to cases in which the relevant conditional ("Necessarily, if {Socrates} exists, then Socrates exists") holds with *metaphysical* necessity (not just "natural" or "normative" necessity) (2012, 38). Investigating *metaphysical* grounding relations then might be thought to be the distinctive work of metaphysics, complementary to the sciences. As Fine writes:

> It is plausible to suppose that the natural in-virtue-of relation will be of special interest to science, the normative relation of special interest to ethics, and the metaphysical relation of special interest to metaphysics. Each of these disciplines will be involved in its own explanatory task, that will be distinguished, not merely by the kind of things that explain or are explained, but also by the explanatory relationship that is taken to hold between them. (2012, 39)

And Fine explicitly connects questions of *metaphysical* grounding to the task of metaphysics, writing, "Questions of ground . . . are *central* to realist metaphysics. Indeed, if considerations of ground were abolished, then very little of the subject would remain" (2012, 41).

So, what are distinctively *metaphysical* grounding relations that metaphysicians might hope to study? Paradigmatic purported *metaphysical* grounding relations include the following:

(1) {Socrates} exists *because* Socrates exists. (Schaffer 2018, 3)
(2) That object is square *because* it has four sides of equal length [connected at right angles]. (Thompson 2019, 107)
(3) The proposition *that Socrates was wise* is true *because* Socrates was wise. (Schaffer 2018, 2)
(4) Socrates was wise or handsome *because* he was wise. (Schaffer 2018, 2)
(5) Socrates was pale *because* he had this specific skin tone. (Schaffer 2018, 2)

As Fine (1994, 2012) insists, the relation in these cases cannot be captured in merely *modal* terms. For in some of these cases (1–3) we could get a necessary *biconditional*: "Necessarily, Socrates exists if and only if {Socrates} exists"—yet (Fine argues) there seems to be an *asymmetry*, in that the existence of Socrates *explains* the existence of {Socrates} and not vice versa.[10] Talk of grounding (and correlatively of essences, real definitions, and the like) was introduced as a way to capture this asymmetry: We can say that {Socrates} is metaphysically grounded in Socrates and not vice versa (even if, necessarily, they exist in all the same possible worlds).

It is true that such explanations are not things one would expect to find in the natural sciences, so perhaps if we think of this as the project for metaphysics, we can avoid any appearance of a rivalry with the natural sciences and find a remaining project for metaphysics. Some

---

[10] Fine insists on the need for an asymmetry that can't be captured in modal terms, using the language of essence rather than grounding, writing, "we want to say that it is essential to the singleton to have Socrates as a member, but not that it is essential to Socrates to be a member of the singleton" (1994, 7).

might still worry, though, about whether the remaining project is very *interesting*, if claims like 1–5 above are the central kinds of truths metaphysicians can aim to discover. I would not want to try to explain to a funding agency why "uncovering" truths like 1–5 above is a valuable project.

5.2 Troubles for the Fundamentality Project

One way to make the grounding project look deeper and more interesting is to link it to the project of determining "what's (absolutely) fundamental": the most basic grounds on which everything else is grounded. But as we have seen in discussing the structural view, we should hesitate to reformulate the project of metaphysics as asking what's fundamental, given important criticisms raised by Barnes (2014) and Mikkola (2017).[11] For if we limit metaphysics to the study of the fundamental, Barnes argues, we rule out the work of feminist metaphysics, which generally begins from agreement, say, that gender is *not* fundamental and goes on to engage in serious and interesting (and apparently *metaphysical*) debates about what gender is: "A major part of the project of feminist metaphysics is to argue that what is real ... goes beyond what is fundamental" (Barnes 2014, 344). As Mikkola puts it, "feminist metaphysics is *not* about fundamentality and it does not consider gender or sex to be fundamental" (2017, 2440).

This problem also generalizes beyond feminist metaphysics. For a great many of the traditional topics in metaphysics concern entities that few would suspect of being fundamental—not just social entities such as social structures, race, gender, geographic entities, money, classes, and the like, but also works of art, artifacts, even moral properties and numbers. To limit the work of metaphysics to answering the question

---

[11] Barnes applies these criticisms to three attempted reconceptions of metaphysics: Sider's view that metaphysics is about "the fundamental nature of reality" (2011, 1), where the relevant debates are substantive only to the extent that the terms employed "carve the world at its joints"; Schaffer's view that metaphysics is about "what grounds what" (2009, 347); and Cian Dorr's view that we can express substantive metaphysical claims only with a "fundamental" use of the quantifier, in which speakers aim to use quantified statements to make claims about the "fundamental furniture of reality" (2008, 23). For replies, see Schaffer (2017) and Sider (2017).

"What's fundamental?" would unduly constrain it away from many of the most interesting topics we might have hoped it would address—and away from projects that could distinguish its work from that of the natural sciences.

Karen Bennett (2017, 230–35) also objects to the idea that the metaphysics should be thought of as the study of "fundamental reality." Among other problems, she aptly notes that thinking of metaphysis as the study of *fundamental* reality lands us right back in the traditional problem of a rivalry with science, for "Physics, too, tries to discover the fundamental nature of reality" (2017, 230), and one might well think that we have more reason to listen to physicists than metaphysicians in claims to have discovered "what's (really) fundamental."

Other problems, by now familiar, also arise in thinking of metaphysics as asking what's fundamental. In Chapter 4 I raised difficulties for using a truthmaker approach to metaphysics to determine what is fundamental. There I noted the problem of the "ontological flexibility of language": that whatever description we give of the fundamental entities, there will be options in ontologically alternative languages we can use in saying what the "fundamental entities" are. How can we decide among these what the fundamental ontology *really* is? The attempt to choose some *uniquely correct* answer from among these alternatives leads us straight back into the epistemological mysteries of metaphysics. The same epistemological difficulties persist if we dissociate the fundamentality project from talk of truthmakers, and aim to ask (without talk of truthmakers), "What is *fundamental?*" One common response to the epistemological mystery (discussed in Chapter 1) is to say that we should simply weigh up the competing options by comparing theoretic virtues, and thereby arrive at the true fundamental ontology. But we have seen reasons for doubting that we can appeal to theoretic virtues to answer serious metaphysical questions like these.[12] Without a better response, the fundamentality project leaves us mired in the familiar problems of rivalry with science and epistemological mystery.

---

[12] For an overview of some of these epistemological difficulties, see also my (2017b, 369–70).

All things considered, then, I think we should reject the idea that the project of metaphysics is determining what's "fundamental," whether we think of this in terms of discovering fundamental *structure*, the fundamental *truthmakers*, or fundamental *grounds*. There may be legitimate questions about what fundamental entities (if any) there are. But these are questions for physics—not questions for speculative metaphysics.

5.3 Troubles for the Layered Picture

One response to these problems that still recognizes the interest of grounding projects is to suggest that the project of metaphysics is not determining "what's fundamental," but rather determining how *all the rest* is grounded in the fundamental—or, more neutrally, asking, "What grounds what?" In that way, we might hope to bring back questions about how social or cultural entities (say) are grounded in the fundamental (and in which intervening layers), and so not abandon all the interesting questions of feminist metaphysics, for example.[13]

Seeing the project of metaphysics as a matter of determining "what grounds what" encourages us to think in terms of a "leveled" or "hierarchical" picture of reality, where, as Louis deRosset puts it, "grounding is the relation that links entities of higher layers to entities of lower layers" (2013, 2).[14] As Schaffer puts it, "Grounding is something like metaphysical causation. Roughly speaking, just as causation links the

---

[13] While Barnes argues that this project is also insufficient to give room for feminist metaphysics (2014, 343), see Schaffer's reply (2017) for defense of the idea that asking "what grounds what" *does* leave room for and provide tools for addressing many of the problems of feminist metaphysics. Nonetheless, I will argue below that grounding approaches also incorporate a functional monist assumption. Work in feminist philosophy has reason to avoid a functional monist assumption, since it leaves out of view the possible roles that gender terms, pejoratives, and other forms of social discourse may play not just in *describing* (a grounded) "social reality," but also in *imposing, reinforcing,* or *renegotiating* the relevant norms.

[14] Such "layered" pictures of reality have also, of course, arisen in earlier philosophical work, particularly in debates about the "emergence" of so-called "higher level" phenomena (especially the mental), and about the relationship between physics and the "special sciences." For articulation of a layered view see Oppenheim and Putnam (1958). For discussion and criticisms of layered models, see Kim (2002) and Heil (2003).

world across time, grounding links the world across levels. Grounding connects the more fundamental to the less fundamental, and thereby backs a certain form of explanation" (2012, 122).[15]

Schaffer himself does not endorse such a fully layered conception of reality, but some have taken this idea to suggest that we can develop a "layered" view of reality. The layered conception invites a picture something like this: Reality is like a big layer cake, or a big cliff with different geological strata. Our task is to discover how many layers there are and how they are related. For cliffs and cakes, these questions make sense: We can count the layers. We can say how the layers are related (they are physically on top of each other, with the lower supporting the higher). We can say of any two parts (the granite and the limestone / the blueberry crème and the raspberries) whether they are in the same layer or different layers. We can say what holds the layers together (layers of silt or icing). As soon as we buy into the levels-of-reality picture, there is a strong temptation to treat questions like these as appropriate, and to try to answer them. But embracing this picture leads us into difficulties as well, for the levels metaphor is misleading and can generate pseudo-questions and pseudo-problems.[16]

And so, once we embrace this picture, we might expect to be able to get answers to questions about how many layers there are, and what is layered on top of what else. Those who defend levels of reality generally say things like: We have a physical layer at the bottom, a biological layer toward the middle, a psychological layer higher up, and perhaps a social or cultural layer on top. But how many layers, precisely, are there? Does the chemical form a different layer than the physical? Are single-celled organisms in a different layer than mammals? Are higher-order thoughts in a different layer than mere feelings or sensations? Are symphonies or novels (as abstract cultural creations) in a different layer than concrete cultural artifacts like forks or events like marriages or 10-kilometer races? The robust realist layered conception makes it

---

[15] For development and defense of a "layered" picture of reality, appealing to grounding explanations to articulate the layered conception, see deRosset (2013).
[16] For fuller discussion of problems with the "layered conception of reality," see my (2014). Nonetheless, as I aim to make clear there, there was something that made the "levels" view preferable to its historical rivals of elimination and reduction.

seem like we should be able to discover answers to these questions by examining the world.[17]

These are questions that I, for one, do not want to have to answer—any more than I want to answer the question of exactly how many layers of reality there are. Suppose we say that when A is grounded on B, then A is on a higher level than B. This will still leave a huge range of cases in which we cannot say whether A is on a higher level than B or not (when neither is grounded on the other). But if in a great many cases we can't say whether A is on a higher or lower level than B (are colors on a higher or lower level than corporations? are corporations on a higher or lower level than footraces?), then the picture that reality has a certain number of layers misleads us.[18]

As Jaegwon Kim concludes his discussion of a layered picture of reality: "I hope it has become clear that these questions [about the relative levels of many different things] don't have clear answers, and there is no reason why we should seek them, to begin with. I think that attempts to construct an overarching levels ontology for the whole of the natural world in which every object has its "appropriate" place are rather pointless if not hopeless" (2002, 16).

But what is most important here is that this "layered" picture of reality also clearly presupposes a form of functional monism about language—that all the nouns at issue in metaphysics aim to refer to and track some parts of a structured reality—the only question being how these parts are interrelated. It thus obscures deeper questions about the way mathematical terms, modal terms, or moral terms, for example, function—keeping out of view the thought that discourse of these sorts may function very differently than terms that aim to track "higher" or "lower"-level "parts of reality," and presupposing that

---

[17] Bennett suggests a more complex layered picture that allows that there are "several different building relations, each of which generates its own notion of relative fundamentality; claims that something is more or less fundamental than something else are implicitly indexed to a particular building relation" (2017, 236).

[18] Jaegwon Kim reaches a similar conclusion for the supervenience conception of levels—that the defender of that view may simply "have to accept the fact that properties and kinds are not always comparable to each other in terms of higher and lower. And if individual objects are ranked in terms of the properties they have, as I have suggested, the same outcome has to be expected for them as well" (2002, 10). Such concerns about incommensurability also lead Schaffer to reject a layered picture.

"placement" questions (about how the numbers or possible worlds or moral duties could be "placed" in the natural world) are appropriate. The analyses to be given in Part II about the functional roles and entry rules of various sorts of discourse will bring this into question.[19] Pressing these questions about what "layer" X is in, for every noun term of metaphysics (numbers, moral properties, modal properties), may turn out to be analogous to pressing the question "What geological layer of the earth is X in?" for every noun of geology: an approach that would lead us to ask not only what layer limestone, coal, and shale are in, but also what layer soil analysis, erosion, thickness, and geological time scale are in.

5.4 Looking for Local Grounding Relations

But perhaps the difficulties arose from tying the grounding conception of metaphysics too closely to ideas of (absolute) fundamentality and a hierarchical picture of reality. Perhaps new projects for metaphysics could emerge from more generally thinking of a project for metaphysics in identifying *local* grounding relations, or answering questions about *relative* rather than *absolute* fundamentality. On this model, metaphysics might address questions such as "What grounds moral properties?" "What grounds the social world?" "What grounds gender?" "What grounds color?" "What grounds modality?"—even if we do not aim to produce a unique account of what's *absolutely* fundamental or a total picture of how reality is hierarchically layered.

There are different ways of thinking about the project of identifying grounding relations. As mentioned above, some (Schaffer 2009; Audi 2012)[20] have thought that identifying "what grounds what" can enable us to offer "metaphysical explanations": where a grounding relation can "back" the relevant explanations. As Schaffer puts it, a metaphysical explanation is "an explanation backed by grounding relations" (2017, 303). So understood, one way of thinking of the task of

---

[19] Relevant here are also criticisms by John O'Leary-Hawthorne and Huw Price (1996) of the so-called "Canberra Plan" championed by Frank Jackson among others.
[20] See discussion in Koslicki (2015).

metaphysics is as giving the relevant (perhaps piecemeal) "metaphysical explanations."

But what, exactly, is metaphysical explanation supposed to be? It is widely held to be at least *analogous* to causal explanation, yet is usually thought to be distinct from it—as Jonathan Schaffer puts it, "By a 'metaphysical explanation' I mean a non-causal explanatory connection" (2018, 303)[21] (though perhaps not just any non-causal explanatory connection: mathematical explanation, for example, may be different [Brenner et al. 2021, introduction]). A metaphysical explanation is supposed to be what is given by a true (non-causal) *in virtue of* claim—so that we can say that certain facts hold *in virtue of* certain others. As Dasgupta puts it, a metaphysical explanation is supposed to provide a way of saying "what underlying facts *constitute* the phenomenon" (Dasgupta 2017, 75). At least in typical cases, a metaphysical explanation (or "grounding explanation") works by appealing to some more fundamental fact "that in some sense non-causally 'gives rise to,' 'produces,' or 'generates' less fundamental facts" (Brenner et al. 2021, sec. 2).[22]

But as soon as we turn to speak of metaphysical explanations, more controversies arise.[23] While Schaffer and Audi hold that

---

[21] Though there is no analog for statistical or probabilistic metaphysical explanations (Wilsh 2016, 15). Bennett (2017) argues for including causation (along with grounding) in the general class of what she calls "building" relations.

[22] Brenner et al. consider grounding explanations perhaps just one kind of metaphysical explanation, acknowledging that there may also be different kinds, such as essentialist explanations and reductive explanations (2021, sec. 2).

[23] Some deny that metaphysical explanations require "backing" by one or more relations in the world at all. Shamik Dasgupta (2017) argues that we should just take "grounding" as a *label for* a certain kind of non-causal, constitutive explanation, and develops a deflationary conception of grounding as such (2017, 76), such as even "the masses" appeal to. Even if we deflate it from its metaphysical associations in this way Dasgupta argues, the notion can track many issues of intellectual importance. Kovacs (2018) and Baron and Norton (2021) also keep the idea that metaphysics can give us "metaphysical explanations" while denying that such metaphysical explanations require "backing" with one or more "worldly" relation, developing instead a unificationist model of metaphysical explanation, inspired by Philip Kitcher's (1981) unificationist model of scientific explanation. Naomi Thompson (2019) develops an alternative pragmatic approach to metaphysical explanations, which likewise does not require a metaphysical "backing" relation. I will largely leave such issues to the side here, leaving untouched the question of whether metaphysical explanation, on these non-backing models, can remain as a legitimate project for metaphysics. Nonetheless, I would offer some general cautions about projects of *unification* in metaphysics, as the very *generality* of

metaphysical explanations must be "backed" by a metaphysical relation of grounding, others have held that metaphysical explanations are instead "backed" by *various* different metaphysical relations, not a single distinctive "grounding" relation. Karen Bennett (2017) argues that there are various "building" relations (including at least composition, constitution, set formation, realization, micro-based determination, grounding, and [most controversially] causation), which nonetheless form a "unified family" with shared features (2017, 236). Both Wilson (2014) and Koslicki (2015) argue that "grounding" seems to be a coarse-grained label covering many *different* relations—perhaps including genus/species, determinable/determinate, truthmaking, and maybe others besides (Koslicki 2015, 340). Wilson (2014) argues that talk of "grounding" obscures important differences across different metaphysical relations that might hold: type or token identity, functional realization, mereological parthood, set membership, determinable/determinate, etc. Koslicki (2015) argues that "the grounding idiom lacks the requisite unity to tie together the collection of data which allegedly exhibit grounding connections under a single relation" (2015, 340)—instead, talk of "grounding" covers and obscures differences among a variety of distinct relations, such as genus/species, determinable/determinate, and so on. She concludes, "by treating a collection of phenomena which is in fact heterogeneous as though it were homogeneous, we have, if anything, taken a dialectical step backward" (2015, 307). If that is the case, metaphysicians interested in issues of dependence or relative fundamentality might do better to make use of a variety of different relations in conducting their analyses, rather than speaking generically of a "grounding" relation (Wilson 2014, 542). And we might see "metaphysical explanations" as potentially "backed" by various different worldly relations.

    I have sympathy with the thought that there are various *different* relations appealed to in standard claims of "grounding," and that we might do better by being more specific. I also have some sympathy with the idea that *many* questions in metaphysics are appropriately

---

metaphysics ensures that the terms in question are used with a wide variety of different rules and functions.

framed as questions about the various different kinds of dependence relations holding among entities of different sorts.

In fact, I addressed such questions myself in earlier work, for example, in discussing what I called (before "grounding" was hip) "existential dependence" relations between fictional characters, works of literature, and readers; between social objects or works of art and human activities; etc.[24] In fact, I spent much of my early career, in my work on the ontology of fiction (1999), ontology of art (2004, 2005), and social ontology (2003a, 2009) drawing out such different "dependence relations"—aiming to articulate the different ways in which, say, works of literature depend on their authors, versus on physical copies of a text, versus on the capacities of readers. In *Fiction and Metaphysics* (1999) I distinguished variations in dependence relations—according to the *times* at which the dependence held (is it just a dependence for *coming into* existence, or a *constant* dependence?) and according to whether the relevant entity depended *rigidly* on a particular individual or *generically* on anything of a specified kind. And, of course, this isn't to deny that there may be still *other* sorts of metaphysical relationships (or "building relations")—perhaps including determination, functional realization, material constitution, part/whole, etc.

I still accept that work along these lines can be very helpful in articulating, for example, some of the relations that hold among entities in the everyday social and cultural world, and between them and mere natural objects. But I also encountered two challenges, which have motivated much of my work thereafter. I turn now to lay those out, as cautions for those tempted to follow the same trail.

If we do take a central task of metaphysics to be identifying various local dependence relations (perhaps of different sorts), two challenges arise. One is the epistemological problem: How can we come to know that such "metaphysical relations" hold? How can we justify the relevant claims and resolve disagreements? One difficulty is that many of the cases of interest in metaphysics involve merely *modal* differences, say, between the dollar bill and the piece of paper, the

---

[24] In this work I was inspired by Husserl's work on foundation, especially as found in his *Logical Investigations*, as well as by Roman Ingarden's (1964) work. See, e.g., my (1999, ch. 2).

statue and the clay—so we can't think that differences between them, or their relationships of dependence, can be discovered empirically. Thompson notes that notions like grounding have an "(at best) underdeveloped epistemology" (2023, 10). Can we give an account of how we can pursue this "project for metaphysics" and come to know what dependence relations hold, without landing ourselves in epistemological mystery?

The other problem is a generality problem. For if we think of metaphysics as addressing questions not only about the ontology of ordinary objects, works of art, social objects, etc., but also about numbers, possible worlds, propositions, moral obligations, etc., it's not clear that the "ontological dependence" framework is fitting, or sets up the right kinds of questions. For such entities have seemed, at least to many, and on a traditional conception, to be completely *independent* of natural objects in the world, and even of our beliefs and practices. To say otherwise invites familiar problems, for example of saying that there would not be numbers in a world without speakers or thinkers, or that whether it is necessary, say, that seals are mammals depends on our thought or language.[25] Of course, we can assert that they are *in*dependent, but that does nothing to help with the familiar ontological and epistemological puzzles of philosophy of mathematics, modality, and metaethics.

Over the years I have come to see that these two problems can be addressed together, by attention to linguistic and conceptual rules.

5.4.1 Clarifying the Epistemology

The best way I know of to understand and clarify how we can come to know the relevant metaphysical relations is to see them as reflections of various linguistic and conceptual rules—and as knowable via extrapolation from mastery of those rules, sometimes combined with empirical knowledge. The classic purported grounding claims (1–5 above) all seem to involve conceptual connections. There are links

---

[25] For discussion of such problems as arise with the "modal conventionalist" view, see my (2020a, 24–31 and 88–90).

between the concepts of an individual and its singleton set, between being square and having four equal sides, between P and a proposition P's being true, between a disjunction and each of its disjuncts, and between being pale(-skinned) and being of certain skin tone (e.g., light beige).[26] So one might naturally think of (at least central cases of) grounding claims as object-language reflections of these conceptual links, and as discoverable via extrapolation from conceptual mastery.

I have developed a detailed story for how we can acquire modal knowledge in this way (see my 2020a, ch. 7) and have also elsewhere begun to suggest how we can understand talk of material constitution as a way of systematizing and giving a common name to certain linguistic/conceptual rules, expressed in the object language (see my 2013). Theodore Locke (2020) and Naomi Thompson (2023) have both suggested that the notion of metaphysical explanation can likewise be developed in a deflationary way that appeals to nothing more obscure than conceptual and empirical work. Locke develops a view along these lines (extending and paralleling my [2020a] normativist treatment of modality), arguing that "metaphysical explanations do not give us a better understanding of a worldly metaphysical order. Instead, metaphysical explanations are conceptual explanations given in an object language using rather than mentioning the relevant concepts or terms . . . metaphysical explanations express and endorse important features of semantic rules of use that cannot be adequately expressed using basic modal claims" (2020, sec. 1). The basic idea is that at least some metaphysical explanations "involve conceptual truths that reflect metalinguistic *conceptual laws*, which are generalized norms that cover important features of concept use that bear on conceptual competency" (Locke 2020, sec. 4.2.1). For example, Locke identifies one kind of metaphysical explanation as involving "real definitions," and he plausibly argues that these "real definitions" endorse and express constitutive rules for our expressions (rather than covering both those *and their consequences*, as modal claims do on my [2020] normative analysis of metaphysical necessity) (Locke 2020, sec. 4.2.2). That is

---

[26] Perhaps this is why there seems to be no "explanatory gap" remaining once we have given the metaphysical ground—why, as Fine observes, "If there is a gap between the grounds and what is grounded, then it is not an explanatory gap" (2012, 39).

what gives us license to say that *what it is* to be a bachelor is to be unmarried (given the relations in rules of use), but to deny that *what it is* to be a bachelor is to be unmarried and for triangles to have three sides (for there is no connection in the rules of use for "bachelor" and "triangle," even though it's true that *necessarily*, if someone is a bachelor then they are unmarried *and triangles have three sides*).

I do not aim here to show how we can reinterpret all of the various purported "metaphysical relations" as reflecting relations among linguistic or conceptual rules—in fact, I think we would do better to just switch to the latter terms in any case. What is crucial here is just the idea that if we can understand the relevant "metaphysical relations" in this way, then they may be rendered epistemically non-mysterious.

It is important to note that this approach to understanding the epistemology of claims of dependence, constitution, metaphysical explanation, and the like does not prevent us from saying that there (really) are the corresponding metaphysical properties and relations "in the world." It really is true, for example, that a particular statue *depends on* and *is constituted by* a lump of clay, though these dependence and constitution claims are object-language reflections of certain kinds of conceptual interrelations and are knowable via extrapolation from our mastery of the relevant concepts and terms—combined with empirical knowledge.[27]

Of course many metaphysicians won't be satisfied with this route to understanding the epistemology of claims about such metaphysical relations—either because they want to appeal to relations of metaphysical grounding, for example, in cases where there aren't (or they don't think there are) relevant interconnections in rules of use of the relevant concepts (say, if you want to say that the presence of certain neurological activity *grounds* phenomenal experience); or because they want to characterize what they are doing as a matter of making "deep worldly" metaphysical discoveries. To them I can only ask that they provide some other clear and compelling story of how such metaphysical relations can come to be known and how we can reconcile debates

---

[27] I spell out details for the modal case, clarifying how the normativist approach may at the same time entitle us to say that there *are* modal facts and properties, and to clarify the epistemology of modality, in (2020a, especially chs. 6 and 7).

about them in a way that will help solve the epistemological crisis in metaphysics.[28]

5.4.2 The Problem of Generality

But what about the second problem: that investigating various "dependence" relations does not help us with many metaphysical problems, concerning numbers, possible worlds, propositions, etc.—where these things are often thought of as *independent* of us, our thought and talk, perhaps of the whole empirical world? For many of these classic problems, asking questions about what "layer of reality" they are in, or how they are grounded, only leads us astray into irrelevant pseudo-questions.

We can do better by seeking a better understanding of linguistic functions and rules. For once we have a fuller understanding of the forms linguistic rules can take (enabling different parts of language to serve different functions), we also can see why the generality problem arises. It arises because there are more kinds of conceptual interrelations than just those that underlie claims of dependence. As I will argue in Chapter 8, understanding those conceptual interrelations can help us make progress on the old problems of metaphysics beyond those having to do with social and cultural objects—including problems of mathematics, modality, and metaethics.

Let me clarify a bit here, though the full clarification will require work done in the second part of this book. One important sort of conceptual interrelation holds when satisfying the application conditions for one term "conceptually guarantees the satisfaction of the application conditions of other expressions" (Locke 2020, 39), for example, "'the ball is crimson' conceptually entails 'the ball is red,'" and "Socrates exists" conceptually entails "{Socrates} exists" (Locke 2020, 39). Such interrelations can entitle us to say that the dress being crimson *metaphysically explains* why it is red, and that the existence

---

[28] An alternative is to avoid talk of metaphysical "backing" relations at all and adopt a unificationist approach to "metaphysical explanation" (see Kovacs 2018 and Baron and Norton 2021). I will leave that option to the side here.

of Socrates *metaphysically explains* the existence of the singleton set. This analysis also enables us to capture the asymmetry characteristic of metaphysical explanation claims, for, as Locke puts it, "the object language asymmetry reflects a conceptual asymmetry between 'the set {Socrates}' and 'Socrates'—namely, satisfaction of the application conditions for 'Socrates' are included in the application conditions for 'the set {Socrates}' as a constitutive prerequisite, but not vice versa" (2020, 43).

So, claims of metaphysical dependence relations or "grounding" may often be object-language reflections of conceptual interrelations between the application conditions for our terms. It is important to note, though, that there are many different relations that may hold among application conditions. Above we looked at cases in which satisfying one set of application conditions *conceptually guarantees* that others are satisfied (as satisfying the conditions for "is red" guarantees satisfying the conditions for "is colored"). Fulfilling the application conditions for one concept may also *require* those for another concept to be fulfilled—for example, fulfilling the application conditions for "church" requires that those for "act of consecration" be fulfilled. As I argued in earlier work (1999, ch. 2; 2014), there are many different sorts of dependence relations that we can and should distinguish, given the differences in relations among application conditions. For example, even in the case of fictional characters, the application conditions for the concept of "(literary) fictional character" may require that the application conditions for the concept of "work of literature" be fulfilled *at that same time* (constant dependence), but only that those for the concept of "act of writing" have been fulfilled *at some prior time* (historical dependence). There are also differences between *generic* dependence cases (in which what is required is only that the application conditions for some *general* term be fulfilled. e.g., that there be some or other reader) and *rigid* dependence cases (those that require that the application conditions for a given *name* be fulfilled—requiring that there be a specific individual). And of course, there are differences in whether the application of one term *entails* the application of another (as the application of "scarlet" entails the application of "red") or *requires or presupposes* the application of another (as the application of "square" *requires* the application of "four-sided").[29]

But an even more important point is this: For certain concepts, it arguably doesn't make sense to think of them as having "application conditions." If so, we can't think of them as standing in conceptual relations of *these* sorts.[30] Consider, for example, terms for what are generally thought of as necessarily existing entities: numbers, propositions, properties (Platonistically conceived), etc.[31] Suppose that terms for numbers may be introduced by trivial inferences such as this:

(1) There are two cups on the table.
(2) The number of cups on the table is two.
(3) There is a number.[32]

In this case, number talk is introduced via trivial inferences from ordinary object talk (from what Carnap (1950/1956, 206–7) called the "thing language"). And so, we might say that in some sense the thing language is "conceptually prior" to number language. Yet there are no *application conditions* for "number" that require that the application conditions for "cup" (or any other "thing term") be fulfilled—that is the sense in which we want to say that (3) could be true regardless of whether or not (1), or indeed any other empirical claim, is true.[33] (This

---

[29] As Naomi Thompson reminded me, talk of "metaphysical explanation" may also come apart from any "underlying relations" (whether in application conditions or "metaphysical relations"), to the extent that what counts as a good *explanation* may be subject to a variety of epistemic, psychological, and pragmatic constraints. See Thompson (2019) for arguments that metaphysical explanations are subject to epistemic constraints. See also Maurin, who emphasizes that explanations are always "a function of the needs, knowledge, and expectations of those to whom the explanation is offered" (2019, sec. 2.2) and argues that explanation gives us no reason to think that a metaphysical relation of grounding exists.

[30] In *Ontology Made Easy* (2015a, 86) I spoke as if all general nouns have application conditions, but I would now revise that. I now think it is preferable to speak of "introduction rules" for talk of things of a given kind, some of which may involve worldly application conditions, and others of which may be introduced by trivial inferences from either a statement or its negation (so that no worldly conditions are required).

[31] For discussion of how these claims of necessary existence can be seen as object-language reflections of a consequence of semantic rules, see my (2020a, 115–17).

[32] For further discussion of such "easy inferences," see my (2015, especially ch. 3).

[33] See my (2020a, 115–17) for further discussion of how reference to necessary existents such as numbers could be introduced via such semantic rules.

is the sense Husserl gave of saying that we could "bracket" questions of the truth of statements like (1) and still come to refer to and know of essences.)[34] In such cases, it would be a mistake to say that the existence of ordinary objects *metaphysically explains* the existence of numbers, or that numbers are *grounded on* or *metaphysically depend on* cups—or any features of the empirical world.[35]

Similarly, one might hold that property talk can be introduced by easy inferences that succeed whether or not the original claim is true, as we can reason as follows:

(1) The barn is red.
(2) The barn possesses the property of redness.
(3) There is a property of redness (possessed by the barn).

Suppose we adopt Platonistic rules for introducing property talk (or interpret our ordinary property talk as following such rules)—that is, rules that allow that properties may exist uninstantiated. Then we can allow that a parallel inference to the same conclusion might be available even if (1) is false. For from "The barn is not red" we can infer "The barn does not possess the property of redness" and "There is a property of redness (that the barn does not possess)." Here again, it would be a mistake to say that the existence of the property of redness is *metaphysically explained by* or *depends on* the barn's being red (or even on there being *any* instances of redness).

Nonetheless, even in cases in which *application conditions* aren't at issue at all, there may be (other kinds of) *conceptual interrelations* among our concepts.[36] For it may be that (nominative) talk of properties or numbers is arrived at on the basis of grammatically licensed shifts from talk of ordinary, perceived objects in the surrounding world; given linguistic rules that license the move from (1) to (2) in each of the above "easy" arguments. In that sense, talk of

---

[34] For discussion and defense of this interpretation, see my (2017b).
[35] Koslicki distinguishes "abstraction" as a separate relation from "construction," "artificiality," and "disunity" (2015, 337–38).
[36] I came to recognize this fairly late myself, and even in (2015a) spoke of (all) nouns as having application conditions. Locke also alludes to other forms of "conceptual priority," including "historical, functional, or theoretical priority" (2020, 44).

ordinary objects (in the "thing language") may be developmentally and conceptually prior to talk of properties or numbers—despite the fact that terms for the latter don't have application conditions at all. I will return to this idea at length in the second half, aiming to also make clear what *functional reasons* make it worthwhile for a language to license these grammatical shifts to introduce new terms.

Conceptual priority in the last sense may well be worth investigating and (as I will suggest in Part II) may shed light on a variety of metaphysical problems. But it doesn't seem anything like the ontological dependence / grounded entity / layered conception of reality that talk of "grounding" and "metaphysical explanation" were originally supposed to capture. It seems closer to the thought that speaking of numbers and properties is not a language game "one could play, though one played no others."[37] In fact, as we will see, conceptual interrelations of *these* kinds seem to arise precisely where we have forms of language that serve functions *other* than tracking worldly features to which we are causally connected.

The point for now is that, while I am happy enough with the idea of investigating various kinds of metaphysical dependence relations, *provided* these can be made epistemologically accessible by seeing them as reflections of certain kinds of conceptual interrelations, I also have come to see that there are *many* kinds of conceptual interrelations, and that our concepts and terms may be introduced via many different forms of rules, to serve many different purposes. Given that, we may do better to identify the specific conceptual interrelations at issue, rather than supposing that we are always dealing with "grounding" or some form of "metaphysical dependence relation," and we should not assume that questions about how a thing is "grounded" are always appropriate. Uncovering how these concepts work, and how they are introduced and interrelated, fits quite nicely with the reconception of the metaphysical project to be developed here—not seeing it as engaged in quasi-scientific explanation, but rather as properly focused on conceptual research and development.

---

[37] To borrow a phrase Robert Brandom uses in characterizing Sellars's account of purely theoretical concepts (2002, 366).

5.5 Conclusions

In this chapter I have considered three interrelated ways of reconceiving the project of metaphysics: first, thinking of it as investigating what's *fundamental* (and what's grounded); second, relatedly, thinking of it as aiming to articulate a *layered picture of reality*, in terms of which we can identify the fundamental entities and the grounding relations that hold together various "layers of reality"; and third, the less ambitious project of identifying various "dependence relations" that might hold locally, among entities of particular sorts.

I have expressed severe reservations about the project of discovering "what's (absolutely) fundamental" or developing a "layered picture of reality." The same reservations don't apply to the thought that we can *often* investigate (local) dependence relations between entities of various sorts. This can be appropriate work for metaphysics—provided we can do so in an epistemologically transparent way. A clear way to do this is to think of claims about various metaphysical dependence relations as giving object-language expressions of various *conceptual* interrelations—which can be part of a deflationary approach to metaphysics (such as that to be developed below). If we go that way, however, given the wide variety of different conceptual interrelations, we will do better to aim to identify and speak directly in terms of the relevant sorts of conceptual interrelations involved.

But a deeper problem persists even if we can identify a variety of metaphysical dependence relations and make them epistemologically accessible. That is, we shouldn't assume that, for any of the entities or facts considered by metaphysics, it is appropriate to ask, "Is it fundamental or grounded? What grounds it (or what is grounded in it)? What metaphysical dependence relations does it stand in to other entities?" and so on. For such questions again rely on a functional monist assumption: presupposing that all the terms at issue in metaphysics aim to track and describe some "parts of reality," such that all we need do is investigate their (metaphysical) interrelations, interdependencies, etc. The same goes for thinking that the project of metaphysics is to provide "metaphysical explanations" backed by relations of grounding or dependence. For if we think it is *always* appropriate to ask, for *any* sort of topic, "What metaphysically explains the

existence of numbers?" "What metaphysically explains modality?"...,
and think of metaphysical explanation as a kind of bottom-up constitutive explanation, we seem to be assuming that all of our noun terms are intended to track features of the world, so that it always makes sense to ask how these various features they track are interrelated, and we can ask what features provide the "constitutive explanation" for numbers or possibilities. Demanding a story of how (the existence of) entities referred to in different kinds of discourse are *metaphysically explained* by others seems to presuppose that all our indicatives have a descriptive function: tracking features of the world, so that we can then go on to ask what "metaphysical glue" keeps them together and provides the needed explanation of some entities in terms of others.

But this has been widely questioned by those offering functionally alternative analyses of various forms of language, including moral, modal, and mathematical language. As I will argue in Part II, if we become sophisticated about noticing the different functional roles of different forms of discourse, and the different ways by which they are introduced (including in ways that reflect certain conceptual priorities), it will become evident that not all of our noun terms are introduced to track some feature of reality, such that it makes sense to ask how that feature of reality is *metaphysically explained by* more "basic features" of the physical world (or if, instead, it is itself "fundamental"). In fact, asking what *constitutively explains* the existence of numbers, moral facts, or modality (or what they exist "in virtue of") may introduce wrongheaded questions that belie misunderstandings about the functions and introduction rules for mathematical, moral, and modal discourse.

This brings us to a more general conclusion about *all* of the past projects in metaphysics considered so far—including the explanatory project, the structure project, the truthmaker project, and grounding projects. Metaphysics traditionally includes questions about all kinds of topics: ordinary material objects, persons, works of art, consciousness, fictional characters, meanings, modality, propositions, numbers, moral facts, races, genders and so on.

But whether any particular project or standard of assessment is suitably applied to a given topic will depend on a prior evaluation of the functions of the discourse in question:

- Is it suitable to ask whether referring to certain entities would add *explanatory power* to our theories? *That depends on the functions of the discourse.*
- Is it suitable to say that we should only make use of terms or concepts if they "carve reality at the joints"? *That depends on what the functions of those terms or concepts are.*
- Is it suitable to adopt a truthmaker constraint, demanding that we identify truthmakers if we are to retain the relevant area of discourse? *That depends on the functions and entry rules of the discourse.*
- Is it suitable to ask what the x's exist *in virtue of* (what "metaphysically explains" their existence)? *That depends on the functions of x discourse, and the rules governing it.* (And we might in any case need more specific questions.)

It may be that *none* of these projects is suitable as a *completely general project for metaphysics*, if we consider metaphysics an area of study that addresses *all* of the usual topics. For the functions of ordinary object discourse, modal discourse, moral discourse, and number discourse (to name but a few) may vary.

I am, of course, well aware that I have not here considered *all* of the possible, or even all of the *actual*, ways of thinking of the project of metaphysics. I have left some prominent options unaddressed, such as thinking of metaphysics as engaged in offering "metaphysical explanations" on a *unificationist* model (rather than thinking of these as requiring metaphysical "backing" relations like grounding), or such as thinking of metaphysics as the study of *essences*. And even if I were to address all of the approaches currently in vogue, new ones would inevitably pop up. I leave it for the reader to examine whether other approaches to metaphysics that have been taken or are developed in the future suffer from the same type of problems described here. For I do not want to spend too long on the critical part, as the overall point of the book is not *destructive* but *constructive:* I hope to show how we can reconceive the work of metaphysics in ways that avoid a rivalry with the natural sciences, that are less epistemologically mysterious, and yet that leave it clearly relevant to human life.

The aim of Part I accordingly has been modest: I have not aimed to definitively prove that none of these conceptions of metaphysics work, still less that no further reconception is possible. Instead, I have aimed in the first half of this book to build a plausible *diagnosis* of where many prominent approaches to metaphysics have gone wrong, in thinking of metaphysics as aiming to make deep discoveries about "reality" (whether about existence, truthmakers, structure, grounding relations . . .), while at the same time thinking of it as completely general, addressing questions about *all sorts* of topics. For this can generate the mistake of assuming that the discourse involved in all of these topics functions in the same way: to describe, track, or explain certain "features of reality." If you have some other favored way of thinking of the project of metaphysics, I ask you only to consider these questions: Does it avoid rivalry with the sciences? Does it have a clear and plausible epistemology? And most important: Does it tacitly rely on assuming that all of the diverse terms of interest in metaphysics (including terms for ordinary objects and theoretic entities, for time, causation, modality, morality, mathematics, mental states, etc.) function in the same way—for example, as aiming to represent, track, or describe "features of reality"?

In Part I I have aimed to motivate changing how we think about and practice metaphysics, by making it evident that *many* prominent approaches to metaphysics illegitimately assume a kind of functional monism about language. A central lesson is that before we can determine whether various metaphysical projects, criteria, or questions are appropriate, we need to assess the functions of the relevant form of discourse, the ways it is introduced into language, and the rules it follows. In short, we need to start a step back, asking such linguistic questions, before we dive into pursuing metaphysical questions and applying metaphysical criteria. Taking that step back is the crucial first step in rethinking metaphysics.

PART II
HOW WE SHOULD RETHINK METAPHYSICS

6
Metaphysics as Conceptual Engineering

In Part I I have argued that we have good reason to rethink metaphysics. For if we think of it on the traditional model, as aiming to discover deep facts about "reality," we end up with a problematic rivalry with the sciences, as well as epistemological mysteries about how these alleged facts could be known in any other way. Moreover, as one can see from past metaphysical work, we end up with an unconstrained proliferation of metaphysical views, without any clarity about how we could tell which among them is "correct." In the present day, staying on this heroic track, and insisting that metaphysics is the "study of ultimate reality," is suicidal for metaphysics, inviting increasing obscurity, irrelevance, and skepticism.

Of course, metaphysics has seen hard times before. In the antimetaphysical days of the early 20th century, Carnap (1931) spoke of "overcoming metaphysics," A. J. Ayer pressed for "the elimination of metaphysics" (1936/1952, 33), and many metaphysical theories of the past were dismissed as disguised "nonsense."[1]

That is not, however, the goal here.

I aim not to reject metaphysics but to rethink it. For there is much in past philosophical work—including that which commonly goes under the heading "metaphysics"—that is worthwhile, important, and can even be world-changing. (I aim to show how in Chapter 10.) What we need is a way to see how the work of metaphysics can be rethought in a way that gives it a legitimate role that avoids rivalry with the sciences,

---

[1] Contemporary metaphysicians often comfort themselves by suggesting that these dismissals of metaphysics relied on a form of verificationism that has long been discredited. In fact, however, verificationism was a component of only a small portion of the critiques of metaphysics from the early 20th century. The critiques developed here also do not rely on verificationism.

Rethinking Metaphysics. Amie L. Thomasson, Oxford University Press.
© Oxford University Press 2025. DOI: 10.1093/9780197787830.003.0006

while making it clear how the work can proceed and why it is important. Doing so will also enable us to sort through past work in metaphysics in ways that distinguish what is central, helpful, and worth engaging in from work that arises from confusion, linguistic mistakes, or misguided questions.

6.1 What Can Philosophy Do?

In the first half of the 20th century, the dominant response to the problems facing metaphysics was to suggest that philosophy is concerned not with knowledge about the *world* but with our *language* or *concepts*. Despite their differences, a response along these lines was held in common by phenomenologists, logical positivists, and ordinary language philosophers alike.

But this consensus didn't last. To many it seemed disappointing to think that we could only do such "superficial" work on the structure of our thought or talk, leaving the "deep worldly" questions of metaphysics behind. Nearly a century later, it might also seem to raise questions about whether a new rivalry between philosophy and the sciences arises—this time, not with physics, but rather with linguistics, psychology, and cognitive science. Those disciplines have come many miles since the mid-20th century in gaining knowledge of how our language and thought work, and one might think they give us the best shot at learning more.

So, we seem left in something of a dilemma. If we think of metaphysics as aiming to discover "ultimate reality," we end up with a rivalry with the natural sciences, epistemological mysteries, and skepticism. But if we think of it as investigating the structure or workings of our language or concepts, we threaten to make its work superficial and to invite a new rivalry with the work of linguistics, psychology, and cognitive science.

The problems for metaphysics are just a local version of problems that philosophy as a whole has faced. As we saw in Chapter 1, philosophy has faced the broader threat of being made redundant by the sciences. Hawking and Mlodinow (2012), for example, declared philosophy dead, with its traditional questions taken over by the sciences.

METAPHYSICS AS CONCEPTUAL ENGINEERING 105

But let's look again at the challenge Hawking and Mlodinow present.[2] The questions they list as best handed over to the sciences are questions like "How does the universe behave?" "What is the nature of reality?" and "Where did all this come from?" These I agree cannot be addressed without the serious empirical work of the sciences.

But other core questions of philosophy are notably absent from their list: How ought I to live my life? What should we treat as fundamental human rights? What form of government would be the most just? How should we reason in order to ensure that we reach a true conclusion if we start from true premises? How should we judge the value of a work of art?

Philosophers working in such core areas as ethics, political philosophy, social philosophy, logic, and aesthetics might be irritated by the generality of the criticism, but not at all worried by it.

What do these remaining questions have in common? They are all *normative* questions: questions about what we ought to do, how we ought to behave, be governed, reason, or evaluate art. The questions Hawking focused on, by contrast (and not surprisingly), are *factual* questions about the history, structure, or nature of the universe (what exists, what it's like, what laws it follows, where it came from).

This distinction was already present in the standard criticisms of psychologism. For Frege (1884, 1893) and Husserl (1900/2000), for example, argued that we must distinguish the *descriptive* question of how people *actually* reason from the *normative* question about how we *ought to* reason. While the former question might be best answered by psychology (or ultimately perhaps by neuroscience), questions about how we *should* reason remain questions for logic.

This idea can be turned into a general proposal: that philosophy is, at least in large part, a *normative* discipline. This has the advantage that we can draw on the familiar distinction between *is* and *ought*: scientific, empirical methods are the best methods by far of telling us what *is* the case. But, taken on its own, this does not tell us anything about what *ought to be* the case—about how we *ought to* speak, think,

---

[2] This section is taken from my (2015b).

reason, or live. And these are practical questions that we must engage with as we decide what to do and how to live.

While this view clearly fits well with much work in ethics and political philosophy, logic and aesthetics, one might still worry that it builds a fortress that leaves large portions of philosophy—including philosophy of science, epistemology, and metaphysics—outside the wall and unprotected.

However, it is easy to see at least large portions of philosophy of science and epistemology in a normative light. Epistemology investigates such overtly normative questions as how we should acquire evidence and draw conclusions, when we should count someone as having knowledge, and how we should reason under conditions of uncertainty.

Philosophers of science investigate such issues as how we should reason based on evidence, what methodologies should be employed or cautions should be heeded in scientific reasoning, what conclusions about the world should be drawn from the empirical results of quantum mechanics, or what conclusions about the mind should be drawn from results in cognitive science and psychology. This of course does not—and should not—make philosophy of science entirely distinct from science. The goal is not to make science and philosophy disjoint, but rather to show a role for philosophical *work*, whether in the hands of scientists or philosophers, or both working together. Scientists, too, are concerned to work out what conclusions about the world we should draw from the evidence. Moreover, philosophers of science and scientists alike may be concerned with normative issues about what conceptual scheme we should adopt to do work in biology, ecology, psychology, or quantum mechanics. Such choices may have to be empirically informed and responsive to the practices and needs of working scientists—and to that extent cannot be done without intimate knowledge of the sciences. But they may also involve the kind of broad conceptual work that involves considering alternative conceptual schemes and integrating conceptual schemes into a wider picture—tasks we might hope philosophers will be well suited to help with.

But what about metaphysics? Though it might seem at first to be the most difficult area of philosophy to preserve from these criticisms, this way of reconceiving the work of philosophy can also show the way to reconceive the work of metaphysics. The earlier view of the options (think of metaphysics as investigating *the world* or investigating *our language and concepts*) leaves out something important. We needn't just be concerned with how we *do* think or talk (though, I will argue, that can also be important). We can also ask how we *should* think and talk. Nor are we constrained to just *use* our existing concepts to investigate the world. Instead, we can work to evaluate and reconstruct the concepts and language we use, and sometimes even to construct new concepts and terms to help us in a variety of endeavors.

So understood, we can rethink metaphysics as engaged in a project of conceptual engineering. For the remainder of this book, I will aim to show how we should understand conceptual engineering, how we can do it, and why it matters both to philosophy and—more broadly— to life.

6.2 A Brief History of Philosophy as Conceptual Engineering

The idea that philosophers can engage in conceptual engineering is typically traced to Rudolf Carnap. Though he did not use that term himself, in 1950 he argued that, rather than thinking of philosophy as a rival to the sciences, we can think of it as useful in clarifying, modifying, and developing concepts for use in the empirical work of the sciences.[3] That is, philosophers may aim to *explicate* the concepts we need to do science: concepts such as "confirmation," "probability," "temperature," and "species." Explication, on Carnap's view, isn't a matter of reporting how our concepts *do* work, but rather *improving them* to make them more useful for scientific theorizing by making them more precise and more fruitful for serving in generalizations and laws. With this, Carnap recognized the possibility of a project of conceptual engineering and took steps to develop a method for

---

[3] The term "conceptual engineering" was introduced by Richard Creath (1990) in discussing Carnap's work.

undertaking it—seeing it primarily as a way of engineering concepts to aid in scientific progress.[4]

Carnap is important, but his work only gives a fragment of the historical story. As I have argued elsewhere (2016b), prior work in something like conceptual engineering (in the *implicit* form of negotiating for how or whether we should use concepts such as *person, necessity, freedom, matter*, etc.) appears at many places in the history of philosophy, including in the work of Locke, Hume, and Berkeley. I will return to discuss these uses of metalinguistic negotiation in Chapter 10.

The idea that philosophy can be engaged in conceptual engineering was also developed *explicitly* before Carnap by philosophers of the Lwów-Warsaw school. Jan Łukasiewicz, for example, argued in a 1905 paper for creating a "noncontradictory, unambiguous, scientific concept of cause" that may differ from the current folk or scientific concepts (1905/2022, 11). In fact, the idea that philosophical work may be directed at improving our conceptual scheme can be found in works of many proponents of the Lwów-Warsaw school, including Kazimierz Twardowski (1901), Maria Ossowska (1931), Alfred Tarski (1944), Kazimierz Ajdukiewicz (1934/1987), and Izydora Dąmbska (1958).[5]

The idea that philosophy often has been and can be engaged in something like conceptual engineering also arose repeatedly from the 1930s to the 1960s among those influenced by Wittgenstein. Wittgenstein himself tended to emphasize the therapeutic task of untangling us from old philosophical problems and conceptual confusions—"the philosopher's treatment of a question is like the treatment of an illness" (1953/2001, 255). And an important method Wittgenstein used in doing so was analyzing conceptual connections and distinctions

---

[4] For an account and defense of Carnapian explication as "conceptual re-engineering for theoretical purposes," see Georg Brun (2016). Brun (2020) also points to Nelson Goodman's work on reflective equilibrium (a central influence on Rawls, who introduced the term "reflective equilibrium" but not the approach [Brun 2020, 929]) as developing a method of conceptual re-engineering that further develops the Carnapian approach to explication.

[5] I am indebted to Krzysztof Sękowski (personal communication) for bringing this part of the history of conceptual engineering to my attention, and for the above references. See also Sękowski and Landes (forthcoming). For further discussion of the metaphilosophical approaches of members of the Lwów-Warsaw school, see also Brozek et al. (2020).

among uses of language (Hacker 1996, 111–12). That work (as I will argue below) can be seen as engaged in a kind of *reverse* conceptual engineering. It was in this light that Wittgenstein wrote, "it can never be our job [as philosophers] . . . to explain anything. Philosophy really *is* 'purely descriptive'" (1958, 18d). Wittgenstein noted that some metaphysical claims are best understood as implicitly objecting to a certain use of an expression or notation (1958, 56–59; see also Hacker 1996 120–21). He did not, however, tend to emphasize the possibility of a *constructive* project of engaging in potentially helpful conceptual change—on the contrary, he insisted, "Philosophy may in no way interfere with the actual use of language; it can in the end only describe it" (1953/2001, 124).

Nonetheless, several of Wittgenstein's students and followers (in more conciliatory mode) saw the open path of thinking that philosophical work can not only free us from old problems but also lead to helpful *proposals*. John Wisdom (acknowledging his influence by Wittgenstein) wrote in 1937, "A philosophical answer is really a verbal recommendation" (1937, 71), while acknowledging that philosophical claims nonetheless "have not a verbal air" and "have not a merely verbal point" (1937, 73).[6] And Wisdom emphasizes that these recommendations can be illuminating. Many of the "surprising" things metaphysicians say, he writes, "*are* false—only there *is* good in them, poor things" (1937, 77).[7]

The most thorough early development I have seen of the idea that philosophical work can be seen as conceptual engineering was by Alice Ambrose.[8] Ambrose was an American philosopher who studied

---

[6] In both of these respects, Wisdom's claim resembles the later idea that philosophical debates are often cases of metalinguistic negotiation (cf. Plunkett and Sundell 2013, and Plunkett 2015 and my 2017a for application of the idea of metalinguistic negotiation to philosophical debates). But in his discussion of *what* further (nonverbal) point they have, Wisdom suggests only that they illuminate "the ultimate structure of facts; *i.e.*, the relations between different categories of being or . . . the relations between different sub-languages within a language" (1937, 73). By contrast, the more recent articles cited above bring out more direct forms of worldly importance that metalinguistic negotiations may have.
[7] Wisdom (1937, 85) also notes that attention to functional differences is important.
[8] I am grateful to Matthew Shields for directing me to her work, and for his work in reconstructing and rediscovering it. See his "Alice Ambrose and the History of Analytic Metaphilosophy" (in progress).

with Wittgenstein in Cambridge, and was one of the students to whom he dictated the *Blue and Brown Books*. Ambrose went on to become the Austin and Sophia Smith Chair in Philosophy at Smith College and served as editor of the *Journal of Symbolic Logic*. In a paper originally published in the *Journal of Philosophy* in 1952,[9] Ambrose argues against the "orthodox" view that "describes philosophy as a pursuit of truth, where 'pursuit of truth' is interpreted... as the attempt to acquire knowledge about our world" (1952/1966, 142). She argues that philosophical views cannot be considered empirical, in part on grounds that "philosophic disputants come to opposite conclusions although the same facts are available to them and no possible further fact can decide betwixt them" (1952/1966, 143). The apparent alternative, thinking of philosophical theories as (in some sense) *linguistic*, she argues, is best developed as the position that "philosophers are neither analyzing concepts nor stating correct usage in giving a view, but are doing something else equally linguistic, namely, *revising language*" (1952/1966, 149, italics mine). She also (with Wisdom) anticipates the idea developed and named much later, that many past philosophical debates often "conceal a proposal for linguistic change" (1952/1966, 149). That is, in contemporary terms, that philosophical debates may often be best interpreted as engaged in (what David Plunkett and Tim Sundell 2013 came to call) "metalinguistic negotiation" (for later developments of this idea, see also Plunkett 2015 and my 2017a). As Ambrose puts it more fully:

> This approach stems from the view that philosophical theories are not, as they appear to be, answers to questions, but are proposals to alter language: that they do not in fact attempt to clarify a concept

---

[9] This paper was first presented at a symposium on Linguistic Conceptions of Philosophy held at Smith College on May 20, 1951. She attributes versions of this view of philosophy to Wisdom and to Morris Lazerowitz, who presents a related though less sympathetic take on philosophical theories (in a more Freudian mode), that "the nucleus of a philosophical theory is a hidden verbal innovation which does one kind of work at the conscious level of our minds and another kind of work at the unconscious level" (1960, 730). Ambrose also mentions that Norman Malcolm describes the skeptic as recommending that we no longer apply "certain" to any empirical statements (151), and presents Max Black (1949, 75–78) similarly as suggesting that we only say "practically know" not "know for certain," though neither Malcolm nor Black subscribed to this general view about the nature of philosophical theories.

or to explain a current usage, but instead, in a concealed way, propose that a word's use shall be modified for philosophical purposes. (1952/1966, 149)

Both Ambrose (1952/1966, 155–56) and Wisdom (1937, 76) also discuss ways in which this approach is preferable to dismissing metaphysical statements as mere "nonsense."

In her wonderful essay "Philosophical Plumbing," Mary Midgley also suggests that the proper and useful work of philosophy can be considered analogous to a certain kind of engineering. There, she likens philosophical work to plumbing, writing:

> Plumbing and philosophy are both activities that arise because elaborate cultures like ours have, beneath their surface, a fairly complex system which is usually unnoticed, but which sometimes goes wrong. In both cases, this can have serious consequences. (1992, 139)

The central job of philosophy, as she saw it, was to understand, repair, and renew our conceptual schemes:

> Conceptual schemes as such are philosophy's concern, and these schemes do constantly go wrong. Conceptual confusion is deadly, and a great deal of it afflicts our everyday life. It needs to be seen to, and if the professional philosophers do not look at it, there is no one else whose role it is to be called on. (1992, 143)

Wisdom, Ambrose, and Midgley all took a broader view of work in conceptual engineering than Carnap—seeing it not merely as a task to be applied to scientific concepts, but as applicable to all sorts of concepts relevant to philosophy and human life. But their work has been largely forgotten—with the only memory of past conceptual engineering traced to Carnap's work in engineering concepts for use in the sciences. It is only quite recently, over the past 20 years or so, that explicit interest in conceptual engineering has revived and spread. In part, the recent interest in conceptual engineering comes from recognizing again that Carnap's approach can be broadened—for it is not only our *scientific* concepts that might be improved. Sally Haslanger

(2000) raised the question of whether social concepts, such as race and gender concepts, might be improved—not to serve our scientific theories, but rather to serve the cause of social justice. This instigated a broadening of conceptual-engineering projects well beyond Carnap's contributions, as it has come to include not only attempts to (re-)engineer scientific concepts, but also social concepts,[10] logical concepts,[11] and other philosophical concepts.[12]

6.3 What Is Conceptual Engineering?

Think of conceptual engineering on analogy to civil or mechanical engineering. Engineers may be involved in constructing new bridges or roadways, or in designing new kinds of machinery or structures to serve new purposes. But it is also engineers we look to when we need to assess our old structures—whether a building remains stable after an earthquake, or what repairs or maintenance an aircraft needs to safely carry passengers. It is engineers we look to for repair or retrofitting—say, in determining what reinforcements a roof needs to withstand a possible hurricane, or a building needs to stand through an earthquake. And it is engineers we look to when we need to engage in *reverse* engineering to determine how a piece of malware works, or how an old engine or machine worked and what it did.

Similarly, conceptual engineering may focus on constructive engineering, or on assessment, repair, retrofitting, or reverse engineering. In fact, if we think of it as fundamentally faced with questions about what concepts and/or language we *should* use (and how we should use them), conceptual engineering must do all of these. Once we see all facets of the project, we can better see the ways in which conceptual engineering may encompass a great deal of the work that metaphysics

---

[10] See, e.g., work by Haslanger (2000) on re-engineering race and gender concepts, Diaz-Leon (2022) on the concept of woman, Dembroff (2020) on gender and sexual orientation concepts, and Cantalamessa (2021) on re-engineering disability concepts.
[11] See, e.g., Kevin Scharp's (2013) work on re-engineering the concept of truth.
[12] See, for example, David Papineau's (2019) suggestions about re-engineering the concept of knowledge, and Justin Garson's (2022) aims to rethink our concept of "madness."

(and other areas of philosophy) has traditionally done well, as well as leaving room for further important work it can do.

Since we have some concepts and language already, we must first ask how our concepts and language work, before determining whether those are parts of language or of our conceptual scheme that we should retain, repair, or replace. Assessing our extant language and conceptual scheme requires undertaking reverse engineering. Matthieu Queloz (2021a) similarly suggests that a good way to begin with terms of our current language is with reverse engineering. That is, we should begin by assessing what terms such as number terms, or a term for "truth," or moral terms *do* that has made them a useful part of the conceptual repertoire—or at least useful for *some*. In doing this functional work, we must not assume that any functions uncovered are *universally* beneficial—like other artifacts (from fences to weapons to pesticides), parts of language may be beneficial to some individuals or groups but not to others, or useful for some purposes without being beneficial overall.

Once we have a good idea of what the relevant *functions* are, we can do better at assessing whether these are functions we should retain or reject. Are they (like number terms) functioning in crucial ways to help us systematize information, reason, and make inferences in science and elsewhere? Or are they (like pejoratives) functioning to derogate? We can also better assess whether the relevant terms and concepts are still serving their functions well (even in changed technological and social circumstances), or if we might do better by changing our concept of truth, or freedom, or death, or marriage, or intelligence.

We also need to engage in assessment to properly do *reparative* or *retrofitting* work in civil, mechanical, software, or electrical engineering: If (for example) there seems to be a problem with an electrical system, we need to examine how the system works so as better to identify and resolve the problem. Much the same goes for conceptual engineering. One symptom that conceptual engineering is needed is when our current concepts—say, our concept of truth, or freedom, or person—seem to lead us into paradoxes, unresolved questions, or unacceptable conclusions. In this light, we can see some traditional philosophical problems as symptoms that we need to do some reverse engineering, and perhaps go on from there to engage in conceptual revision and reconstruction. Paradoxes and puzzles have often driven work in conceptual engineering throughout the history of philosophy. The truth paradoxes, for example, have led to a great deal of work on conceptual analysis and re-engineering of "truth" (most recently, in work by Kevin Scharp [2013]). Gilbert Ryle (1949) was motivated to re-examine the "logical geography of mental concepts" by noting the paradoxes and difficulties their use led us into. Kant (1781) was motivated to re-examine how to understand fundamental concepts such as causation and necessity by attention to the "antinomies." Berkeley (1713) argued for revising our conceptual scheme to do away with the concept of "matter" based on the paradoxes and difficulties the use of that concept led to.

Where there appear to be puzzles and paradoxes, we have two options: We might, through a kind of reverse engineering, come to better understand the functions the concept serves and the rules it follows, and thereby untangle it in a way that enables us to understand why the original paradoxes or perplexities arose, and yet that relieves the puzzlement.[13] Wittgenstein's "therapeutic" approach to philosophy can be seen as pressing for this sort of role for philosophical work, as "showing the fly the way out of the fly-bottle" (1953/2001, 309). Or we might (if that work fails to disentangle the concept but instead reveals deep problems) aim to re-engineer the concept, or even to do away with it entirely.

But reverse conceptual engineering needn't be prompted by paradox. It also can arise from attempts to simply understand, globally or locally, how our conceptual scheme works. Are certain concepts essential for experiencing a world at all? Or for considering individuals as agents? Or for our moral practices to make sense? Such forms of global reverse conceptual engineering, aiming to understand how our conceptual scheme as a whole works, include work by Kant, Husserl, Strawson, and others. Or it may engage in more local investigations into relations among our concepts—for example, asking about the

---

[13] Sometimes this untangling may be done by way of work in linguistics as, for example, work in systemic functional linguistics may show that certain terms enter language as grammatical metaphors, and may reveal that certain paradoxes result from harmless shifts in grammatical category. See Halliday (2009, 131). See also discussion in Chapter 8 below.

relations between our concepts of liberty and necessity (as Hume did), or agency, personhood, action, and responsibility (as so much work in moral philosophy, action theory, and free will does). So conceived, in short, a great deal of traditional and historical work on philosophical paradoxes and puzzles, as well as work in conceptual analysis, ordinary language philosophy, moral psychology, and phenomenology, can all be considered as work in conceptual engineering—primarily on the reverse-engineering side.

But our philosophical work isn't limited to understanding and evaluating our extant language and concepts. As Carnap saw for scientific concepts, Quine saw for logical concepts, and Haslanger saw for social concepts, we may also engage in reparative and constructive conceptual engineering. We sometimes need to engage in conceptual research and development when concepts fail to fulfill their functions, whether these are extant functions or new or altered functions. Carnap's own task of explication (1950) falls under the latter heading, for in explication terms acquire the function of serving in a precise set of well-connected concepts for a scientific theory, which will be useful in formulating universal laws. Meeting these higher standards requires us to explicate certain of our familiar concepts—such as "probability," "confirmation," "heat," or "fish." At times, empirical discoveries may demonstrate the need for conceptual reform. For empirical discoveries may show that the concept *never could do* what we asked it to, or that *given certain empirical changes in the world*, it can no longer do what we (now) need it to. For example, as Carnap points out, "fish," as used for "sea creature" generally, turned out to be inept for forming biological generalizations, and so we did better to replace it with a narrower version (Carnap 1950, 6). More recently, discoveries of the great diversity in evolutionary history among things called "fish" (even using the new concept) have led some to suggest that we should reject the concept of "fish" altogether.[14]

Even Quine, when responding to accusations that philosophy has lost contact with people, cites a central contribution as introducing and developing formal logic: "A striking trait of scientific philosophy [in the

---

[14] https://medium.com/illumination/there-is-no-such-thing-as-a-fish-eca04 8dd6163.

last hundred years] has been the use, increasingly, of the powerful new logic. This has made for a deepening of insights and a sharpening of problems and solutions" (1981, 191). Various developments of formal logic can easily be seen under the heading of constructive conceptual engineering—as ways of developing new formal linguistic tools with which we can unravel old puzzles and paradoxes and sharpen our analyses.

But conceptual engineering isn't limited to assisting with the work of the sciences or logic—it has also increasingly been seen as relevant and useful to social and political questions, such as what we should do with the parts of our conceptual scheme that concern gender or race. As Anthony Appiah (1994) has made beautifully clear, "race," as used by Thomas Jefferson and Matthew Arnold (and many of their contemporaries and followers) turned out to name nothing like a natural kind that could support the generalizations and inferences about cultural and intellectual characteristics that these influential thinkers sought to make. Noticing that race concepts never really could do what they purported to do is a powerful prompt for conceptual change.

Other concepts may have once functioned well but are no longer able to do so, in a new environmental, social, or technological context. A good example of this sort (discussed by Bernard Gert et al. 2006) is the concept of *death*. We need the concept of death in determining when we may cease medical interventions, commence inheritance and funeral proceedings, etc. But given the expense and wide use of end-of-life medical procedures (as well as technologies for artificial respiration and organ transplantation), we now need the concept to be far more precise in order to serve these functions well. Along similar lines, David Papineau[15] has argued that while the concept of knowledge may have served our ancestors well enough in distinguishing who was and wasn't "in contact with the facts" (e.g., about where the food is), in the current context (he argues) it does harm by prioritizing perceptual over statistical evidence, for example in court rulings.

We often need to consider reconstructing our old concepts in a changed context. For example, in the current social and technological

---

[15] https://aeon.co/essays/knowledge-is-a-stone-age-concept-were-better-off-without-it.

context, what concepts do we need of intelligence, privacy, information, mind, disease, disability, or death? In other cases, the crucial changes are in the context of our current *knowledge*, especially as scientific knowledge develops. How should we readjust our biological concepts and species concepts, in light of ongoing discoveries? (Consider the debates in biology and philosophy of biology about which species concept[s] to use.) How should we think about the mind, about beliefs, desires, or emotions, given what we now know about the brain and its relation to other bodily and environmental systems?

Another type of situation in which conceptual reform is called for is not when a term fails to fulfill a function but when it fulfills a function we do not endorse or do not think should be fulfilled. Consider, for example, the functions of exclusion and derogation often served by pejoratives, which mediate between descriptive application conditions and exit rules that endorse problematic norms of regard and treatment.[16] This kind of conceptual reform may call for eliminating old concepts rather than introducing new ones.

Other needs for conceptual research and development arise when we aim to engage in what David Chalmers has called "ex nihilo" conceptual engineering, designing new concepts to serve some new, perhaps scientific, technological, or social, purpose.[17] For the first, think of Wilhelm Johannsen's 1909 introduction of the concept of a gene (a concept that has been much re-engineered since) to engage better in explanation of inherited traits. For the second, think of terms such as "website," "bug," "server," "app," etc. that have been introduced to keep up with and enable communication about our new technology. For the third, think of the introduction of terms like "homophobia," "genocidal rape," and "human rights."

Once we understand conceptual engineering broadly in this way to include both reverse engineering, assessment, repair and retrofitting, and constructive engineering, it is easy to see how it can unify our

---

[16] David Braddon-Mitchell (2020) similarly suggests that we think of concepts as having not only causal inputs, but also direct connections to behaviors, negative affect, and so on.

[17] Philosophical purposes might also be added here. Consider, for example, Edmund Husserl's introduction of a range of new terminology ("noesis," "noema," "hyle," ...) to serve work in phenomenology.

understanding of a great deal of past philosophical work—including past work in metaphysics, phenomenology, ordinary language philosophy, epistemology, philosophy of science, social and political philosophy, and even applied ethics.

6.4 Avoiding the Problems of the Traditional Conception

In Chapter 1 I described three central problems that arise for the traditional concept of metaphysics as aiming to discover "ultimate reality": that it leads to problems of a rivalry with the sciences, a proliferation of views that leads to a despairing skepticism, and epistemological mysteries about how we could ever come to know which views are correct.

Rethinking metaphysics as conceptual engineering—including both reverse and (re)constructive engineering[18]—can give us ways to avoid or rethink all of these problems.

6.4.1 Rivalry with the Sciences

If we think of philosophy as engaged in conceptual engineering, it no longer faces a rivalry with the sciences. It may work hand in hand with the sciences, say, with physics, in asking how we should think of space and time, or with biology in asking what concepts of species or gene we should use, or more broadly in asking how we should understand confirmation, evidence, and inference. Or it may work on concepts that are not specifically the province of science but play central roles in human life—concepts such as art, freedom, responsibility, consciousness, or person. But as long as we see it on the normative side, as addressing questions about what concepts or language we *should* use (and how we should use them), these are clearly questions that are not addressed by the empirical work of the sciences alone (though they often must be *responsive to* that work, to do their job well—more on

---

[18] Machery (2017) refers to roughly these projects as "descriptive" and "prescriptive" conceptual analysis.

that in Chapter 9 below). That, of course, concerns the *(re)constructive* side of conceptual engineering, rather than the reverse-engineering project that asks descriptive questions about how our language or conceptual scheme *does* work.

The latter, descriptive kind of work, as I have mentioned above, might overlap with the work of linguistics, psychology, and cognitive science—fields that have all progressed a great deal since the heyday of phenomenology and ordinary language philosophy in the first half of the 20th century. In this case, while there is a potential for rivalry, I think the right response is to work *with* it (rather than working in isolation from or rivalry with it). Questions about how our concepts *do* work (especially local questions about our concepts of responsibility, freedom, reference, or innateness [Machery 2017, 241–44]) are being addressed by experimental work—whether we label this as work in experimental philosophy or psychology.[19] Even questions about what (if any) basic concepts enable us to perceive a spatiotemporal world at all, and about whether there are any innate concepts, are interestingly addressed by work in developmental psychology (see, for example, Carey 2009).[20]

Work in linguistics may also be crucially helpful to reverse-engineering work. In Chapters 7 and 8 I will aim to show how work in systemic functional linguistics helps with unraveling old metaphysical problems, showing how they arose from mistakes (often about the functions and rules of different parts of language) and how we can avoid them. It may also be helpful in our (re)constructive-engineering projects, in determining what functions our terms have served, so that we can better evaluate whether to retain, revise, or reject them; and in finding ways to *implement* the changes we think are needed. In all of these ways, the picture of metaphysics I will develop here sees not a

---

[19] Of course, questions abound about what methodology we should use for this work, and what conclusions we should draw from its results, but those questions can be left to the side here. For discussion of how we can "naturalize" conceptual analysis, see Machery (2017).

[20] Again, whether we should accept the results is a matter of some philosophical controversy (see Hirsch 1997). I will also leave open questions about whether this work is relevant to philosophical debates done in transcendental terms, such as work done by Kant and Strawson about what concepts are necessary to be able to experience a world at all.

rivalry between the work of metaphysics and that of psychology and linguistics, but potential for a fruitful *collaboration.*

6.4.2 Proliferation and Skepticism

Rethinking the work of metaphysics as work in conceptual engineering also enables us to reconsider the problems of proliferation and skepticism. As I discussed in Chapter 1, if we think of metaphysics as aiming to discover facts about "ultimate reality," the fact that metaphysical views (on pretty much any topic) have tended to increasingly proliferate can undermine our confidence that we have any hope of determining *which is right*, and finding out the *real facts of the matter.* And this, in turn, tends to lead to a despairing skepticism about whether such facts can be known (Nozick 2001; Bennett 2009; Machery 2017), and even to suggestions that we would do better turn our attention to more tractable pursuits.

But the proliferation of views is only a problem if one joins traditional metaphysicians in thinking of the task of metaphysics as discovering some *deep truth* about what (really) exists, what (really) is fundamental, what the modal properties of things of various kinds (really) are, and so on. For only if we think of metaphysics as aiming to discover the "real facts" does it seem problematic when we get conflicting views about what those facts are, and no clear prospect of resolution.

Suppose we instead think of it as a task in conceptual engineering—particularly on the *prescriptive* (re)constructive side of things. While factual questions about how many protons are in the nucleus of a carbon atom had better close in on a single answer, engineering questions are fundamentally *practical* questions. If we ask how we should build a new bridge over the Connecticut River, we might get a myriad of different answers—but these aren't conflicting reports about some underlying fact, but alternative *proposals.* It may, in fact, be useful to get a range of alternative proposals, reflecting alternative constraints and purposes for the bridge. (Is it to be a pedestrian bridge, a road bridge, a rail bridge? What is the budget? What constraints are there about how long we can take to build it, or what materials we can reasonably acquire, or what modifications we may make to surrounding land or structures?) Where constructive engineering is concerned, a proliferation of answers is not an embarrassment that should lead us to skepticism and to giving up the project. Instead, it provides a richness of available *options* that may reflect different ranges of assumed functions or purposes, different sets of constraints, etc. And even when we narrow it down to a single purpose and set of constraints (say, a pedestrian bridge for under a million dollars), we may end up with two or more different viable options. But having options in such cases is a *good thing* that can enable us to meet our goals in different ways—not an embarrassment that leads to skepticism.

6.4.3 Epistemological Mystery

I have often argued that if we think of metaphysics on the traditional model, as discovering deep facts about (fundamental) reality, we end up with epistemological mysteries about how such facts could be discovered—particularly when metaphysicians insist that these questions cannot be settled merely *empirically*, but that they also are not matters for conceptual analysis. And I have long sought to develop a clear way of answering questions about what exists (2015a), or about identity and persistence conditions (2020a), in ways that make use of nothing more mysterious than empirical and conceptual work.

What happens if we rethink metaphysics as conceptual engineering? On this reconceived model we can recognize several kinds of questions: empirical questions, conceptual questions (which may also be factual questions *about concepts* and, seen as such, are empirical questions), and *practical* questions.

The reverse-engineering work, as I will draw it out below, involves empirical work on our concepts and language, including both investigating the rules of use for our expressions and their interconnections, and questions about the functions of the relevant forms of language. All of that, in principle, may be conducted empirically—I will aim to do some of this below in employing work in systemic functional linguistics.[21]

But what of the normative (re)constructive conceptual work? At bottom, the questions driving such work concern what terms or concepts we *should* use, and how we *should* use them. These are at bottom not *factual* questions but *practical* questions. It is not that there are deep facts to uncover but rather that there are difficult *decisions* to make. The vast majority of questions in conceptual engineering as such, however (like the vast majority of questions in civil engineering or mechanical engineering), are engaged practical questions about what will best serve some *established or tacitly agreed upon* needs or purposes. As long as certain practical purposes are clear and established (as I will argue in Chapter 9) it may be a factual matter for empirical discovery whether any given proposal will suit the purposes well, or how well competing proposals may fare at serving the relevant purposes. In that way, our decisions in (re)constructive conceptual engineering may be non-arbitrary, and open to clear and reasoned defense.

But questions remain about what purposes we *should adopt*, how we should weigh competing purposes or values, etc.—the most basic form of which is *What shall we do?* These are matters for practical *decision*.[22] They are *difficult practical quandaries*, not factual questions where it is *epistemologically mysterious* how we could discover the answers. Thinking of them as matters for discovery is a form of what Jean-Paul Sartre called "bad faith."[23]

---

[21] There are underlying issues here about how rules or norms may be empirically discovered, which I will not be able to address here. Linguists and anthropologists of course regularly address these questions in broadly empirical terms, as they aim to determine the grammatical rules of a previously unstudied language, or the cultural (say, gift-giving) rules in play in a certain culture. See also the work of Bicchieri and Mercier (2014) for an empirical approach to studying and changing norms. Further discussion will have to be left for elsewhere. Thanks to Joshua Gert for raising these issues.

[22] They can, of course, be rephrased in ways that ask about what the "best" decision would be, or what is "morally right" or "practically best." But these hypostatizing reformulations are derivative ways of framing the issue, which tend to mislead us into thinking of them on the model of factual discoveries.

[23] I owe to Lewis Gordon the insight that resisting the idea that conceptual engineering is possible, and treating our concepts as fixed and immutable, is a form of bad faith (from a conversation with my class, in spring of 2022).

Thinking of philosophy as conceptual engineering rather than worldly discovery also enables us to avoid the feeling there are deep but unknowable answers to philosophical questions, so we should just give up trying. We must decide what to have for dinner, even if there is no prospect of discovering a "right" answer to that question. If we don't decide, we go hungry. Similarly, we must go on using some conceptual system. The worst thing we could do would be to give up thinking seriously about which concepts we should use and how we should use them.

6.5 Should We Engineer Concepts or Language?

I have argued that we should change the way we think of metaphysics—thinking of it primarily as a matter of *conceptual engineering*. So far I have been speaking of engineering our *terms or concepts*, usually without specifying which. But if we are to think of metaphysics as a form of conceptual engineering, should we think in terms of engineering *concepts* or *language?* Both are good projects. I will primarily take a linguistic approach here, and will begin by explaining why I find it helpful to do so—while also emphasizing that it does not rule out work done in psychological mode, but provides a useful complement to it that can reach new territory.

So far there has been little consensus in the burgeoning conceptual-engineering literature about whether we should think in terms of engineering language or concepts (see Isaac 2021 and 2023). Manuel Gustavo Isaac (2021, 291) argues that if we see the target of conceptual engineering as language rather than concepts, that makes "conceptual" engineering a misleading misnomer—and one that undermines its own goals if it leads people astray (2021, 6). I do not see that as a decisive worry, however, for conceptual engineering has long been presented as a way to understand, evaluate, and modify how we *think and talk*. Both of those projects remain—particularly since, at least for a great many of the scientific, social, and philosophical concepts of interest in philosophy and conceptual engineering, we think *in* and *using* language. And when we take interest in conceptually engineering philosophically interesting terms such as "person," "freedom," "cause," etc., we are not interested in their phonetic or typographic structure, but rather (as we might naturally put it) in the *concept they express*. In short, in thinking about words and how to engineer them, we *are* thinking about concepts, so it is not misleading.

Approaching these issues linguistically does not prevent us from also discussing them in conceptual terms. Talk of concepts is, perhaps among other things, a way of talking about what a term in one language and its appropriate translations in another language have in common ("they express the same concept"). As a result, we can aim to shift up from any conclusions we reach regarding particular terms of English, Spanish, Igbo, Chinese, or Tagalog, to ask about to what extent those conclusions carry over to good translations of those terms in other languages (acknowledging that we can abstract away from phonetic or typographical issues, which aren't of primary interest).[24] When we reach conclusions for how or whether we should re-engineer "woman," that may tell us something about what we should do with "Frau" or "mujer" too.[25] But beginning from the linguistic level also reminds us to be appropriately cautious in such generalizations. For given the holistic nature of natural languages, and the ways in which languages are embedded in a way of life, often what look like apt (or best possible) translations may have limitations and subtly different inferential roles, or may overlap only in restricted contexts.[26] In short, talk about concepts can still be undertaken, even if we begin by thinking about language—since we can still begin from linguistic analysis, and then investigate where it is legitimate to abstract from accidental features of the linguistic formulation in question to apply the same analysis and results to appropriate translations. But it also serves as a reminder to not generalize too quickly, and to attend to subtle differences in the use of terms that are commonly intertranslated—which may demand

---

[24] Except perhaps with regard to implementation—as new words that are hard to pronounce for speakers of a given language may be less likely to catch on, and new words that sound like an old word may create confusion (see Koslow 2022).

[25] Though, as one anonymous referee aptly suggested, we can't just *assume* that the relevant suggestions will be equally apt across languages, given their different sets of inferential connections and the varying social contexts in which they are used.

[26] One important example of this (as Italo Lins Lemos, Jerzy Brzozowski, Gabriel Andersen Eugênio, and Cristian Santiago Kraemer reminded me) is the very different sets of "race" concepts used in Brazilian Portuguese versus in English.

that sometimes conceptual-engineering projects go differently when we work with different languages.

In fact, though I will focus on language here, I do not think we need to choose between thinking in terms of engineering concepts or engineering language; we can fruitfully ask questions using either set of terms. Edouard Machery, who has perhaps done the most to develop a psychological approach to conceptual engineering, similarly acknowledges that "Historical, anthropological, or sociological linguistics" may do work complementary to his (2017, 240).

Work on concepts is undeniably relevant and interesting. One can see some historical work (say, in Kant, or in Strawson [1964]) as doing a kind of reverse-engineering work that addresses transcendental questions about the structure any conceptual scheme would have to take (in order for us to experience a spatiotemporal world at all). And one can see some recent work in psychology (Carey 2009) as asking parallel evolutionary questions about how our evolved conceptual scheme actually functions. There are also good reasons to think that infants and (other) non-linguistic animals may have certain concepts without language, though we may build upon and enormously add to such conceptual schemes as we acquire language. A complete reverse-engineering project that traced the development of our color concepts, object concepts, or even moral concepts might need to move stepwise to track the abilities gained by having nonverbal concepts (perhaps just reliable responsive dispositions), versus by coming to modify the concept through various linguistic forms that may be developed later.[27] Some work directly on conceptual engineering focuses on developing a naturalized approach to conceptual analysis that can be of use in both *descriptive* reverse-engineering projects and in *prescriptive* (reconstructive) conceptual-engineering projects (see Machery 2017, 239–44). I find work on conceptual engineering, conducted in the psychological mode, both interesting and promising.

---

[27] So, for example, we might separately articulate the functions of being able to reliably discriminate red things, versus having a fully inferentially articulated concept *is red*, versus developing it into linguistic forms where it can not only be expressed in an adjective but be expressed in noun form, enabling us to speak about *the property of redness*. (For more on such grammatical metaphors, see Chapters 7 and 8.)

But there are also good reasons to work in linguistic terms, and here I will focus on the linguistic approach. One reason to work with language is that it enables us to avoid questions about what concepts are, and to avoid some historically prominent ways of thinking of concepts that would block our very ability to see conceptual engineering as possible. Platonists about concepts, who think of concepts as timeless and changeless, obviously can't even acknowledge the possibility of conceptual engineering—at least not if we think of it as altering our concepts.[28] The same goes for any view of concepts on which a concept has its intension or extension essentially. Herman Cappelen attributes this view to Mark Richard, expressing it as follows:

> *You can't improve on a concept by changing its intension and extension because that very idea is incoherent.* Concepts have their intensions and extensions *essentially.* So a change in intension or extension always involves abandoning a concept, and can never be an improvement of the old concept. Insofar as conceptual engineering rests on the idea of changing a particular concept's intension and so extension, the entire project is incoherent. (Cappelen 2018, 104)

If we are Platonists about concepts, thinking of them intensionally, as functions from worlds to extensions, it will indeed be hard or impossible to see how a given concept could be *changed*. More generally, as Sarah Sawyer puts it, "so long as we assume that concepts have their intensions and extensions essentially, it will not be possible for them to be revised" (2020, 391).[29]

---

[28] One could instead think of it as conceptual replacement—provided one thinks new concepts can be created. If not, the perhaps the best we could hope for is a kind of conceptual shuffling that involves shifting which concept (of a preexisting range) is expressed by a given term.

[29] For this reason, she recommends that we separate out the idea of *concepts* from that of *linguistic meanings*, and treat the primary focus of conceptual engineering to be to change *linguistic meanings*. Concepts, she suggests, we should think of as individuated by relations to "objective properties in the world," which enables them to fix a stable subject matter. By contrast, she suggests that we understand linguistic meanings as supervening on use and capable of change over time—including change for the better, as we get a better view of the subject matter and engage in conceptual engineering (2020, 387).

By contrast, it is natural to think of language as a human construction and as changing and evolving historically. That is, we can naturally think of languages as abstract cultural artifacts.[30] Doing so fits well with work in historical linguistics and enables us to rely on some of that work in beginning to understand processes of word formation and meaning change over time—natural processes that we can make use of to increase our chances of success at implementing recommendations in conceptual engineering. Allison Koslow (2022) makes the case that we can draw on work in *historical* linguistics to better understand how language *does change* over time, and what the natural processes of linguistic change are, so that we can better make use of these in determining what sorts of change in conceptual engineering are more and less likely to succeed, and how to make use of these natural processes of change in implementing the recommendations of conceptual engineering.

Of course, one doesn't *have to* think about concepts on a Platonistic model. We can, instead, make use of a psychological understanding of concepts. The most prominent contemporary psychological approach treats concepts as "bodies of information about some category of referent" (Isaac 2021, 10), which are activated to be used in categorization, action-planning, induction, and deduction (Isaac 2021, 11). Such a view of concepts, Isaac argues, has better prospects for allowing concepts to change over time, and enables us to make use of empirical work in psychology in understanding concepts. Machery similarly has developed an understanding of concepts as "psychological entities, not abstract entities" (2017, 210), namely "bodies of information about individuals, classes, substances, or events" consisting in those belief-like states about the entities represented that are retrieved "by default" (quickly, automatically, and across contexts) to play a role in our cognition and language understanding (2017, 210).

Such an understanding of concepts is a helpful improvement over the Platonist approach and may be useful for various projects in conceptual engineering and for investigating at least some of our concepts. But, at least as described here, it also has limitations that are important

---

[30] For development of the view that languages, and words, are abstract artifacts, see Kaplan (1990), Irmak (2019), and my (2021b).

for our philosophical purposes. For as Machery and Isaac articulate it, this psychological way of thinking about concepts is inherently *representational*—as Isaac puts it, it treats concepts as "bodies of information about some category of referents" (Isaac 2023, 2152). That is, it focuses on concepts *of certain kinds of things* (dogs, triangles) as carrying information about them. As Machery puts it, "Concepts are about entities, and can characterize these more or less accurately" (2017, 210). And on this model, as Machery develops it, descriptive conceptual analysis (of the sort involved in reverse-engineering projects) consists in describing a subset of the belief-like states "about the members of the extension" of the concept (the subset retrieved by default from long-term memory) that "specify properties of members of the extension of the concept" (2017, 212).

Thinking of concepts in this way takes on a representationalist presupposition that, as I have argued in Part I, has led earlier conceptions of metaphysics astray. It has also led us into pseudo-problems about properties, numbers, modality, morality, and other perennially problematic philosophical concepts—all of which can be reassessed if we give up the functional monist assumption, and no longer assume that the sole and universal job of concepts is to carry information about objects in the world we refer to. For some of the most interesting and promising treatments of modality, morality, numbers, etc. are treatments that *do not* involve treating the relevant terms or concepts "representationally," as ways of carrying bodies of information *about* certain worldly referents.[31] If we simply think of concepts as mental representations of certain referents that carry "bodies of information" about those referents, then we leave out of view a range of interesting and promising neo-pragmatist approaches to concepts (such as moral, modal, and number concepts) that have been central in provoking metaphysical problems.

Moreover, some of these concepts, in their philosophically interesting (problematic) form, rely on being expressed in a

---

[31] For general discussion of the problems of the so-called "representationalist" assumption, see Price (2011). For particular problems with this approach to morality, see Blackburn (1993); for modality, see my (2020b) and (2023b). Other applications of a nonrepresentationalist, neo-pragmatist approach may be found in Gert (2023).

certain *grammatical* form or category. For example, Quine notoriously claimed to have no problem with assertions that houses and sunsets *are red*, but rejected the "ontological commitments" that seemed to come with talk of *the property of redness*. Yet, if we speak in terms of concepts, there is a temptation to simply speak of *the concept of redness*.[32] But examining only concepts considered in noun form (*the concept of x*) elides this distinction, and may also overlook important functional differences between adjectives and their nominalizations. (Much the same goes for determiner uses of number terms [e.g., in "there are two geese"] versus nominal uses of number terms [e.g., in "two is an even number"]).[33] (I aim to make good on this claim in Chapter 8.) Working in the first instance with language enables us to more visibly preserve these differences.

This brings us the most important advantage of working with language rather than concepts, if we aim to engage in conceptual engineering in part to shed light on old philosophical problems. When we philosophize, we must use language, and we can use language to articulate questions (say) about what modality is, how we can know moral facts, or whether there are numbers. Language, however, is a public, social construction, which clearly serves many other purposes than just enabling an individual to represent the world. Language is used socially and interpersonally, to greet, insult, command, and establish social roles and dominance relations; language is used to express our attitudes and emotions; language is used to show paths of reasoning, to generalize, to make inferences and show connections of ideas, and to impose, renegotiate, and challenge rules. If we focus on language, we can consider the full *range of linguistic functions* that may be served by different terms of philosophical interest and do so in ways that enable us to drop the presupposition that all language (or all concepts) simply serve to "represent" and carry "bodies of information" about worldly features. By contrast, we tend to think of concepts as "internal" ways of "representing the world," rather than as carrying all the social and

---

[32] Perhaps, as Matthieu Queloz suggested to me, it is an avoidable temptation, as one could differentiate between *the concept red* and *the concept of redness*.

[33] I don't mean to suggest that there is no way to develop a psychological view of concepts that could handle these phenomena. I simply don't know of one yet; and linguistics provides helpful and clear inroads.

interpersonal functions a well-developed public language serves. The individuality and privacy of concepts (as we tend to think of them on a psychological model) tends to lead us away from thinking in terms of these sorts of public, social, and interpersonal functions that are carried by a public language and studied by linguistics. But I will aim to make the case that we cannot fully understand many terms of philosophical interest without appreciating these other sorts of functions language serves in human life.

So, for present purposes, I will speak first and foremost about understanding, engineering, and changing *language* rather than *concepts*. Working with language enables us to make use of empirical work in linguistics, not only in understanding linguistic *change*, but also in understanding the notion of *function* that conceptual engineering relies on. For, as I will argue next, work in systemic functional linguistics can provide helpful inroads to understanding the functions of various parts and aspects of language.

6.6 The Work to Be Done

I have argued that rethinking metaphysics as conceptual engineering enables us to avoid the problems of rivalry with science, of landing in a skepticism that can come from noting the proliferation of metaphysical views, and of epistemological mystery. On the new model, we can think instead of the work of metaphysics as work in conceptual engineering—including reverse engineering, assessment, and forward-looking (re)constructive engineering.

But how, exactly, can we undertake conceptual engineering in a clear, non-arbitrary, and non-mysterious way? We need a *method* to clearly and non-arbitrarily evaluate old terms and concepts, as well as to develop and evaluate new proposals in conceptual engineering. For both sides of this task, the notion of a *function* plays a central role. For we may evaluate extant terms or concepts (as one would evaluate extant machinery) by identifying their functions and determining whether they successfully fulfill those functions, and whether those are functions we should aim to serve, going forward. As I will argue in Chapter 8, we can also use the appeal to functions in unraveling old philosophical problems and paradoxes and in identifying category mistakes. And in designing new terms and evaluating proposals for changing our concepts or language, we must attend to how well they (would) serve their relevant functions, and if these are functions we should promote. As I will argue in Chapter 9, attending to functions enables us to make evaluations and decisions in conceptual engineering that are clear and non-arbitrary.

The first step, therefore, to developing a clear and non-arbitrary approach to conceptual engineering is to address this question: How can we identify linguistic functions? I turn to address that question next in Chapter 7, with the help of empirical work in systemic functional linguistics. On that basis, I will then turn in Chapter 8 to show how this work on functions helps us diagnose and dissolve old problems in metaphysics. In Chapter 9 I will show how we can make use of the appeal to functions in undertaking *constructive* projects in conceptual engineering in a way that enables us to better evaluate proposals in ways that are neither arbitrary nor mysterious.

Finally and most importantly, we need to show *why it is worthwhile* to undertake this work—why work in conceptual engineering, so conceived, matters to philosophy and matters more generally to human life. I will conclude in Chapter 10 by showing why conceptual engineering, as conceived above, matters, and why its work is never finished. And this makes philosophy a perennial part of human life.

7
Identifying Linguistic Functions

I have argued that we should rethink metaphysics: taking it not to be the "study of ultimate reality," but rather to be concerned with conceptual engineering.[1] The key to doing a conceptual engineering project well—whether it is a matter of assessing our old concepts and terms, modifying them, or designing new ones—is to consider the *functions* the relevant parts of language have served or are to serve. For in that way we can better assess whether our extant terms or concepts, or proposed innovations, serve their functions well. More deeply, we can explicitly evaluate whether those functions are ones we should endorse and pursue.

But how can we identify the relevant linguistic functions?

Many people are skeptical that we can make sense of the idea of linguistic or conceptual functions—expressing a worry that one can just "say anything," make stuff up, about what the function of a word or concept is. This is a reproach often leveled against neo-pragmatist proposals that begin by identifying non-descriptive functions of, say, moral or modal terms. The skepticism reflects worries about a lack of a clear methodology or standards for determining the functions of a word or concept. Herman Cappelen goes further, bluntly stating: "I don't think concepts have purposes and certainly not words" (2018, 181), and arguing that the appeal to function doesn't "do any work." Why? In response to proposals for how to understand functions,[2] Cappelen asserts that the only functions that can be identified for words are "denotational" functions:

---

[1] Parts of this chapter draw on work in my (2022).
[2] Here Cappelen is responding to my proposal for how to understand functions, as well as to proposals by Haslanger (2000) and Brigandt (2010).

Rethinking Metaphysics. Amie L. Thomasson, Oxford University Press.
© Oxford University Press 2025. DOI: 10.1093/9780197787830.003.0007

The reason "salmon" is useful for us is that it can be used to talk about salmons (or denote salmons). The reason "freedom" is useful is that it can be used to talk about freedom. We care about salmons and freedom and so we have words that enable us to talk about them. ... However ... beyond these disquotationally specified functions, there's variability. We can use "freedom" in speech acts that have as their aim to undermine freedom or promote it or discuss it or disparage or make fun of it or ... There's no limit to what we can go on to do with this term. (2018, 187)

This reflects a more widely held view that the most that can be consistently said about linguistic function is disquotational: "the function of 'F' is to refer to the Fs" (Cappelen 2018, 187). On this view, there is nothing about linguistic functions we can say except, perhaps, that language serves to represent or describe the world in certain ways: biological discourse describes the life forms, mathematical discourse describes the numbers, moral discourse describes the moral facts, and so on. "If the goal is to find functions that are more substantive and informative than the disquotationally specified functions, then it will be unsuccessful," Cappelen predicts (2018, 187).

Here I aim to address these concerns and to take some steps toward showing how we can find a better approach to understanding functions, in part by making use of work in systemic functional linguistics. I aim to show that the idea that pieces of language have functions is not hopeless, and that the claim that all that can be said about function is disquotational not only is plainly inadequate but also leads us philosophically astray. I will argue that we can do better by looking to work in linguistics for a framework to address questions about what functions language, and its various parts and subsystems, serve. Once we can see the functions of some philosophically interesting aspects of language (as I aim to show in Chapter 8), we can better assess whether we should eliminate or revise various parts of language—and thus make better assessments of various old philosophical problems and of various proposals in conceptual engineering.

7.1 How (Not) to Think About Function

Despite frequent skepticism of the idea that our concepts or language have identifiable functions, I do not think it is at all hopeless to investigate linguistic functions. And given the potential usefulness of the notion, we should not give up so easily. Linguistic structures are artifacts, and identifying functions of other artifacts is not hopeless, nor is it unempirical work in which you can just say "whatever you like" or "anything goes." On the contrary, identifying functions of artifacts is central to the work of such sciences as anthropology and archaeology.

Nonetheless, the critic's concerns deserve to be taken seriously, as ways of showing us what routes *not* to take. One thing we can learn from the skeptics and critics of the idea of linguistic functions is that we should not collapse the *function* of an entity with the ways in which it is *used* on particular occasions.[3] As we have seen, Cappelen resists the idea that anything useful (beyond the disquotational) can be said about function by noting that we can *use* a term like "freedom" in many ways, to do many things. Even J. L. Austin (who one would expect to be sympathetic to identifying different functions or uses of language) expressed concerns, writing:

> Certainly there are a great many uses of language. It's rather a pity that people are apt to invoke a new use of language whenever they feel so inclined, to help them out of this, that, or the other well-known philosophical tangle; we need more of a framework in which to discuss these uses of language; and also I think we should not despair too easily and talk, as people are apt to do, about the *infinite* uses of language. (1961, 234)

---

[3] It is also crucial to distinguish a stable *function* from variable *uses* if we are to avoid the notorious Frege-Geach problem (Geach 1965) in proposing non-descriptive approaches to an area of discourse. That is, if we can identify a stable function, and identify meaning with the rules a term follows that enable it to fulfill those functions, then we may be able to identify a stable sense of meaning that remains even in embedded contexts where the term is not *used* to perform the characteristic speech acts with which it is associated. (For work on this approach, for the case of modal terms, see my 2020a, chs. 2 and 3, drawing on work by Michael Williams [2011].) See also Joshua Gert (2021) for a discussion of how to develop a neo-pragmatist semantics that can solve the Frege-Geach problem.

I shall aim to develop more of a framework here—one that begins with the idea of *functions* rather than *uses*. For the fact that we *do* many different things with something, of course, does not tell us that it lacks a more unified *function* or *functions*. Artifacts from pennies to forks to chairs may be used for all sorts of purposes, yet this does not interfere with their having a unified function. The same goes for biological entities such as hands and mouths, which are *used* in an endless variety of ways. Nor should we even require that a type of entity be *typically* or *often* used in a certain way, in order for that to be its function: a safety valve on a nuclear reactor may never be used to stop a catastrophic reaction, if none ever begins.

But how can we identify something like stable linguistic *functions*, across the endless varieties of *uses* to which language is put? One tempting route for pennies or forks would be to appeal to their *intended* functions. But clearly the sense of function we need to address linguistic functions can't be identified with *intended* functions. For the vast majority of our natural language words and concepts (perhaps excepting those that are intentionally created in de novo engineering efforts) are not intentionally created, and so can't be said to have as functions whatever functions their creator(s) intended.

A better start, as I have argued elsewhere (2020a, 444–45), is to look to notions of system function and/or proper function. To ask about system functions (roughly as Cummins (1975) understands them) does not involve asking about *intended* functions, but instead involves asking what each part contributes to the subsystem in question, and what those subsystems in turn contribute to the overall capacities of the total organism or system. So, for example, in biology we might ask what stomach acid contributes to the digestive system, and what the digestive system contributes to the functions of the organism as a whole. In the case of language, this approach would involve asking about what roles a given part of language or linguistic structure (say, modal verbs) play within larger linguistic subsystems (such as the modal system), and what these systems contribute to the functioning of the linguistic system as a whole. There is also the option of thinking of linguistic functions in terms of proper functions (in roughly Millikan's (1984) sense). This approach, too, avoids collapsing function with uses and gives a notion of function separate from *intended* function. Addressing functional questions about language in terms of proper functions would encourage us to ask to what the relevant aspect of language *does* (or what prior tokens of it have done) for us (or for some people or groups of people) that has made it useful (for them) and has led to its perpetuation in our language.[4] The system function and proper function approaches to addressing functional questions are generally not in conflict. For identifying what a type of item does within a system that makes it useful is one way to get at why it might have been preserved and perpetuated in our culture or language.[5] Investigations of functions of other cultural artifacts tend to combine these approaches, appealing to what the entity *can do* and *has done* that might have been useful (to someone) within its embedded system, that would explain its presence and perpetuation. If software engineers are presented with a piece of malware and aim to discover its function, they begin by figuring out what this bit of inserted code *does*, or what it *can do* within the systems where it becomes embedded. Archaeologists, similarly, in discovering a new artifact, employ reconstructive methods in experimental archaeology—trying to rebuild a similar tool to discover what it can do (can it be used in butchering? can it survive fire?) as a crucial step in discovering what its function may have been (Renfrew and Bahn 2016, 322–32) in the wider system of life of which it formed a part, and why it might have stuck around in that culture.

If we are looking for something like *system* functions, we ought to start at the level of *language*: beginning from questions about the functions *language* serves, not about the functions served by individual *words*. For if we can identify the functions served by language, we can better identify the roles played by various parts of the linguistic system. This requires a change from the standard approach in

---

[4] It is important to note that these functions needn't be beneficial to all or benign; there is room here for critique. More on this below.

[5] Moreover, as Karen Neander (1995) argues, we have reason to bring the two approaches together. For we can resolve notorious indeterminacies in how we describe system functions if we appeal to "by-relations" (saying, e.g., that the stomach digests food *by* releasing acids) that require a proper-functional analysis. Thanks to Justin Garson for a helpful discussion of these points. As he has pointed out to me, conflicts between proper-function accounts and system-function accounts tend to arise only where there has been a recent change in what something functions to do—but that seems unlikely for the broad, high-level linguistic functions at issue here.

conceptual engineering, which just asks directly after the functions, say, of our race or gender terms, or a truth predicate, without beginning from a more global inquiry into the functions of language and broader linguistic structures. (We can still get to these questions, but we might do better by taking a longer route.)

Nonetheless, if we take a broad approach and begin by asking about the functions of language, serious objections have been raised to the idea that we can speak of language as having a function. Robert Brandom makes the point as follows:

> I think it is a mistake to think of [linguistic practice] as having a point at all. Linguistic practice is not for something. It does not, as a whole, have an aim or a goal. It may and does, of course, fulfill many functions. But none of them is its *raison d'être*. Language is certainly not a tool for the expression of thoughts intelligible as such apart from their relation to such a means of expression, as Locke, in the company of most of the Cartesian tradition thought. For that conception of contentful thoughts is mythological. Neither is it a means to secure some other end specifiable in advance of engaging in linguistic practice—not adaptation to the environment, survival, reproduction, nor co-operation—though it may serve to promote those ends. Even if in a causal, evolutionary sense, those functions explain why we came to have language, once we did have it, our transformation into discursive creatures swept all such considerations aside. For discursive practice is a mighty engine for the envisaging and engendering of new ends—thereby transforming the very concept of an end or goal, giving it for the first time its proper, practical-rational, sense. (2000, 363)

I join Brandom in rejecting the picture according to which there is some preconceived purpose (specifiable in advance) with language made, like a tool, to serve that function. That is a picture that fits best with an intended function model, which I have already rejected. Another important point Brandom makes here is that language may enable us to generate new ends, serving new purposes we would not have dreamed of prelinguistically.[6] As we will see, the model from

[6] And of course this is not unique to language—other forms of technology, too, have ways of generating new goals or ends to be served, as our massive computer technology

systemic functional linguistics that I will defend not only is consistent with this thought but enables us to *demonstrate* it. For example, it will enable us to show the ways in which the development of grammatical metaphors enables us to develop theories and bureaucracies in ways that were not otherwise possible—"engendering new ends" rather than serving any end that could have been preconceived. The picture to be developed below also does not treat language as in the service of a *single* goal or with a single raison d'être. Nonetheless, I will try to show that a closer look at the functions served by different parts of the linguistic system (identifying also the functions added by different parts, aspects, or developments of the linguistic system, and isolating the multiple functions served by each clause) can be extremely helpful, both in disentangling ourselves from old philosophical quandaries and in making new progress in conceptual engineering.

On the model to be developed here, language is a multipurpose tool. Indeed language is such a multipurpose tool that identifying the functions of language might seem hopeless. Huw Price (2011, 138), however, has a helpful suggestion about where to begin. He notes that in inquiring about the functions of a multipurpose human instrument (such as string), we would do well to begin by recognizing "that string has certain core properties—length, thinness, strength, and flexibility, for example" that are exploited in, and enable, many or most of its various uses. Given that language is itself a multipurpose tool, we might aim to take a similar approach here—aiming to identify certain *core properties* of language that enable it to fulfill many and varied purposes.

If we think of language as a human cultural artifact, we can ask what functions it serves, and has served, which have made it such an enduring feature of an enormous range of different human cultures. And we can turn to work in empirical linguistics to help us with these questions about what functions language serves, how its different parts and aspects contribute to serving those functions, and what its "core properties" are that enable it to fulfill these many and varied functions.

has generated new purposes for new technological developments, say, to debug programs, update apps, maintain cybersecurity, etc.

7.2 Systemic Functional Linguistics

In addressing questions about the functions of language, I will follow the spirit of Price's "subject naturalism"—the view that "philosophy needs to begin with what science tells us *about ourselves*" (Price 2013, 5). That includes what science tells us about language, how it works, and what functions it serves in human life. And so we might turn to work in anthropology and linguistics for help with these questions. Work in systemic functional linguistics has focused on exactly these questions, as it begins from the idea that "language has evolved in the service of certain functions" (Halliday 1973, 14). Systemic functional linguistics goes on to ask questions about ways in which the functions of language are reflected in the *structure* of language (Malmkjaer 1991, 159). As Michael Halliday (a central figure of systemic functional linguistics) writes, "The internal organization of natural language can best be explained in the light of the social functions which language has evolved to serve. Language is as it is because of what it has to do" (2009, 96), and "The internal organization of language is not accidental; it embodies the functions that language has evolved to serve in the life of social man" (2009, 107). Work in systemic functional linguistics is well placed to address both questions about the functions of language and about how these are served by the ways in which languages are structured.

Systemic functional linguistics may be unfamiliar to many philosophers, who (if they have background in linguistics at all) have been more attuned to work in the Chomskyan tradition. Systemic functional linguistics has been more influential in anthropology and education than in philosophy.[7] And it focuses on a different range of questions about language than those addressed in the Chomskyan tradition—questions about the functions language serves in human social life and culture, and about the ways language is structured that enable it to fulfill these functions: the very questions that we need to address here.[8] As Halliday puts it, "I would defend the view that

---

[7] In fact (except for some of my own recent work) I have seen zero references to it in philosophy.

[8] Bavali and Sadighi (2008) argue that systemic functional linguistics is not a rival to familiar work in the Chomskyan tradition. On the lack of rivalry, see also Halliday

different coexisting models in linguistics may best be regarded as appropriate to different aims, rather than as competing contenders for the same goal" (1964, 13).

Systemic functional linguistics does share some common roots with philosophy. One early source was work in the Prague school of linguistics from the 1920s and 1930s, led by Vilem Mathesius, and with Roman Jakobson centrally involved. Jakobsen in turn was influenced by Husserl's *systematic* approach to language in the third and fourth of the *Logical Investigations*,[9] where Husserl identified linguistic laws of "compounding" that establish which meaning categories can be sensibly conjoined.[10] Husserl also identified laws of "modification" that govern the ways in which one meaning category can be transformed into another, "as in the cases of nominalization, in which verbs, adjectives, adverbs, etc. are used as nouns" (Aurora 2015, 12). The emphasis on *function* developed under the influence of the anthropologist Bronislaw Malinowski, who insisted that we must study meaning by analyzing the functions of language in its culture, and whose work on language influenced both Wittgenstein and the English linguist J. R. Firth. Firth, who drew on work by Wittgenstein and Ryle (Bateman 2017, 14), and repeatedly refers to Wittgenstein's focus on types of speech function (Firth 1962, 10), was the teacher of Michael Halliday. Halliday in turn was influenced not only by Firth but also by Sapir, Whorf, and work in the US anthropological tradition. Halliday's work played a central role in developing systemic functional linguistics in its modern form, which I shall draw on here.[11]

While this is not the place (nor am I the author) for a full-scale introduction to systemic functional linguistics,[12] I will suggest that some of its central insights may be extremely useful in seeing how we can think

---

(2014, 56). For further discussion of the place of systemic functional linguistics in the history of linguistics, see also Bateman (2017).

[9] See Aurora (2015). Roman Jakobson "explicitly considers Husserl's phenomenology [especially the third Logical Investigation] as one of the main sources underlying Prague structuralism and Russian formalism" (Aurora 2015, 14). Husserl also gave a lecture to the Prague Circle (invited by Jakobson) on November 18, 1935.

[10] As I draw out elsewhere (2002), this Husserlian work also influenced Ryle's later work on linguistic categories and category mistakes.

[11] For a brief historical overview, see Malmkajaer (1991, 141–46).

[12] Interested readers are instead referred to Eggins (2004) and Halliday (2009), as well as work in two recent handbooks, *The Routledge Handbook of Systemic Functional*

about function in language in a way that is helpful both for assessing proposals in conceptual engineering, and elsewhere in philosophy.

7.2.1 Functions in Developmentally Early Language

A good place to begin investigating linguistic functions is by examining developmentally early language. For, as Halliday puts it, "The functional origin of language is most evident in the language of young children" (2009, 85), since it is functionally simple, with each utterance typically serving a single function.

One way to investigate what a cultural technology does for us is to take a contrastive approach—asking what children can do in learning (early) language that they couldn't do (or couldn't do so easily or so well) without language. So, what can children first learning a basic form of language *do* that they couldn't do (as effectively) otherwise? Halliday identifies six micro-functions (typical uses) in early childhood language (1975, 19):

1. Instrumental: language as used to satisfy material needs (to get goods or services) ("Milk!")
2. Regulatory: language as used to control the behavior of others ("Mama, come.")
3. Interactional: language as used in greeting, parting, calls to others, and responses to calls ("hi," "bye bye," "Sissy!!")
4. Personal: language as used to express the child's personal feelings "of interest, pleasure, disgust and so forth" (1975, 20) ("Yuck," "Yay!" "Oops")
5. Heuristic: language as used to investigate the environment ("What that?")
6. Imaginative: language as used in play and pretense ("Let's pretend...") (2009, 85)

As a somewhat later development, Halliday also identifies

Linguistics (Bartlett and O'Grady 2017) and the *Cambridge Handbook of Systemic Functional Linguistics* (Thompson et al. 2019).

7. Informative/representational: language as used to communicate information about the world—to someone thought not to know (1975, 21). ("I got a lollipop! [at school today].")

This connects well with work on language disabilities and language delays (indeed Halliday's central concern was improving language education). As speech therapists emphasize, a core problem for children who do not acquire language (or acquire it very late) is not so much that they can't state truths about the world but that they can't make their needs known and can't acquire control over their world—leading to frustration and behavioral problems. As always, one way in which we can study what something *does* is to note what we can't do (so well) when it is *missing*.

It matters little for present purposes if this is an optimal or complete categorization of functions in early language development. The important point here is that this work on language development is a powerful *reminder* of the *many* functions language serves, even for a toddler—and anyone who has spent time around linguistically developing toddlers can easily confirm this from personal experience. It also gives a powerful reminder of how relatively late and peripheral the "informative" or "representational" function is in language development.[13] And this makes it clear that, even if we narrow our focus to the relatively simple protolanguage of early childhood, the idea that all that we can say about linguistic function is the disquotational mantra, "The function of F is to pick out the Fs," is completely inadequate. Serving to "pick out the Fs" (properly understood) may be a relevant part of the story for *some* terms the child learns.[14] For example, basic nouns

---

[13] It is also important to note that the "representational" function described in systemic functional linguistics needn't embody all the presuppositions of philosophical forms of (what Price 2011, 5, calls big-R) "Representationalism" that see our statements as "standing for" or "mirroring" the world.

[14] In saying this, I do not mean to endorse a merely *local* form of expressivism (endorsed, e.g., by Simon Blackburn [2013]) as opposed to the *global* expressivism defended by Price (2013). For the distinction between the introduction rules and functions governing words like "dog" or "pig" on the one hand, and those governing terms for properties and numbers (for example) on the other hand can also be captured by Price's distinction between terms that are (and are not) "e-representational." Those congruent terms that are introduced observationally to serve a heuristic function seem to be "e-representational" in the sense that their "job . . . is to covary with something else—typically some *external* factor or environmental condition" (Price 2011, 20). For

(like "dog" or "pig") acquired observationally and used in service of the heuristic function enable the child to inquire and learn more about dogs and pigs, and eventually (in the service of representational function) to communicate information about dogs and pigs. But if the thought that "yuck" is used to pick out the yucky stuff (rather than to express disgust and refusal) is hardly plausible, the thought that "oops" is used to pick out the oopsies is less plausible still, and the thought that "hi" is used to pick out the "hi's" is so bizarre as to be incomprehensible. Even here, with the simple language of early childhood, we need a far broader view of the diverse functions language serves.

But if the functional pluralism that marks even very early language is so obvious, why have philosophers often missed it, focusing exclusively on the ability of terms ("F") to "pick out" the Fs, or of sentences to express propositions? Interestingly, Halliday makes note of this mistake in ways that suggest that it's not just a philosopher's mistake. While the representational (or "informative") function—to communicate a content that the speaker thinks is unknown to the addressee—is relatively late for the child, it comes to dominate the adult's "conception of the use of language" (Halliday 1973, 27). Adults generally tend to think of language only in informational or ideational terms:

> Language is, in addition to all its other guises, a means of communicating about something, of expressing propositions. . . . This is the only model of language that many adults have; and a very inadequate model it is, from the point of view of the child. (Halliday 1973, 8)

The representational function is not "one of the earliest [functions] to come into prominence; and it does not become a dominant function until a much later stage in the development towards maturity" (Halliday 1973, 8). Although it may never be the dominant function, "it does, in later years, tend to become the dominant *model*" (Halliday 1973, 8). This is a model that not only is dominant in the adult's

---

discussion of the global versus local expressivist debate, see the full range of essays in Price (2013). For a defense of a form of global pragmatism against concerns that it can't properly address discourse about ordinary objects, see my (2019).

conception of language generally, but has become ossified in dominant philosophical conceptions of language and presuppositions about its functions.[15]

7.2.2 Functions in Mature Language

Having identified a range of functions served by the language of early childhood, we can go on to ask another contrastive question: Why do children *go on*? What can we do, in speaking a *mature* language, that speakers of early childhood protolanguage cannot do (or cannot do so well)? What (additional) functions does mature language serve?

Systemic functional linguistics provides a very interesting answer. Mature language is distinct from the language of early childhood in that it enables speakers to *serve more than one function* at a time, with each utterance. While "It is characteristic... of the utterances of the very young child that they are functionally simple; each utterance serves just one function," when we get to mature language, this changes: "Every adult linguistic act, with a few broadly specifiable exceptions, is serving more than one function at once" (Halliday 1973, 26).

The core feature that enables adult language to serve more than one function at a time is the introduction of grammatical form—which brings in a level "intermediate between meanings [content] and sounds [expression]" (Halliday 1973, 26; cf. Halliday 1975, 45). Linguistic form, or grammar, "allows for meanings which derive from different functions to be encoded together, as integrated structures, so that every expression becomes, in principle, functionally complex.

---

[15] Linguist Gerard O'Grady (personal communication) has also suggested to me that this may be in part because, previously, the evidence used in linguistics was written language, often made up for the purpose and disconnected from use. A distinctive feature of work in systemic functional linguistics is the way it addresses larger pieces of text in use, including use in real conversational contexts. As Suzanne Eggins puts it, in systemic functional linguistics there "is a common focus on the analysis of authentic products of social interaction (texts), considered in relation to the cultural and social context in which they are negotiable" (2004, 2).

Grammar makes it possible to mean more than one thing at a time" (Halliday 1975, 48; cf. Eggins 2004, 119).[16]

This makes it clear why we might get ourselves befuddled if we begin by asking about *the function* of a particular word or utterance. Each utterance (of a mature language) generally serves *more than one function*. A better place to start is at the *systemic* level, where we ask instead about the *functions* (plural) served by language, and the structures within language that enable it to simultaneously serve these different types of function.

What are the functions served by language? Again, we might generate a long miscellaneous list if we tried to simply enumerate all the things language can be and has been *used* for. Rather than focusing on the huge range of individual purposes served by different *uses* of language, Halliday helpfully starts from a more abstract level, identifying three "metafunctions" of adult language, all of which are typically served simultaneously in each utterance (indeed, in each clause) of adult language (1973, 34)—and each of which covers a wide variety of different *uses*. These metafunctions Halliday labels the "ideational," "interpersonal," and "textual." I shall begin by describing them here in the terms from systemic functional linguistics, and then go on to discuss their philosophical significance.

The **ideational metafunction** Halliday earlier sometimes called the "representational" or "informative" metafunction (1973, 29), though I will follow his settled use of calling it "ideational" here. Calling it "ideational" highlights the functions of language in communicating ideas. The ideational metafunction is the linguistic function of informing, or "packaging of content meaning" (Eggins 2004, 211). It is related to the earlier informative/representational function, and originally

---

[16] The relevant notion of meaning used is of "meaning potential"—what a speaker can do, linguistically (Halliday 1973, 44), where this is a subset of general behavioral options (1973, 47). So, the thought is that grammar enables us to (linguistically) do the same thing, in different ways—and often by combining the primary goal with other functions. "So a category like that of 'threat' . . . will be realized in the language system through a number of different grammatical options" (1973, 49)—each of which may realize "more delicate options in the meaning potential" (1973, 50). For example, a gangster might say, "I'll kill your dog if you don't pay your debts" or (adding subtlety and plausible deniability) "You sure owe me a lot of money. It'd be a shame if something was to happen to your dog."

develops out of the personal and heuristic functions of early childhood language. Put in philosophical terms, the ideational metafunction is a matter of encoding and communicating a (propositional) content—whether about the observable world, the speaker's experience, or abstract matters (Halliday 1973, 31). Nearly all uses of adult language (except, e.g., simple greetings or exclamations) serve ideational functions.

A separate strand of meaning is carried by the **interpersonal metafunction,** covering the social, interpersonal, and expressive functions of language. The interpersonal metafunction is what enables language to serve as a *social* tool. It covers a "whole range of particular uses of language" to "express social and personal relations, including all forms of the speaker's intrusion into the speech situation and the speech act" (Halliday 2009, 103). The interpersonal meaning component enables speakers to take up or show their relation to the listener or reader, and to take on social/conversational roles (like questioner or commander). For example, a speaker may take the position of questioner or respondent, commander, peer or superior, etc. Speakers may also use interpersonal functions to "intrude" into the speech situation in various ways, *showing* their attitudes, judgments, level of certainty, etc. (even while they are *saying* something about the world). For example, if I say, "They *might* serve tacos there" rather than "They serve tacos there," I show my hesitancy, while still communicating content about the restaurant. In English, these interpersonal functions are typically carried by the mood and modal systems (Halliday 1973, 33; cf. Eggins 2004, 172–84). Interpersonal functions, like ideational ones, are typically carried in each clause of the adult's language, and are analyzed as separate strands of meaning. As Halliday summarizes it: "the ideational and the interpersonal [metafunctions] together determine a large part of the meaning potential that is incorporated in the grammar of every language. This can be seen very clearly in the grammar of the clause, which has its ideational aspect, transitivity, and its interpersonal aspect, mood (including modality)" (2009, 10).

In addition to the ideational and interpersonal functions, there is the **textual metafunction,** which enables speakers (or writers) to organize a text in ways that connect it to the surrounding conversation, utterances, or writing. As Eggins puts it, "the clause is also making meanings about how this bit of information relates to other bits of information near it in the conversation" (Eggins 2004, 212). By making use of textual functions, a clause make evident how what we are saying hangs together, what the theme and relations among ideas are, and how the parts of a text are interrelated into a whole (Eggins 2004, 11–12), creating a "flow of meanings" (Halliday 2009, 241) that indicate "the cohesive relations between the clause, its context and its purpose" (Eggins 2004, 298). These textual functions may (for example) be served by logical/connector words ("but," "since," "therefore," "so," etc.), and by word order making clear what is the point of departure (Theme), versus what is the new information about it (Rheme) (Eggins 2004, 296).

These three metafunctions of the linguistic system (Halliday 2009, 316) are "modes of meaning that are present in every use of language in every social context," and most texts simultaneously serve all three types of metafunction (Halliday 2009, 316). Grammatical structures give us a variety of grammatically distinct options for how to use language to pursue (some of) our primary goals, whether those are informing, threatening, commanding, etc. Mastering the grammatical options enables mature speakers to jointly serve these three metafunctions in subtle ways that are inaccessible to young children, and often also to beginners at speaking a language foreign to them. Textual analyses given in systemic functional linguistics analyze each of these three strands of meaning separately. In examining an individual utterance, we can again seek a contrastive explanation: we can ask why the speaker used *this* formulation, rather than one of the other (grammatically) available options—and how that enabled the speaker to fulfill specific ideational, interpersonal, and textual functions. And that may enable us to identify what the relevant mode of expression—rather than one of the alternatives—more generally *enables* speakers to do.

An example may help make this clearer. Consider, for example, the following speech situation. Suppose you are at the home of an acquaintance and want a cup of tea. Without language, you might have to resort to grabbing the tea and commandeering the kettle. If you were only capable of early childhood language, you might have but one linguistic option: say, "Tea!" in a demanding tone. But you probably won't do that. As a mature speaker, you have various mood options. You could utter a straightforward imperative, "Give me tea." But that involves taking on the social position of commander, which may not be appropriate. You could instead utter an indicative, "I want tea." But this still might seem too direct to be polite, so you can soften it by uttering a modal formulation instead: "I would like some tea" or an interrogative "Do you have any tea?" or combine the two for a modal interrogative, "Might you have any tea?" Or you could even use a worldly indicative, not directly presenting your own desires at all, and also not commanding. Instead, you might present yourself as if you are only commenting on the world, saying just: "Some tea would be lovely." By choosing among such alternatives, and making use of the options for mood and modality that language provides you with, you can not only express the ideational content (roughly: I want tea) and work to acquire tea, but also serve interpersonal functions that establish the appropriate social relation with your interlocutor at the same time, and show your attitude toward tea and toward your host.[17]

The textual metafunctions can be seen in a longer dialogue, where we can also make evident the connections among ideas. Suppose now you have your tea, and you really want some milk for it. Again, you've got a range of linguistic options. In response to the host's apologetic, "Sorry, it's gone a bit dark," you might reply, "*Since* the tea is strong, I would like some milk to go with it." Here, "since" serves a textual function of making evident the relations between ideas as part of the flow of conversation; but the text also communicates the *ideational* content that you want milk, while the modal form ("would like") serves the *interpersonal* function of establishing a polite request relationship to your interlocutor. In this way, we can see how a simple everyday text may serve all three metafunctions at once.

Of course, you have other options as well. You could explain your desire for milk in more general terms, saying, "It's the *strength* of a tea that matters to whether I prefer milk with it," now introducing a nominalized adjective ("strength" from "strong") to put the focus of attention on that quality of the tea, in order to both *justify* your

---

[17] For a further exemplification of such options, see Eggins (2004, 118–19).

preference and enable your interlocutor to make *general inferences* about when you will and will not want milk. Introducing new noun terms like these enables us to do new things with language beyond conveying a certain propositional (ideational) content and (interpersonally) establishing appropriate social roles. I will have more to say about the roles of these so-called "grammatical metaphors" below.

The variety of grammatical options available to speakers also accounts for what I called in Chapter 4 the "ontological flexibility of language," which enables us to describe the "truthmakers" for a sentence like "The barn is red" in many different ways (a point that, as we saw there, makes trouble for the project of identifying a unique set of *truthmakers*). We can now see this "ontological flexibility" as reflecting the diverse *grammatical* options that are available to speakers of a mature language—and we can see why this flexibility is not accidental or a defect, but rather would be built into a language for good *functional* reasons.

7.3 Ideational Functions

As we have seen so far, if we begin by zooming out to ask what functions *language* serves, we see that mature language serves three sorts of metafunctions: conveying propositional content; establishing appropriate social roles and interactions and expressing one's own attitudes; and enabling a flow of information that makes evident relations among the parts of extended conversations and texts. It does not matter much for our purposes exactly how these metafunctions are labeled, or even if we should divide them as exactly three (or if, say, the so-called "interpersonal" metafunctions should be relabeled and/or subdivided [say] to distinguish separate social role, expressive, and regulative functions; or if the ideational metafunction should be divided into experiential and logical components [Halliday 2014, 361–62]). What matters for our purposes is that distinguishing these different sorts of metafunction enables us to get away from the philosophical mistakes that arise from assuming that all that can be said about functions is denotational (that the function of "F" is to represent or denote the Fs). These mistakes arise from focusing only on the *ideational* functions that (outside of work in the pragmatist tradition) have been the center of attention in philosophy.

The ideational metafunction of communicating propositional content has been the primary focus of philosophical attention. It also seems to coincide with the small-r, "internal" sense of representation identified by Price (2011), on which something "counts as a representation, in this sense, in virtue of its ... role, in some sort of cognitive or inferential architecture" (2011, 20). For only expressions with propositional content can figure in all the characteristic logical inferences.[18] Standard propositional logic takes propositions as input and gives propositions as output—and the ability to figure smoothly in inferences to be used in reasoning is one chief advantage of language expressed in propositional form.

Having an ideational content in this sense must be distinguished from the idea that the relevant language is *congruent* language, *observationally introduced*.[19] Early childhood language contains "congruent" meanings: nouns for things, verbs for processes, and so on (Halliday 2009, 117). An early utterance like "man clean car" is congruent.[20] Congruent meanings are "evolutionarily and developmentally prior" to non-congruent meanings (Halliday 2009, 117).[21] Basic "congruent" nouns such as "stick," "car," "hole," and "ball" are acquired in response to observations of interest in the environment, "In contexts of observation, recall, and prediction" (Halliday 1975, 27). Such terms seem to be something like those Huw Price identifies as "e-representational." That is, they are terms that have the job "to *co-vary* with something

---

[18] Of course, this is not to deny that some non-propositional forms of language may figure in some forms of reasoning, as, for example, one can develop a logic of commands.

[19] Roughly, from the idea that it is "e-representational" in something like Price's sense (2011, 20).

[20] For a history of the use of the term "congruent" and discussion of criteria for congruence, see Taverniers (2003 and 2017). Taverniers (2017, 360–61) notes that one cannot use probability of occurrence as a criterion for congruence, as incongruent modal expressions ("Could you pass me the sugar?") are used more often than (congruent) commands ("Pass the sugar")—perhaps given constraints of politeness.

[21] This is not to say that *in each case*, the congruent form of expression is learned before related incongruent expressions or occurs more frequently. For in some cases, incongruent expressions have become "domesticated" and taken the dominant role (Taverniers 2003, 10), for example, as (in contemporary American English) "take a bath" is more typical than "bathe," and "make a mistake" is more typical than "err."

else—typically, some *external* factor or environmental condition" (Price 2011, 20). As Halliday puts it, these terms function to contribute to the child's learning about the environment (1975, 27–28). In early declaratives, congruent terms are used in statements that communicate ideational content about the observed world.

But not all language that carries ideational content is congruent—and not all should be thought of as directly tied to worldly observations. Even sentences that are very far removed from observation may carry ideational content, as in the example used by Halliday: "The perception of an inadequate retirement program consistently surfaces as a primary cause of our recruiting and retention problems" (2014, 713).[22] So having ideational content should not be confused with "tracking" or "representing" the world in a way that implies a direct perceptual connection or "mirroring" the world.

7.4 Interpersonal Functions

Another important result from the work in functional linguistics is that it identifies some of the structural features of language that enable it to fulfill these distinct types of metafunctions simultaneously. For then we can identify the roles of systems of *mood* and *modality*, as well as the roles of *grammatical metaphors*. One reason this matters philosophically is that it turns out that a great majority of those expressions that have been philosophically interesting and often problematic are expressions that arise in the mood or modal system, or that are introduced as grammatical metaphors. As I will argue in Chapter 8, if we can properly identify the functions of the relevant terminology and thereby do our *reverse* engineering well, we can avoid a range of philosophical mistakes (giving a better philosophical account of moral or modal discourse, for example), and make better decisions in conceptual engineering, about whether to retain, reject, or revise central parts of our linguistic scheme.

---

[22] This piece of text is packed with grammatical metaphors—more on these and their significance in section 7.5.

Let us begin with moral and modal terms. Basic moral and modal expressions ("One *shouldn't* lie," "That *might be* Jane at the door," "Squares *can't* have more than four sides") are formulated using *modal* terms—which (as we have seen) primarily contribute *interpersonal* functions to the language. That gives us a good idea of where to look in reverse engineering these philosophically interesting parts of language. For we can see that the right place to begin might *not* be to assume that the function of moral discourse is simply to denote the good or right actions, or that the function of modal discourse is simply to talk about the possibilities or to describe other possible worlds. If we assumed that, we might then be driven into metaphysical investigations about the natures of these things described (the right actions, the moral properties, the possible worlds), and to the full range of metaphysical tangles that have resulted from these investigations. (I will have more to say about this in Chapter 8.)

Instead, with the functional picture outlined more clearly, we might begin by asking what social, regulative, or expressive functions the relevant parts of language serve. And this may make *non-descriptive* accounts of this terminology show up as reasonable options—accounts that don't simply tell us that the function of moral terminology is to denote things that are morally right/wrong, or that the function of modal terminology is to denote the possibilities and necessities. This kind of work can thereby enable us to better develop and defend neo-pragmatist accounts of moral, modal, or other forms of language that deny that such language should be seen as originating from the need to serve a *representational* or *descriptive* (ideational) function. Such accounts include, for example, work in metaethics by Hare, Blackburn, and Gibbard; and non-descriptive approaches to modal expressions, such as one can find in the work of Ryle, Sellars, Brandom, and myself.[23] And we might even be able to see the simultaneous *ideational*

---

[23] Unfortunately, there is not space here to do the relevant reverse-engineering work on moral or modal language. I have aimed to make a start at work on metaphysical modal language (as serving a regulative function of mandating, conveying, or renegotiating semantic rules) elsewhere (2020a), though I had not yet found the material on systemic functional linguistics to work from. For a later, more fine-grained application of these ideas to *modal* discourse, building on work in systemic functional linguistics, see my (2023b). For an initial approach to *moral* discourse through this framework, see Warren and Thomasson (2023) and my (in progress).

functions that are served by being able to formulate moral and modal claims as indicatives carrying content in propositional form—giving us the means for more fine-grained functional assessments than simply those that ask about the function of (all) moral or modal discourse.[24] I will return to this thought in Chapter 8.

7.5 Grammatical Metaphors

The framework from systemic functional linguistics also enables us to see that many other philosophically interesting terms enable us to serve new kinds of functions. For a great many terms that present philosophical difficulties fall in the category that systemic functional linguists refer to as "grammatical metaphors."

In the current philosophical context, the terminology of "grammatical metaphor" can be problematic. For it might be taken to suggest that it involves *merely metaphorical speech*, to be interpreted in a fictionalist or simulating way, or as if it's *merely pretending*. I want to explicitly reject those interpretations, and I do *not* think it's appropriate to read what Halliday and others in the systemic functional linguistics literature call "grammatical metaphors" in this way.[25] Once we see the actual idea here, we can distance ourselves from that interpretation. The term "metaphor" derives from the Greek *metaphora*, a transfer or carrying-over.[26] While familiar (lexical) metaphors carry over one *semantic meaning*, transferring it for another (if we shift from

---

[24] Though they may still be expressed in propositional form and come to serve an ideational metafunction, the crucial point here is that moral or modal claims (even expressed propositionally) originate from forms of speech introduced to serve interpersonal functions, and thus have introduction rules that differ in crucial ways from congruent, observationally acquired language introduced to serve an ideational function.

[25] Those familiar with my other work will see why: For I think that it is a mistake to think of nominalizations to speak, say, of properties as *merely pretending*, rather than as giving rules for what it takes to speak of properties, *in the only sense that has sense*. For details of the argument for a deflationist rather than fictionalist interpretation of such nominalizing discourse, see my (2013). Macarthur and Price similarly endorse a pragmatist *quietism* about metaphysical issues—which means they are normally "happy to stand with the folk and affirm the first-order truths of the domain in question," contrasting this with an anti-realist fictionalist approach (2007, 99). For a similar reaction to fictionalism, see Blackburn's (2005) response to David Lewis.

[26] Thanks to Manuel Gustavo Isaac for pointing this out in conversation.

speaking of a "sharp knife" to "sharp words"), *grammatical* metaphors carry over a term from one *grammatical category* to another (if we shift from saying "He has a knife" to "He knifed someone," or from "The barn is red" to "The property of redness is possessed by the barn").[27] As Halliday puts it, "In grammatical metaphor, one grammatical class takes over from another" (Halliday 2009, 126). By way of these grammatical metaphors, "a meaning that was originally construed by one type of wording comes instead to be construed by another" (Halliday 2009, 117).

As we have seen, children begin by learning congruent terms. But we depart from congruent formulations as we acquire more mature language[28] and learn to use grammatical metaphors.[29] So, for example, we shift from speaking of washing the car, to say we will "give the car a good clean," speak of "a carwash," "the cleaning of the car," and so on. The most obvious grammatical metaphors, at least in English, involve nominalization. But grammatical metaphors are not limited to cases in which another form of speech is converted to a *noun*. The shift can also go in other directions, as we might transform the noun "knife" to a verb that enables us to say, "She knifed someone." Grammatical metaphors may be introduced from language that is ideational (as we move from saying "She washed the car" to "She gave the car a wash"), or from language that is interpersonal (as we move from saying "It might rain tomorrow" to "There is a possibility of rain tomorrow")—thus linguists identify two kinds of grammatical metaphors: ideational and interpersonal (including in the latter both metaphors of mood and modality).[30] They also involve shifts from a wide range of grammatical categories (e.g., we may move from saying, "She lit the match, *so* the stove ignited," to "She lit the match, and that *caused* the stove to ignite";

---

[27] The terminology, thus, should not be taken to suggest that the resulting statements are anything less than literally true, and should not be confused with "fictionalist" proposals about how to understand discourse about properties, numbers, etc.

[28] Children typically process grammatical metaphor fully only after age eight or nine (Halliday 2009, 46).

[29] This also seems like a way of making good on the idea that there are optional additional frameworks that can be added onto the "thing" language, in Carnap's (1950/1956) terms.

[30] See Taverniers (2003, 5). For more details on the shifts in the modal system, and the relevance of this for philosophical work on modality, see my (2023b).

or from "It might rain tomorrow" to "There is a *possibility* of rain tomorrow").[31] Nonetheless, the examples of primary interest here will be nominalizations.

Nominalizations and other grammatical metaphors enable us to do new things with language. Though using grammatical metaphors may also sound more "learned" and be used for rhetorical effect, the primary motivation for nominalization is "a functional one: by nominalizing we are able to do things with the text that we cannot do in unnominalized text" (Eggins 2004, 95). Everyday grammatical metaphors (e.g., shifting from saying, "She bathed" to "She took a bath," or from "They danced" to "They did a dance"), enable us to qualify and quantify processes. That in turn enables us to say things such as "she had a *relaxing hot* bath" or "there are *three* folk-dances in the second act" (Halliday 2009, 135).[32] Consider how difficult it would be to describe the bath or count the dances without grammatical metaphors. As Eggins notes, with nouns, we can expand our clauses to do many things that we can't do with other parts of a clause (like verbs), viz.: count, specify, describe, classify, qualify (Eggins 2004, 96). This enables greater lexical density: that is, a greater proportion of content-carrying words (main verbs, nouns, adjectives, adverbs) in the text.[33] It also (as Thomas Hofweber noted [2005a, 2005b], and Eggins [2004] argues) can help us organize texts rhetorically, putting the focus on different parts of information.

While everyday language contains some grammatical metaphors (such as those above), grammatical metaphors get much more numerous, sophisticated, and layered when we develop scientific theories and bureaucratic systems—since they play a critical role in enabling scientific theorizing and in enabling us to establish and run bureaucratic systems. Grammatical metaphors "seem to represent tendencies common to the elaborated discourse of science and technology,

---

[31] Whether the grammatical metaphor is introduced from a congruent verb or adjective, or from another part of speech, such as a modal term, may make important differences in the ways we articulate their introduction rules, in what epistemological story is appropriate, etc. But such investigations will have to be left for another occasion.
[32] Halliday also shows that parallel nominalization constructions appear in Chinese to similar effect (2009, 135).
[33] Non-content-carrying words include prepositions, conjunctions, auxiliary verbs, and pronouns.

government and bureaucracy, in all languages" (Halliday 2009, 138). There is historical evidence that use of grammatical metaphors explodes with the development of science, technology, and bureaucracy. As Halliday puts it:

> Grammar has always had this potential for "cross-coupling." But it came well to the fore in the classical languages of the iron age, such as Chinese, Sanskrit and Greek, where it became the resource for creating abstract, technical objects . . . hundreds of verbs were nominalized as technical terms, and these nouns, together with their associated nominal group constructions, formed the core of a new, typically written, mode of discourse. (2009, 119)

We might even suspect that it is no mere coincidence that these coincide with the origins of philosophy as we know it, across traditions. For many philosophical questions cannot be formulated without a rich vocabulary of grammatical metaphors.

In scientific theorizing, grammatical metaphors play a central role in enabling us to construct extended theories, showing how diverse observations are interrelated in generalized explanations. For an example of how they may aid us in generalizing and theorizing, consider how they might be introduced when playing "snap circuits"—a simple toy that enables children to learn how electrical circuits work. In working with the circuits, my daughter and I observed that the fan spun clockwise when the positive end of the motor was connected to the negative end of the battery unit. It did the same when the negative end of the motor was connected to the positive end of the battery unit. We also noticed that when the connections were negative-negative or positive-positive, the fan spun counterclockwise. But that's a mouthful, full of disjunctions. To generalize, it is useful to introduce the new noun term *polarity* (along with other nominalizations), enabling us to state the principle we had uncovered far more succinctly: Connecting ends of opposite polarity causes the fan to spin clockwise. Connecting ends with the same polarity causes the fan to spin counterclockwise.

While we can see the use of grammatical metaphors even in developing and stating such simple generalizations, they play even more essential roles in developing sophisticated scientific theories. They enable us to "pick up where we left off" in communicating information to experts. So, for example, after a long section explaining how spin components fluctuate, a physics book may refer back to "the random fluctuations in the spin components of one of the two particles," enabling the author to "package the knowledge" that has been developed over a long preceding text and present it as to be "taken for granted" as we move to the next step (Halliday 2009, 45). If I "have to say every time that particles spin, that they spin in three dimensions, that a pair of particles can spin in association with one another, that each one of the pair fluctuates randomly as it is spinning, and so on, then it is clear that I will never get very far" (Halliday 2009, 45).

Halliday emphasizes that the function of much grammatical metaphor is to enable theory construction:

> It is no exaggeration to say that grammatical metaphor is at the foundation of all scientific thought. You cannot construct a theory—that is, a designed theory, as distinct from the evolved, commonsense theory incorporated in the grammar of everyday discourse—without exploiting the power of the grammar to create new, "virtual" phenomena by using metaphoric strategies of this kind. (Halliday 2009, 119)

"Such discourse evolved as the language of technology and science" and was "moulded by the demands of the physical sciences into its modern form" (Halliday 2009, 125), and "specialized technical discourse cannot be created without deploying grammatical metaphor" (Halliday 2009, 125).[34] Halliday notes that "this metaphoric shift from the clausal to the nominal construal of experience seems to be a characteristic of scientific discourse in every language" (2009, 123 n. 21).

But that is not all that grammatical metaphors contribute. For they are essential not only to formulating *theories* that provide *explanations* in ways *generalize* over observations, present causal links, and connect ideas in ways that take us from one explanation to another, and

---

[34] Martin (1990: "Literacy in science: learning to handle text as technology," cited in Halliday 2009, 125) has shown that specialized technical discourse cannot be created without deploying grammatical metaphor.

enable us to make generalized inferences. They are also essential to constructing *bureaucracies*—where we impose generalized systems not of *explanations* but of *requirements* and *permissions*. In developing a bureaucracy, we do not just impose orders on individuals—we establish *general* requirements (and permissions) on *anyone* who meets certain conditions. This ability to set generalized requirements and permissions is essential for moving from "the rule of man" where we are ruled by the individualized power and commands of a Hobbesian sovereign, to the rule of law—where we are governed by laws that apply to everyone. To layer up the requirements into a full bureaucratic system, we must introduce new nominalizations for categories of people, situation, objects, requirements, and entitlements. So, we can also move from speaking of where someone lives, to introduce nominalized talk of *permanent residents* who are *homeowners* and *taxpayers*, and go on to speak of their resulting civic and tax *obligations*, and the *debts* that may result and fines incurred for the late *payment of debts*. Take a look at any contract in your own files, or any legal judgment, to see how packed bureaucratic and legal prose is with grammatical metaphors.

In sum, we can identify at least the following functions that are served by having a language that enables us to form grammatical metaphors. Doing so enables speakers to

- Quantify and qualify processes, events, attributes, etc. (These may also enable us to make quantities measurable—so we can say not just "This is long" or "That is hot" but "The pendulum has a *length of four feet*" or "the mixture a *heat of 425 degrees*.")[35]
- Increase lexical density: with a higher proportion of content-carrying words and more efficient communication of information
- Organize texts rhetorically, showing connections among ideas, formulating arguments, putting the focus on different parts of information
- Enable the flow of information and the construction of theories, forming ordered chains of generalized explanations

---

[35] Carnap (1950/1962) draws out the important uses that introducing quantitative concepts may have for the sciences.

- Expand expressive power in ways that, once introduced, can't always be fully "unpacked" and eliminated into more basic forms of speech
- Organize and run bureaucracies("Homeowners will receive a tax deduction") by instituting impersonal and layered systems of permissions and requirements

Turning back now to our work on function, we can see more clearly why it would be a mistake to think that all that can be said about function is disquotational—say, that the function of "length" is just to pick out the lengths, the function of "fluctuation" is just to pick out the fluctuations, or the function of "tax obligation" is just to pick out the tax obligations. For these functions do not just include *ideational* metafunctions (though of course in a harmless sense they do enable us to speak of the lengths or the tax obligation, and express propositions regarding them—we can simultaneously fulfill an ideational metafunction). More crucially, these grammatical metaphors enable us to serve new kinds of functions that enable us to construct unified theories and bureaucracies.

7.6 Conclusions

As I have argued, we need good ways of thinking about and identifying linguistic functions, in order to better undertake reverse conceptual engineering, and in order to assess proposals in (re)constructive conceptual engineering.[36] I have tried to show that analyzing linguistic functions is not hopeless, nor should we think that the most that can be said is the disquotational "The function of 'F' is to pick out the Fs." On the contrary, the disquotational view is clearly inadequate and (as I aim to show below) prone to lead us philosophically astray.

---

[36] This, of course, is not the *only* use of functional assessments of language. Those working in systemic functional linguistics have not been concerned with conceptual engineering (or any philosophical issues), but rather with goals such as helping children with developmental delays, or learners of a second language, by identifying what is functionally lacking and how these needs can be met.

I have also aimed to redirect our ways of thinking about function, away from thinking in terms of uses or intended functions, and toward a notion of *system* function that begins by assessing the functions of language as a whole, and uses that in identifying the functions that various subsystems, parts, and features of language serve. If we take that path, we will begin our investigations not by asking about the functions of this or that individual *word*, but rather by asking questions about the functions of *language* in human life. We can then work from there to determine what roles various linguistic subsystems (such as the mood system or modal system) play in fulfilling these functions. Moreover, as I will aim to show, we can ultimately make finer-grained distinctions of the different layers of functions that may be added in grammatically distinct terminology that is still "about the same subject." I have also tried to show that we can make progress on all of these questions by turning to work in systemic functional linguistics.

Of course, looking to *system functions* in *language* is not the only way of thinking about function. The everyday notion of "function" may be developed and understood in different ways for different purposes. If we are evaluating the success of engineering prototypes, the notion of *intended* function may be most relevant. In biology, proper or *etiological* function may be most relevant. Even in doing conceptual engineering, more than one notion of function may be relevant. In fact, as I go on to discuss in Chapter 9, more than one notion of function may be *needed* to get a complete picture. System function accounts in general seem to rely on a deeper notion of function that addresses the needs or desires served by the system in question. It is interesting to determine the function of a coil in a heating system, but that relies on a deeper understanding of the functions of heating systems, and why we would want such systems to be included in our homes and offices. We may similarly need to go beyond *linguistic* functions to account for the functions of non-linguistic *concepts* that precede the development of our language (historically), or the acquisition of language (individually).[37] We may also need to go beyond understanding the functions contributed by various formal features of language (such as having a

---

[37] For discussion of prelinguistic concepts such as "object," "agent," and "number," see Carey (2009).

modal system, or the ability to nominalize), to also (with Matthieu Queloz) address questions about what different material concepts contribute to our ability to serve various human purposes.

Here I mean only to emphasize the ways in which the systemic account of linguistic functions can contribute to our philosophical work—including our work in conceptual engineering. For linguistic forms that are well studied by systemic functional linguistics— including the mood and modal systems and grammatical metaphors— play a central role in *metaphysical* problems. As I will turn to show next in Chapter 8, by better understanding these linguistic functions we can disentangle ourselves from many of these old problems. In short, one reason to focus on the formal-linguistic-system-function account here is that it is particularly relevant for disentangling us from various metaphysical problems. Metaphysical problems tend to arise from mistakes that come about by not noticing the plurality of linguistic functions.

Moreover, systemic functional linguistics gives us a sophisticated view of the functions served by different linguistic forms in ways that enable us to move beyond traditional questions raised by neo-pragmatists, say, about "the function of moral discourse" or "the function of modal discourse." Instead, we can move step by step to address much more fine-grained questions, distinguishing the functions of basic modal discourse (involving such terms as "can," "must," and "might") from the functions added by more sophisticated verbal constructions that speak about "the possibility that . . ." or even of possible worlds.[38]

In short, while this work on linguistic functions is complementary to much other work on functions, it is a particularly relevant way of examining functions if our aim is to reexamine and dissolve a range of classic problems in metaphysics. For, as the work of Part I already suggested, a great many of these problems arise by failing to notice and take seriously the range of different functions that different parts of our language serve. I aim to show this relevance next—demonstrating how these functional analyses may enable us to do reverse conceptual engineering work better, in ways that enable us to re-evaluate many

---

[38] See my (2023b) for details on modal discourse and my (in progress) on moral language.

past metaphysical problems, identify pseudo-problems, and provide a better evaluation of what to do with many of our old concepts. While this is only a preliminary glance at this work in linguistics, I hope that it has been enough to build on in ways that show its philosophical importance.

8
Reverse Engineering
Unraveling Metaphysical Problems

In Part I I argued that five prominent approaches to metaphysics all suffer from the same metaphysical malady: assuming that all discourse functions in the same way.[1] Now that we have an approach to understanding linguistic functions in hand, I can clarify what that assumption is and make clear why it leads us astray. I can also make clear how the above work on function enables us to engage in productive work in reverse engineering. For by identifying the functions and entry rules of many concepts that have been perennially problematic in metaphysics, we can disentangle ourselves from many old metaphysical problems.

Metaphysics is concerned with all sorts of topics. As we have seen, it is this *generality* that gives metaphysics a claim to do *more* than the natural sciences can. For metaphysicians (thinking of their work as aiming to study "ultimate reality as a whole") ask about the nature and existence of not just of physical objects and events, but of properties, numbers, thoughts, moral requirements, or possible worlds. In thinking of their work in this way, metaphysicians tend to impose a single model on all this language—a model derived from taking as the paradigm congruent, observationally acquired, world-tracking discourse.[2] But, as we have seen, different parts of language serve different types of functions, and not all serve world-tracking functions.

This enables us to see why it is a mistake to think of work on all of these topics as the "study of ultimate reality"—as if all these forms

---

[1] Portions of this chapter draw on work in my (2023b), other parts from my (2022).
[2] Or (sometimes) taking the terms introduced to refer to the explanatory "posits" of natural science as the paradigm. Language to refer to unobserved explanatory posits may function differently from observationally introduced language but is likewise unsuited to be a general model.

Rethinking Metaphysics. Amie L. Thomasson, Oxford University Press.
© Oxford University Press 2025. DOI: 10.1093/9780197787830.003.0008

of discourse are aiming to track worldly features. It also enables us to see why adopting some approaches to metaphysics across the board—such as requiring that any entities "posited" add "explanatory power" to our theories, asking all discourse to track deep worldly "structure," or demanding worldly "truthmakers" for all of our claims—is misguided. For these each may (at most) be suitable criteria for a limited area of discourse. But it is inappropriate to generalize such criteria to all forms of language of interest in metaphysics.

The work on function not only enables us to better see why past approaches to metaphysics went wrong. It also enables us to do work in reverse conceptual engineering in a way that enables us to make new progress on unraveling old philosophical problems and puzzles, and to make better evaluations in conceptual engineering about what aspects of our old linguistic and conceptual scheme need revising, and why.

In this chapter I take on some of this reverse-engineering work. Some of this work can be seen as making good on the Wittgensteinian suggestion that the philosopher's treatment of metaphysical questions should be *therapeutic*—a way of showing the fly the way out of the fly-bottle. This therapeutic work can be done much more thoroughly with a more developed theory of linguistic function to hand.[3] For that enables us to better see the shape of the bottle, see why we became disoriented, and see how to avoid the relevant problems. More directly, it can be seen as developing the neo-pragmatist project that has shown up in work by Robert Brandom, Richard Rorty, Huw Price, David MacArthur, David Braddon Mitchell, Joshua Gert, Michael Williams, and others.[4] For as neo-pragmatists such as David MacArthur and Huw Price have put it, "pragmatism begins with questions about the functions and genealogy of certain *linguistic* items. . . . It begins with linguistic behaviour, and asks broadly anthropological questions: How

---

[3] There are historical connections, too, since (as mentioned in Chapter 7) Wittgenstein was influenced by the anthropologist Bronislaw Malinowski, whose work was also foundational for systemic functional linguistics. But with nearly a century of further work on linguistic function now to hand, we can engage in diagnoses in a far less impressionistic and more systematic fashion.

[4] Which, of course, itself was inspired by work in the pragmatist tradition that developed in both Cambridge, Massachusetts, and Cambridge, England. For a wonderful and insightful history of this "Cambridge Pragmatism," see Misak (2016).

are we to understand the roles and functions of the behaviour in question, in the lives of the creatures concerned?" (2007, 95).[5]

There are signs of trouble everywhere in metaphysics—puzzles and paradoxes, and difficulties that arise in addressing topics such as numbers and properties, modality and morality. These troubles lay down a trail of clues that reverse-engineering work may be needed. With the help of the work above on function, we can now undertake that reverse-engineering work.

Many of the most formidable problems of metaphysics include problems about events, processes, properties, numbers, truth, causation, etc. All of these are *grammatical metaphors*—terminology introduced via grammatical shifts from other forms of speech which (as detailed in section 7.5) enable us to qualify and quantify processes and events, and to generalize in ways essential to formulating theories and bureaucracies.[6] Central problems of metaphysics also include questions about "the nature of" modality, morality, and mind. These forms of language originate from the mood and modal systems, which add *interpersonal* functions to the language. As I will argue, reverse engineering the relevant terms reveals that many of these most formidable and perennial "metaphysical problems" arise from mistakenly treating these areas of discourse on the paradigm of congruent, observationally acquired discourse.

There is not space here to work through the details of every metaphysical problem. My goal is not to definitively dissolve every metaphysical debate, but rather to begin to construct a linguistic platform that can enable us to climb out of the weeds to get a good overview of the territory. In the service of that goal, I will develop some examples of prominent and perennial philosophical problems—some to do with abstract objects, and others to do with modality. Doing reverse-engineering work to identify some of the functions these terms serve, and the rules by which they are introduced to language, enables us

---

[5] For an overview of the neo-pragmatist approach and examples of how it may be applied to many problems, see Gert (2023).

[6] It is worth noting, however, that grammatical metaphors also should not all be treated together, as their entry rules may work in different ways, deriving from different parts of language (some from congruent nouns, verbs, connectives, etc.; others from basic modal language, or from determiner uses of number terms, etc.).

to show how faulty assumptions about language lead metaphysics into treating existence questions as "deep, theoretical" questions, when they can actually be answered easily. It also enables us to show that these faulty assumptions lead metaphysics into category mistakes—engendering problems and questions that arise from false presuppositions about how the relevant forms of language work. But where category mistakes are built into questions, we do better to diagnose where the relevant questions go wrong, than to try to answer them straightforwardly. Those sample diagnoses may suggest how various further "metaphysical problems" might be reassessed in light of the functional analyses given here—demonstrating the relevance and value of undertaking work in reverse engineering that begins by assessing linguistic functions.

This helps make the case that appreciating functional pluralism in language and developing a more explicit way of analyzing and assessing the functions different parts of language serve may lead metaphysics—and perhaps philosophy more broadly—away from misguided old tangles into fruitful new directions.

8.1 Reassessing Metaphysical Criteria

In Part I, I discussed four recent ways of thinking of the "general project of metaphysics": the explanatory project, the structure project, the truthmaker project, and the groundingproject. I argued that a problem underlying *all* of these projects is this: Metaphysics is traditionally concerned with all kinds of topics (ordinary objects, numbers, properties and other abstracta, persons, works of art, consciousness, possible worlds, moral facts, etc.), but each of these "completely general" metaphysical projects involves imposing some completely general standards (e.g., that the entities referred to add explanatory power to our theories, carve reality at its joints, have truthmakers, etc.). I argued at the close of Part I that determining whether any general task or criterion can be applied to a given topic depends on the *functions* of the relevant form of discourse.

Now that we have a better idea of what functions govern different aspects of discourse, we can better make those assessments. In fact, we can see that they are all inappropriate to adopt as *general* standards.

Consider the explanatory project, which addresses questions about whether there *are* things of a given kind by asking whether "positing" or "quantifying over" the relevant entities would add new *explanatory power* to our theories. I suggested back in Chapter 2 that we should not accept an "explanatory power" criterion across the board, since not all the noun terms of interest in metaphysics function to "posit" would-be "explainers" for our theories. The work from systemic functional linguistics can now confirm this—for we have seen the range of other functions served by "grammatical metaphors" such as terms for numbers and properties—confirming that these are not introduced to "posit" explainers, but rather add a range of other functions to the language—including enabling us to generalize in ways that make it possible to develop scientific theories and bureaucracies.

The structural conception faces a similar problem: we should not, for example, worry that "Necessity and possibility do not carve at the joints" (Sider 2011, 266), given that that is not the role of modal discourse at all. Nor should we conclude that "If modality is not fundamental, then it must be nonfundamental," so that we "need a reduction of modality" (Sider 2011, 268), to be provided by a "metaphysical semantics" for modal claims that shows "how what we say fits into fundamental reality" (Sider 2011, 112). Instead, as we have seen from systemic functional linguistics, modal discourse contributes distinctive *interpersonal* functions to language (and does so in quite useful ways), and aims to track neither fundamental features of reality nor non-fundamental "features of reality" that need to be reduced.

Those who accept a truthmaker approach make a similar mistake. For they insist that we provide some *truthmakers* to correspond to any truth one accepts—implicitly treating all true claims as serving to track and describe features of "reality" that can explain what makes it true. But approaches to dispositions, possibilities, or moral facts are not aptly criticized as "cheating" if they fail to "provide the truthmakers." Instead, the difficulties of identifying truthmakers for these claims are symptomatic of the fact that these forms of modal discourse don't aim to *track worldly features* at all.

Projects of identifying "what grounds what" or what "metaphysically explains" the existence of various kinds of fact similarly founder on those cases in which the function of the terminology is not to track "parcels of reality" so that we can then ask whether these are fundamental, or grounded in something more fundamental. For as we have seen, grammatical metaphors (including terms for abstract objects) and modal terminology enter language to serve other sorts of functions. We should not expect them to refer to "parcels of reality," in a way that it makes sense to ask what more basic "features of reality" these parcels are grounded in.

In short, given the above work on function, we can now make good on the diagnosis from Part I: All of these "completely general projects for metaphysics" falsely presuppose a single model for all of the language of interest in the various topics of metaphysics. The explanatory project treats it all on the model of language for explanatory posits in scientific theories (and to witness the impact of this model, notice the ubiquity of language of "positing" and "explanation" in metaphysical debates on all topics over the past 75 years). The other projects, along with the traditional conception of metaphysics as aiming to tell us about "the nature of reality as a whole," treat all language on the model of the congruent discourse we use to describe, track, and communicate about observational features of our world. But all go systematically wrong by trying to apply a single model of language, or a single criterion, to "all discourse whatsoever," including discourse about properties, numbers, and other abstracta, and to moral, modal, and mental discourse. Before adopting any across-the-board "metaphysical criteria," we must take a step back to assess linguistic functions.

8.2 Re-Evaluating Metaphysical Debates About Abstracta

By the same token, before assessing whether a given part of language presents genuine ontological, epistemological, or other philosophical problems, or whether we should retain, modify, or eliminate it, we should take a step back to assess linguistic functions. Here I will address two types of discourse that have long been thought to present formidable problems: discourse about abstract entities such as properties and numbers, and modal discourse (including discourse about necessity, possibility, possible worlds, possibilities, chances, etc.). Such discourse has long been thought to be so problematic that there have been calls to just deny that numbers, properties, modal facts, properties, or possible worlds exist.

With the above work on function in hand from Chapter 7, we are now in a position to better reverse-engineer how such areas of discourse work, and better understand what functions they serve. And that, in turn, will enable us to re-evaluate many traditional metaphysical debates and problems.

Let us begin by considering classic metaphysical problems about abstract entities such as numbers and properties. The first such problem is this: *Are* there such things?

In my earlier work (2015a) I have argued that we *should* accept that there are. Indeed, I have argued that such questions are *easy* to answer—and in the positive. For there are "trivial" or "redundant" inferences that entitle us to infer from an undisputed truth, say, "The barn is red," that "the barn has the property of redness." And from that, we can conclude that *there is a property of redness* that the barn has—and so answer the ontological question "Are there properties?" with a simple "yes."

Here are some other examples:

- There are two cups on the table; the number of cups on the table is two; there are numbers.
- May was born on a Monday; the event of May's birth occurred on a Monday; there are events.

There surely *appear to be* redundancies in saying, "The barn is red, *and* the barn has the property of redness," as well as in saying, "There are two cups on the table, *and* the number of cups on the table is two," and so on for the other cases. Ontologists like myself (2015a) have emphasized these redundant inferences and have defended the idea that they are valid inferences that enable us to answer existence questions. But others have denied that such "easy inferences" are legitimate, holding that *more must be required* of the world for there to "really" be properties, numbers, or events (for otherwise, wouldn't such turns of phrase just be redundant, and silly to have in our language?).

One way to address these debates is to use work in linguistics to better understand the functions of the relevant parts of language, and the rules by which these forms of speech come to be introduced. In the easy inferences above, we begin from a basic congruent, observational sentence—used primarily to communicate *ideational* content about the world experienced: The barn is red, there are two cups on the table, May was born on a Monday.[7] But a fully developed grammar enables us to shift a congruent part of speech in the first sentence (say, "red" as an adjective) to use "red" as a noun—introducing what Halliday calls a "grammatical metaphor." While the original statement served an ideational function of communicating propositional content (about the observable world), this grammatical shift enables us to (also) fulfill new functions by introducing grammatical metaphors.

This analysis gives us new reason to accept that the "easy" inferences really *are* perfectly valid inferences licensed by the rules that introduce these new forms of speech. In most cases, what we have in the second statement are new noun terms ("property," "number," "event," etc.), introduced from what (in the first statement) played a different grammatical role (adjective, determiner, verb). The work in systemic functional linguistics gives further empirical support to the idea that easy arguments in ontology simply follow from the grammatical shifts that are licensed as part of mature language.

Still more interestingly, the functional analysis enables us to see why speakers would choose to use linguistic forms that involve grammatical metaphors and, more broadly, why we would *want* a language with so much built-in capacity for redundancy. For, as we have seen in Chapter 7, grammatical metaphors add a range of important new functions, including quantifying and qualifying attributes, processes,

---

[7] Grammatical metaphors, however, can also be introduced from other parts of speech, including from parts of speech serving primarily interpersonal functions (such as modal statements). Accordingly, Miriam Taverniers distinguishes "interpersonal" from "ideational" grammatical metaphors (2003, 5 and 12). I will return to these below, and (if we are to unravel metaphysical problems) it will be important to bear in mind the different routes of entry that grammatical metaphors can take.

and events; organizing texts rhetorically; expanding expressive power; and enabling us to formulate generalized explanatory questions and to construct complex and layered theories and bureaucracies.

Given all of the useful roles grammatical metaphors play, it would be a mistake to try to eliminate the discourse on grounds of some "ontological qualms" about accepting "an ontology of properties or numbers." And if we do accept the discourse, with the standard redundant rules for introducing talk of properties, numbers, etc. to our language, then we can easily answer "ontological" questions such as "Are there properties, are there numbers...?" Yes there are.[8]

But if we accept that there are properties or numbers, don't we have to face up to those ontological qualms and all of the associated metaphysical problems?

Not so fast. For the answers we have given to *linguistic* questions about the functions of the discourse, and the rules by which it enters language, may enable us to see which "metaphysical" questions are genuine and which involve pseudo-problems that arise from false presuppositions.

So, what sorts of reasons have been given for denying the existence of numbers, properties, and other abstracta? In some cases, they have been denied on grounds that such "posited" entities would not *add explanatory power to our theories*—but we have already seen why that criterion should not be generalized to apply to these cases, where the relevant grammatical metaphors play important roles *quite different* from those played by terms for explanatory posits. Others have thought we should say no, since accepting that there are such entities would raise formidable philosophical problems: "placement" problems about how such entities could "fit" in with the natural world, or problems with accepting odd or spooky entities that *have no spatiotemporal location*. Others have thought that accepting such entities

---

[8] Of course fictionalists might want to retain the discourse but reject the idea that there are (or "really are") such things. I have argued extensively elsewhere, however, that treating discourse as fictional or pretenseful requires a contrast between what it takes for the term to succeed in applying (e.g., for there to be a bear) and what conditions are met instead (e.g., there is only a stump that we pretend is a bear). But there is no contrast in these cases—the conditions required for there to be numbers or properties *are* met. As a result, there is no basis for thinking of this talk as merely fictional or pretending. For full discussion see my (2013), revised as Chapter 5 of my (2015a).

would be philosophically problematic in other ways—for, at least if we think numbers or other pure abstracta would have to be outside the causal order, we would be unable to refer to them or gain knowledge of them.

If we now look back at these (alleged) problems, our reverse-engineering analysis enables us to show that they are based on mistakes. More specifically, we can diagnose many such "metaphysical" problems and questions as category mistakes. This again both draws from and broadens Price's observation that reductionist metaphysics "may be guilty of a category mistake" in failing to note the functional diversity of different aspects of language (2011, 78), as well as his suggestion that Rylean category mistakes may be best understood as arising where there are crucial functional differences between different forms of language (2009, 332–34). Price also prefigures a point I will try to develop here: that important functional differences in language "will turn out to line up with what, viewed from a different angle, present as some of the 'hard cases' of contemporary metaphysics—the status and nature of morality, modality, meaning and the mental, for example" (2009, 334).

As Michael Halliday emphasizes (2009, 131), when grammatical metaphors are introduced, that brings with it the potential for absurdities and internal contradictions:[9] the hallmarks of what Gilbert Ryle identified as "category mistakes" (1949, 16–18). Huw Price (2009, 330–35) argues that what Ryle identifies as category mistakes are best seen as arising from failures to note functional differences. One way to develop the suggestion that category mistakes are involved here is to make use of Ofra Magidor's analysis of category mistakes. Magidor (2013) argues that category mistakes are infelicitous because they suffer from pragmatic presupposition failures.[10] Magidor says "a wide range of expressions (including most verbs, adjectives, adverbs, and prepositions) are presupposition triggers" (2013, 145). "Two is green," for example (on her analysis), triggers the false presupposition that

---

[9] Halliday's example here is "The fifth day saw them at the summit," which introduces absurdities since, of course, days cannot see (2009, 131).
[10] That is not to say that *all* presupposition failures lead to category mistakes (Magidor 2013, sec. 4.3).

two is colored (2013, 132); "John drinks procrastination" triggers the false presupposition that procrastination can be imbibed.

I would suggest that using a term in a certain grammatical category can also trigger presuppositions—where the relevant presupposition is a *metalinguistic* one about the function and rules of the term. For example, using a noun term can trigger the metalinguistic presupposition that the term (like a congruent, basic noun, observationally acquired) has the function of tracking objects in the environment, and follows the same kind of *rules of use* (requiring introduction via a causal connection with features of the environment). Such *metalinguistic presupposition failure*, I want to suggest, is one source of category mistakes and is behind many alleged "metaphysical" problems that lead to a wide range of philosophical puzzles and paradoxes.

As Magidor makes clear (2013, 122), questions can also inherit presupposition failures (consider: "How old is John's sister?" when John has no sister; or "What color is the number two?"). When that is the case, no straightforward answer to the question will be true. The proper response is not to straightforwardly answer such questions, but rather to show what the presupposition is and why it is faulty in ways that render the questions out of place.

Many of the metaphysical questions pressed for properties and numbers, I would suggest, rely on inappropriate tacit presuppositions about how the language functions (especially: assumptions that it all functions like congruent nouns). We do better to unravel the mistaken presupposition, not to attempt to answer the question straightforwardly, or to treat it as a "deep metaphysical puzzle" to which no good response has been found. Consider, for example, ontological "placement problems" about how the "things referred to" in our talk of properties or numbers can be "placed" in the natural world, or problems about how there could be such "odd" things that lacked a spatiotemporal location. The use of noun terms triggers a presupposition that these terms function like our basic congruent nouns—tracking features of the environment, so that we can reasonably ask how the "things referred to" can be "placed" in the natural world, or how they could exist without having a spatiotemporal location. But once we see that the origins of these noun terms are totally different, and the entry rules for the language require no such connection, we can see that such questions arise out of faulty metalinguistic presuppositions.

Similar category mistakes lie behind many of the alleged "barriers" to accepting that there are numbers, properties, or other abstract objects. For example, accepting that there are abstracta has often been thought to be problematic because we can't stand in a causal relation to such entities, and so (the argument goes) we couldn't refer to them, or acquire knowledge of them. But these alleged barriers again come from presupposing that our noun terms for properties or numbers function like congruent, observationally acquired nouns. It is plausible that such congruent nouns as "dog" or "tree" are ones that we learn ostensively, and that causal connection plays at least some role in determining what sorts of thing they refer to.[11] It is also plausible that our means of acquiring (empirical) knowledge of such entities requires a causal connection to them.[12] But we should have no expectation that the same should go for nouns that enter language as grammatical metaphors. Instead, we come to be able to refer to them through grammatical shifts that can be articulated in redundant inferences such as those I have identified above.

There *is* a legitimate question in the vicinity: How we can come to have mathematical knowledge? And we might hope that a good story about how the terms enter language will help in answering it.[13] But we will only think there is a great *barrier* to such knowledge if we tacitly accept the false presupposition that number terms share the functions and entry rules of congruent nouns, observationally acquired.

In this way, reverse-engineering terms for abstracta such as numbers and properties can both justify us in holding that questions about their existence can be answered easily, and also show us why many of the "metaphysical problems" that have been thought to arise for accepting

---

[11] Though I do not think we should accept, in any case, *pure* causal theories of reference. See my (2020a, ch. 4) for details.

[12] The parenthetical (empirical) is meant to signal that we may have knowledge, say, of their modal properties via other means—such as mastery of the relevant forms of language, and ability to make the rules (and what follows from them) explicit in the object language. For details, see my (2020a, ch. 7).

[13] I take Wright and Hale's work (2001, 2009) to be working on this track.

their existence are based on category mistakes that arise from failing to notice the origins and functions of talk of properties and numbers.

8.3 Re-Evaluating Metaphysical Debates About Modality

Like discourse about abstract entities, modal discourse has long been thought to provoke "insuperable problems" about what the discourse could refer to, and how we could come to know the relevant truths. As Brandom puts it, "Hume (and, following him, Quine) took it that epistemologically and semantically fastidious philosophers faced a stark choice: either show how to explain modality in non-modal terms or learn to live without it" (2008, 96). But here again, understanding linguistic functions enables us to reverse engineer the relevant forms of discourse, in ways that can enable us to re-evaluate the alleged problems.

Modal discourse is a complex area of language,[14] and I will not have the space or expertise to cover all the details here, though I have done some additional work on moral and modal discourse elsewhere.[15] Here I only aim to say enough to make clear how work in systemic functional linguistics enables us to reassess old metaphysical debates about modality.

Modal language is often said to come in three "flavors." These include deontic and ability modals; "alethic" physical, metaphysical, and logical modalities; and epistemic modals.[16] A complete account of modality should make clear what these varieties have in common, while also clarifying the differences among them. Many theorists have focused on just one "flavor" of modal discourse—as Sellars (1958) and

---

[14] Halliday estimates that the "actual number of systematic distinctions that are made in this corner of the language [modality] runs well into the tens of thousands" (Halliday and Matthiessen 2014, 696).

[15] On moral discourse, see Warren and Thomasson (2023), and Thomasson (in progress). On metaphysical modal discourse see Thomasson (2020a and 2023b—of which only the latter was written after I discovered the relevant work in systemic functional linguistics).

[16] Linguists classify deontic and ability modals as "root" modals (and though they have been of less interest in linguistics, it seems physical, metaphysical, and logical modalities would be categorized as "root," too) and contrast these with "epistemic" modals (Cournane 2020, 3).

Ryle (1949, 121) focus on statements of scientific laws, Yalcin (2011) develops an expressivist approach to epistemic modal discourse, and I have focused on claims of *metaphysical* necessity and possibility (2020a). We might nonetheless hope to find some unity across these stories that address particular flavors of modality.

In earlier work (2020a), I suggested that the *unity* behind various forms of modal discourse was that all serve to convey, mandate, or renegotiate rules or norms in useful ways,[17] while the *variety* can be captured in terms of the different *sorts* of rule or norm that are in question. Metaphysical modals, as I have argued (2020a), are concerned with conveying, enforcing, and renegotiating *semantic* rules ("Squares must have four sides of equal length"), which also regulate what sorts of *material* inferences we are entitled to or prohibited from making. Logical necessities regulate what logical *forms* of inference we are permitted and required to make, across different suppositions, as Greg Restall (2012) argues. *Deontic* modals (you *should* or *ought to* or *must* do X) can be seen as serving to regulate behavior according to *authoritative, prudential,* or *moral* rules or norms. Other root modals can be understood as having parallel regulative functions, where the relevant rules or norms vary. Ability modals can be understood as giving something like Rylean "inference tickets": To say, "I can reach that shelf" or "I can skate" is to not describe something one is doing at the moment, but to license the interlocutor to make certain (empirically grounded) inferences about what the speaker would do, in certain circumstances: It is to say what we *may* infer and may not infer (don't infer that I won't be able to get to the cake if you put it on that shelf!).

In each of these areas, modal discourse has provoked endless "metaphysical problems"—for example, regarding what the truthmakers are for our claims of possibility and necessity, whether there are chances, probabilities, or possible worlds, how they are related to non-modal facts and properties, how they could be credence-guiding, and how we could come to know them. In metaethics, parallel problems have

---

[17] Namely, by enabling us to express rules or norms in the indicative mood, in ways that enable us to better reason with and from them, while making the regulative status explicit, making our ways of reasoning with them explicit, and enabling us to express permissions as well as requirements (Thomasson 2020, 63).

arisen about what the truthmakers are for our moral claims, whether there are moral facts and properties, how they could fit in with a world of natural facts and properties, how they could be action-guiding, and how we could know them.

But again, before diving headlong into these "deep metaphysical puzzles," we should take a step back, to ask how modal discourse functions. For starting with the earlier questions about linguistic functions can show us things about the later "metaphysical" questions: how they may arise from mistakes generated by failing to appreciate the diverse functions areas of language can and do serve, and the correlated diverse rules that govern different areas of language, and why this failure might lead us astray into paradoxes, pseudo-problems, and irrelevant debates.

The first important thing to notice, given the prior work from systemic functional linguistics, is that discourse of all of these "metaphysically puzzling" varieties develops from the mood and modal systems, which serve primarily *interpersonal* functions (Halliday, 1973, 33; cf. Eggins 2004, 172–84). So, if we ask, "Why would we have a language with a mood or modal system?" the answer is that it enables us to establish and make evident social roles and relationships, show our attitudes, get people to behave in certain ways, and so forth. Modality is "a complex area of English grammar which has to do with different ways a language user can intrude on her message, expressing attitudes and judgments of various kinds" (Eggins 2004, 172).

The mood system emerges early in language learning (before the modal system), and mastery of it enables the child to speak in various grammatical moods—uttering declaratives, interrogatives, imperatives, exclamatives, etc. A proto-mood system can be observed in early language development, around 19 months (Halliday 2009, 14).[18] In a mature language, mood options enable speakers to take up a range of social relationships to their interlocutors, including

---

[18] As Halliday puts it, the child studied distinguished utterances with a "pragmatic" "doing" function, from utterances with a "mathetic" or learning function, by using a rising and falling tone respectively (2009, 14).

questioner/respondent (with interrogative form), commander/commanded (with imperative form), etc. Among other things, a *mood* system enables speakers to use language to take on the task of regulating behavior, by uttering imperatives.

Use of a *modal* system, in its initial form employing auxiliary and semi-auxiliary modal verbs, emerges somewhat later (around age two to three). What does a modal system give speakers that they would lack if they had only a mood system at their disposal? We can identify at least four further advantages gained by using a modal system (rather than just a mood system). A first is that it enables speakers to fulfill regulative functions without overtly taking on the role of commander. So, as a professor, I can utter the imperative to my students: "Read Kant's *Groundwork*." But I could also use a modal verb instead, saying, "All students of Philosophy 1 *must* read Kant's *Groundwork*." This has the advantage not only of being more polite (I am now not barking orders, but impersonally laying out the requirements), but also of being explicitly *generalized*, making it clear that the regulation applies to any *students of the class, given their role*, not just to whoever happens to be hearing my command. Shifting to a modal formulation also enables speakers to present their regulations *impersonally*, as "not 'just their own' but [as having] some objective status" (Eggins 2004, 175).

A second advantage gained by using modal verbs in regulating behavior is that it introduces variability in *force*, enabling us to "temper" what we say. Modal terminology introduces *degrees* by the processes of "modalization" (moving from "Henry James wrote 'The Bostonians,'" to "Henry James *might have written* 'The Bostonians'" [Eggins 2004, 173]); and "modulation" (moving from "Clean your room" to "You *should* clean your room"). Both modalization and modulation are "grammatical resources for tempering what we say" (Eggins 2004, 181). Modalization introduces attitudes toward *propositions*, so that we aren't limited to *it is* or *it isn't*. Instead, we can more subtly say: it *might* be, it *could* be, it *must* be . . . Modalization enables speakers not just to assert or deny, but to express their judgment of the certainty, likelihood, or frequency of something (Eggins 2004, 174). So, by shifting from "Henry James wrote 'The Bostonians,'" to "Henry James *might have written* 'The Bostonians,'" I *show* my uncertainty while still *talking about* the author and text (Eggins 2004, 173).[19] Modulation, by contrast, enables speakers to express attitudes toward *proposals*, expressing degrees of *obligation* and *requirement* (Eggins 2004, 179) and thereby enabling us to attempt to direct behavior in more subtle and graded ways than we can manage using imperatives. So, rather than commanding, "Clean your room," we can stringently insist, "You *must* clean your room" or more mildly suggest, "You *should* clean your room" (Eggins 2004, 179). Like modalization, modulation introduces degrees, in this case, degrees of attitudes toward *proposals*, so we aren't limited to the "Do x" or "Don't do x" of imperatives. Instead, we can say: You *may* do it, you *should* do it, you *must* do it... (Eggins 2004, 180).

A third advantage of introducing modal formulations (rather than using the imperative mood) is that we can aim to regulate behavior while using the *declarative* mood. And that in turn enables us to reason with and from these expressions in ways that are not available with imperatives. We can say, for example, "If students *must* read Kant's *Groundwork*, then this is going to be a hard class," whereas it isn't even grammatical to say, "If: Read Kant's *Groundwork*, then . . ." By making this shift to using the declarative mood, statements with modal verbs express their propositional content in a grammatical form that enables us to reason with them and from them in all the ways characteristic of declaratives, enables us to categorize them as true or false, etc.— thereby fulfilling additional *ideational* functions alongside their *interpersonal* functions.[20]

---

[19] This way of thinking about epistemic modal language is cohesive with Yalcin's (2011) interesting arguments that we should not (with descriptivists) take these to be *describing* the epistemic states of agents or some body of evidence.

[20] An interesting upshot of this analysis is that it both shows that early prescriptivists, who took moral language to share important features with imperatives, were *onto something*, and yet also makes it clear why more was needed to fully understand moral discourse. Carnap wrote that "a value statement is nothing else than a command in a misleading grammatical form" (1937, 24). Stevenson suggested that ethical judgments are "social instruments" (1937, 31) and have "a quasi-imperative force" (1937, 19), and their "major use" is "not to indicate facts, but to *create an influence*" (1937, 18), though, unlike an imperative, "it enables one to make changes in a much more subtle, less fully conscious way . . . [for] the ethical sentence centres the hearer's attention not on his interests, but on the object of interest" (1937, 26). Hare famously argues that "the language of morals is one sort of prescriptive language" (1952, 1). These prescriptivists were onto something (if the above analysis is correct) since modal language (of which moral *shoulds*, *musts*, and *mays* are one distinctive species) can be seen as a more sophisticated

A fourth advantage of introducing modal (rather than just mood) terminology is that, as Ryle observed (1950/1971, 244), while we can issue *commands* (using the imperative mood) without modal terms, having modal terms also enables us to give *permissions*.[21] These last two features bring advantages in enabling us to lay out generalized systems of rules and permissions: rules that apply to *everyone* (who meets certain stated conditions), from which we can reason about what follows from these requirements, and where *permissions* may also be expressly given or revoked.

But while modal discourse enters language in the form of auxiliary and semi-auxiliary modal verbs, other modal expressions are introduced as grammatical metaphors.[22] The grammatical metaphors associated with simple property and number talk are introduced by grammatical transformations from congruent, observational discourse (as we move from "The barn is red" to "The barn has the property of redness"). By contrast, the grammatical metaphors having to do with possibilities, necessities, probabilities, chances, moral obligations and requirements, etc., are not introduced by transformations from congruent observational discourse, but rather by transformations from more basic forms of *modal* speech—these are "interpersonal" grammatical metaphors.[23] Indeed, grammatical metaphors may be

way of taking over some of the interpersonal functions of the mood system (especially of imperatives). But we can also see why saying that alone is insufficient, given the developments of modal language that enable it to fulfill a range of other functions that imperatives cannot reach—including functions in reasoning, even in embedded contexts (this difference can be seen to lie behind the infamous Frege-Geach problem [Geach 1965]). I only have space to gesture toward these implications here; fuller discussion will have to be left for elsewhere.

[21] With perhaps this exception, suggested to me by Jamie Dreier: "Go ahead and do X (if you want to)" is a way of giving permission without a modal verb. But this, being still in the imperative form, doesn't enable all the same sorts of reasoning as the modalized "You may X"—for example, the former cannot be embedded in the antecedent of a conditional ("If go ahead and do X…" isn't grammatical), while the latter can.
[22] While modal auxiliary verbs are typically shared across flavors of modality ("You must not kill," "A square must have four sides," "It might snow tonight"), in English the terms introduced as grammatical metaphors are often distinct for different flavors of modality ("Killing is wrong," "Squares necessarily have four sides," "There is a chance of snow tonight"). Perhaps this is another use of the grammatical metaphors—as ways of making these distinctions explicit.
[23] For the distinction between ideational and interpersonal grammatical metaphors, see Taverniers (2003, 5).

iterated, undergoing what Taverniers (following Louise Ravelli) refers to as a "pragmatic recursion" that takes us progressively further from congruent discourse, as we might move from saying, "they feel secure" to speak of "their secure feeling," and then to speak of "their feeling of security" (2003, 23). I will have occasion to note some of these progressions for moral and modal speech below. Note that given these progressions, non-congruence is said to come on a *scale* rather than in a simple dichotomy of congruent/non-congruent expressions.[24] The relevant forms of grammatical metaphor (unlike the modal auxiliary verbs) also tend to vary across different flavors of modality, so for now (to reduce confusion) I will focus on the grammatical metaphors introduced from *alethic* modals.

"Objectified" modal expressions such as "it is possible that" and "there is a possibility that" are learned later, between ages six and 12 (Papafragou 1998, 22). What functions are added here—why go on to learn other modal formulations, using not just modal auxiliary verbs but introducing modal adjectives ("is possible," "is necessary") and nouns ("a possibility" "a necessity") on the basis of easy ontological inferences from more basic forms of modal speech?

These late developments in modal language, into modal adjectives and nominalizations, play a central role in prompting familiar metaphysical perplexities. It is only with this sort of modal vocabulary that we can even ask questions such as these: What are modal properties? How are the modal properties of an object related to its non-modal/categorical properties? How can two objects (the statue and the clay) have all the same *non-modal* properties and yet have different modal properties (one being incapable, the other capable of surviving dramatic changes in shape)?[25] What are possibilities, or chances? What are possible worlds? Are there any? So, if we have interest in these philosophical problems, it is particularly useful to be able to understand these forms of modal discourse, their functions, and the ways they enter language.

---

[24] Halliday develops diagrams that exhibit such chains of metaphorical shifts vertically, making evident the "chain of metaphorical realizations" (Taverniers 2003, 27).
[25] This, of course, is the so-called "grounding problem" (for discussion, see Bennett 2004).

Modal predicates and nouns enter language via grammatical shifts from more basic modal statements that use modal auxiliary verbs. These grammatical shifts can be articulated in the form of trivial inferences. So, for example, we can make a trivial inference from "It *might* rain tomorrow" (using a modal auxiliary verb) to "Rain *is possible* tomorrow" (introducing a modal predicate) or to "There is *a possibility of* rain tomorrow" (introducing a modal nominalization).[26] Like other grammatical metaphors, these interpersonal grammatical metaphors add functions beyond the interpersonal and ideational functions introduced by auxiliary modal verbs. With modal auxiliary verbs, we can say, "It might rain" or "It might snow." But by introducing modal predicates and nouns, we can introduce graded comparisons, saying, "Snow *is more possible* than rain tomorrow" or "*The possibility of snow* is greater than *the possibility of rain*"—introducing what Carnap (1950/1962, 9) called "comparative concepts."[27]

We can even go on from there to introduce what Carnap called "quantified concepts," saying, for example, "the possibility of snow is 70%; but the possibility of rain is only 20%" (1950/1962, 8–15). As Carnap emphasizes, quantitative concepts are particularly useful in developing precise scientific theories, enabling us to formulate precise general laws. So, for example, we might have classificatory concepts of "warm" and "cold," but we can only formulate the ideal gas laws if we have introduced a *quantitative* concept of *temperature*, defined in ways that make it measurable (Carnap 1950/1962, 13). Similarly, we can only get precise probabilistic meteorological, physical, or medical theories if we introduce quantified modal concepts. Only then can we say not just "Taking the drug *might* help you avoid pulmonary complications" but rather "Taking the drug reduces *the possibility of* pulmonary complications by 42%."[28] Of course, more should

---

[26] Talk of "potential" and "potentialities" similarly involves a grammatical metaphor, introduced from more basic talk using modal auxiliary verbs like "can." For example, "The student could become a great painter" becomes "the student has the potential to become a great painter" (Halliday 2009, 45).

[27] Carnap noted that these comparative concepts are more useful for scientific inquiry than merely "classificatory concepts," though not as desirable as quantitative concepts.

[28] Such precise probabilistic theories can be better confirmed, figure in more precise scientific theories, and also can be better used in making decisions (whether to take the

be said about what it takes to *successfully* introduce such quantitative concepts. Carnap held that to do so, we must not just nominalize, but give *rules* for assigning the relevant numerical values, defined by "exact rules of measurement" (1950/1962, 14).[29] In the case of "temperature," for example, this was initially given in terms of the volume of mercury in a thermometer (Carnap 1950/1962, 13); in the case of probability, Carnap linked this with long-term relative frequency (1950/1962, 19). Moreover, Carnap suggests that such quantitative concepts would only be *retained* if they turn out to figure fruitfully in general laws (some quantitative concepts of psychology, for example, have turned out not to do so) (1950/1962, 14). In any case, the point here is not to lay out the conditions needed to successfully introduce quantitative concepts, but rather to note that the ability to introduce grammatical metaphors is a necessary precondition for introducing such quantitative concepts at all.

Talk of possible worlds, similarly, is a matter of introducing a new layer of grammatical metaphor, by making trivial inferences from talk of what's possible. David Lewis himself originally suggested this (long before he presented his famous inference to the best explanation arguments for possible worlds), writing:

> I believe there are possible worlds other than the one we happen to inhabit. If an argument is wanted, it is this. It is uncontroversially true that some things might have been otherwise than they are. . . . But what does this mean? Ordinary language permits the paraphrase: there are many ways things could have been besides the way they actually are. . . . I believe things could have been different in countless ways; I believe permissible paraphrases of what I believe; taking the paraphrase at its face value, I therefore believe in the existence of entities that might be called "ways things could have been." I prefer to call them "possible worlds." (1973, 84)

---

medication) and bureaucratic evaluations (whether the drug should be approved, covered by insurance, etc.).

[29] Perhaps this is why parallel quantitative concepts have not been developed out of *deontic* modal talk.

As Lewis showed, adding talk of possible worlds (beyond sentential modal operators) adds expressive power to a language, for example, enabling us to formulate global supervenience claims (1986, 12–17). That is, introducing talk of possible worlds, like introducing modal adjectives and nominalizations, can be done via trivial inferences from more basic forms of modal speech, and is useful because it adds expressive power to the language in ways that contribute to our ability to generalize and theorize.

This work on the functions of various forms of modal discourse now puts us in a position to re-evaluate traditional philosophical puzzles about modality. For simplicity, I will focus on the problems supposed to arise for *metaphysical* modal discourse, though this should give some good suggestions about how parallel problems for other forms of modal discourse (including deontic modal discourse) might be re-evaluated as well.

Consider these problems commonly raised for modality:

1. Are there (really) modal properties, modal facts, or possible worlds?
2. If there are such things, how are they related to "natural" properties or relations?
3. If there are such things, how could we come to know about them, given that modal features of the world seem not to be empirically detectable, and that possible worlds seem to be, in principle, causally disconnected from us?[30]

Given the above linguistic story, we can see that all of these diverse problems arise, at least in their most troubling or worrying form, by treating modal discourse of various forms *on analogy to congruent, observationally acquired discourse*—discourse that has the function of tracking features of the world as we perceive it, and that enters

---

[30] Compare the list of problems Daniel Nolan lists as arising for possible worlds (and motivating fictionalism about possible worlds): "What are they? Where, if anywhere, are they supposed to be? How are we supposed to discover facts about them?" (2022, sec. 0).

language via observations of the environment.[31] By making clear the very different *functions* of modal discourse and the different *rules* by which modal discourse (of various forms) enters language, we can undermine the idea that there is a valid analogy here. We can thereby also challenge the idea that these are major problems that should lead us to deny that there are modal facts or properties, or deny that we could know them.

As we have seen, congruent language comes early in language development, through observation of the environment. Children begin by learning congruent nouns ("goat," "tree," "ball"), verbs ("run," "jump," "wash"), and adjectives ("brown," "tall"), used to track and learn about features of their environment. This early congruent, observationally acquired language tends to become our paradigm of how *all* language functions.

But it is crucial to notice that not all terms are congruent, and that not all terms enter (or are even *supposed to* enter) language observationally or via causal relations. Moreover, while basic declaratives using congruent terms may serve to describe the world in the sense of aiming to track and co-vary with features of the world, not all declaratives do that. For example, as we have seen, we might begin with imperatives that serve an interpersonal, regulative function ("Read Kant") and transform them into declaratives with modal verbs ("Students *must* read Kant"). The latter serve additional ideational functions, carrying propositional content that we can reason with in all the ways characteristic of declaratives. And that's useful. But that does *not* mean that these terms function or *should* function (like congruent terms for sticks and cars) to track special (modal) features of our environment. In fact, these interpersonal grammatical metaphors are not even *derived from* observational, congruent discourse (in the way that some property talk is, such as talk of the color properties). Let us see why this should lead us to reconsider some alleged metaphysical problems about modality.

---

[31] Roughly, what Price (2013, 36) calls discourse that is representational in the "e-representational" sense. Other problems, as we will see, arise from taking it as analogous to discourse about unobserved explanatory "posits."

8.3.1 Are There Modal Properties, Facts, or Possible Worlds?

Understanding the functions and introduction rules of non-congruent modal predicates and nouns helps dispel objections to thinking that there "really are" modal properties, facts, or possible worlds, and helps relieve us of old metaphysical problems about how such things could "fit" into a physical world.

First, consider debates about whether there (really) are modal properties or facts, or possible worlds. I have argued (2020a, ch. 6) that we can answer such questions "easily" and in the positive, by trivial inferences. For example, from "It might rain" we may infer to "There is a possibility of rain," or "It's a fact that there is a possibility of rain tonight" and that inference is guaranteed to succeed, provided the initial statement is true.[32] Given the rules for introducing modal nouns such as "possibility" and "chance," we can similarly give an "easy" answer to the questions "Are there possibilities?" and "Are there chances?" Talk of possible worlds, in turn, is licensed via trivial inferences from more basic forms of modal speech. If we can legitimately say that there could have been talking donkeys, then we are licensed to infer that there is a possible world in which there are talking donkeys.[33]

In short, once we understand the functions of the relevant forms of discourse and the rules that enable us to introduce such discourse to fulfill these functions, it should seem far more natural and less problematic to accept that we can make harmless "easy" inferences to conclude that there *are* such things. For we can see why it is useful to have a language that permits such easy inferences and that introduces these grammatical metaphors that serve a variety of new functions.

But what about all of the *objections* to accepting that there are possibilities, necessities, possible worlds, chances, or modal facts?

---

[32] I realize of course that this leaves a remaining question of how we should understand the truth of basic modal statements. I have elsewhere given a story for the case of metaphysical modal discourse (2020a) but will have to leave the rest for another occasion. Those who have doubts that such trivial inferences succeed are referred to my (2015a), where I respond to many common objections to the claim that they do.

[33] For a technical development of a pleonastic account of possible worlds, including showing what is needed to introduce talk of possible worlds as complete and maximal, see Steinberg (2013).

These arguments, too, can be re-evaluated based on our improved understanding of the functions of the discourse. Debates about possible worlds typically proceed by asking whether our best overall theory quantifies over possible worlds, whether the theoretical benefits of "positing" possible worlds outweigh the costs. David Lewis explicitly develops his argument for possible worlds in these terms, writing, "The benefits [in theoretical unity and economy] are worth their ontological cost. Modal realism is fruitful; that gives us good reason to believe that it is true" (1986, 4). Now it is easy to see, if we are positing black holes, why one might ask whether positing black holes provides a better overall physical theory or not, what the posit explains, etc. The function of introducing a term like "black holes" presumably is to enable us to refer to entities that can play a causally explanatory role in our cosmological theories. But if the above linguistic story about the functions of possible worlds talk and the rules for introducing it is correct, then it is misguided to attack or defend the existence of possible worlds on these grounds. For on this model, talk of possible worlds does not aim to posit some entities that should explain our observations—and (as argued in Chapter 1) we should reject across-the-board use of an explanatory approach to metaphysics. There is no *need* to make an "inference to the best explanation" argument for "positing" these things, or to enter protracted arguments about whether they add "explanatory power" to our "theories." The entry rules alone license us to introduce terms for possible worlds, and to say that there are such things—and these terms don't fall short in fulfilling their *actual* functions even if they don't themselves serve as *explainers* in our theories.

Doubts are often raised about the existence of possibilities (say) because it is thought that they would be problematic, as they would seem to be entities that are not observable. But given the above story about the functions and introduction rules for modal predicates and nouns, we can also begin to see why such debates are otiose. True enough, our paradigmatic congruent predicates ("is red," "is furry," "is cold," . . .) are observationally introduced and are used to refer to trackable, perceptible features of the world. We can introduce a predicate like "is red" in the presence of a red ball, and we can track the presence of redness perceptually.

By contrast, predicates such as "is possible" enter language not through direct observation, but rather via grammatical shifts that take us from modal verbs, which primarily serve interpersonal functions (as in "It *might* rain"), to say instead "Rain *is possible*." And this grammatical shift does not introduce a new predicate to track newly discovered features of the world, but rather adds new functions to our linguistic repertoire (so that we can, for example, go on to ask comparative questions such as whether rain is *more possible* than snow). Since the discourse does not aim to track worldly features, it needn't be a problem if we can't introduce it via observation, and can't think of it as describing observable features of the world.

Why should we think that it's a general rule that we should accept the existence only of *observable* properties or accept any similar constraints? Once we have the pragmatic linguistic story in hand, we can see that the relevant principles that are often thought to raise problems for saying that there are possibilities, properties, and many other "disputed" entities arose and looked natural by considering only the paradigm of *congruent*, observationally acquired discourse. We can then place the onus on the skeptic to say why these are good principles to apply *across the board*, even once we understand how other forms of discourse are introduced to language, what functions the relevant forms of discourse serve (often serving them perfectly well), and why these functions are useful.

Much the same goes for modal nouns. Congruent nouns like "platypus" are introduced observationally, in the presence of visible creatures, and enable us to track and investigate platypuses. Here it makes sense to say: If no one has ever actually had causal commerce with a platypus, the term may be problematic; there may be a "block" in the chain of reference (to use a phrase of Donnellan's [1974, 23–24]), and we should perhaps say that it turns out that platypuses, like unicorns, don't exist. But while terms like "a possibility" and "a chance" are *grammatically* parallel to "a platypus," they are introduced via a completely different route, via different rules, to serve completely different sets of functions. Modal nouns are not even supposed to track a new "kind of thing" that we could observe and investigate in the ways we investigate platypuses. Instead, as we have seen, introducing these nouns adds new functions to the interpersonal and ideational functions served by other forms of modal discourse—they are not new nouns (like "platypus") introduced to pick out previously unnoticed or unnamed things in the world, so their failure to do so is not a problem.

8.3.2 How Are Modal Properties Related to Non-Modal Properties?

The pragmatic linguistic story can also help us see ontological "placement problems"[34] in a new light. These "placement problems" ask what sorts of things modal properties could be, how they could "fit into" the natural world, and how they would be related to non-modal (say, physical) properties. For at least some kinds of modal properties (e.g., *metaphysical* modal properties) this is thought to raise particularly troubling questions, since it seems we can't even say that metaphysical modal properties *supervene on* natural properties. For the statue and the clay (for example) have all the same physical properties, and yet different metaphysical modal properties—as the clay could survive radical changes in shape while the statue could not.[35] Such ontological puzzles arise when we think of modal adjectives and nouns on the model of congruent adjectives and nouns and wonder what "features of reality" we could be responding to or tracking with these

---

[34] The terminology of "placement problems" comes from a discussion in Price (2011, 6); these sorts of problems were identified earlier by Frank Jackson, who called them "location problems" (1998, 3).
[35] Why should supervenience hold for one kind of modal property (say, physical or nomological modal properties or dispositions, which do seem to supervene on the "categorical" non-modal properties of the world), yet not for another (say, metaphysical modal properties)? I will have to leave full discussion of this for elsewhere. Here I can only suggest that this has to do with different introduction rules for different sorts of modal claims, given differences in their functions. Suppose, say (with Carnap 1950/1962, 19), that talk of probabilities is introduced via observations of long-term relative frequencies, in order to enable us to better predict future observations, adjust our credences and behaviors, etc. Then it makes sense to have rules that allow no variation in the probabilities attributed without variation in past observations. But if, by contrast, claims of metaphysical modality reflect rules of use *for our terms*, then we are not constrained to assign "possibly survives a crushing" in the same way to a statue versus a lump of clay, even if all the physical properties instantiated in a given region remain the same.

terms, and how those features relate to supposedly less problematic "natural" properties.

But thinking that such terms must "refer to" odd features of the world—so that it's surprising that these modal features wouldn't supervene on physical features in the way the observable macro-level properties of water supervene on its micro-level properties—results from thinking of these terms on analogy with observationally acquired congruent adjectives like "liquid" or "transparent." In the latter case, it makes sense to ask how these observed features arise from underlying microphysical features. But modal predicates and nouns aren't introduced to track observable properties. Pressing metaphysical questions like "How are modal properties grounded in the natural properties of the world?" or "What are the truthmakers for modal claims?" or "Where, if anywhere, are possible worlds supposed to be?"[36] again involves category mistakes. For such questions make sense only on the metalinguistic presupposition that terms for modal properties function like terms for observable properties—to track observable features of the world. Since that is a false presupposition, we should not attempt or expect to find a good answer to these questions, but instead reject them along with the false presupposition that provokes them.

8.3.3 How Could We Come to Know About Modality?

The puzzles of modal epistemology arise from a similar source. If *metaphysical* modal properties don't supervene on physical, or observable, properties, then it makes sense to think that we can't come to know them through ordinary observation or other empirical methods.[37]

---

[36] As Nolan describes a problem that motivates fictionalism about possible worlds (2022, sec. 0).

[37] There has been a recent surge in the development of empiricist approaches to modal epistemology (for examples, see Vetter 2015; Williamson 2007; Bueno and Shalkowski 2015; Leon 2017; and Roca-Royes 2017). As I argue elsewhere, however (2020a, 150–65), such approaches hold promise for explaining our knowledge of *empirical* modalities (empirically grounded counterfactuals, dispositions, etc.)—but not for explaining our knowledge of specifically *metaphysical* necessities and possibilities (which include many modal claims of *philosophical* interest), since these are cases in

But then modal skepticism seems to threaten. For example, Robert Nozick argues that to have justified beliefs in a given domain, we must have a reliable faculty for forming beliefs of that sort, the existence of which is best explained in terms of natural selection. But, he argues, where metaphysical modal beliefs are concerned, "we do not appear to have such a faculty, and it is implausible that evolutionary processes would instill that within us" (2001, 122). He argues that we have no good explanation of why we should have developed a reliable faculty for detecting metaphysical necessity, and that as a result we should be skeptical about claims that we have such knowledge—and even about the claim that there are such necessities (2001, 125). Nozick concludes that "there are no interesting and important metaphysical necessities" (2001, 120–21).

These doubts about metaphysical modal knowledge rely on a generalized picture according to which knowledge of things of any kind K requires a good explanation of why we should have a "reliable faculty for *detecting*" Ks. This demand is plausible for knowledge of Ks, where "K" is a congruent noun, observationally acquired (we have a reliable faculty for detecting goats but not auras). But once again we should not expect it to generalize to a requirement for acquiring knowledge about *any Ks whatsoever* (where "K" is *any* noun term). Terms for metaphysical modal properties and possible worlds are unlike congruent adjectives and nouns that are introduced observationally to detect and track features of our environment. For, as we have seen, these forms of language are introduced as interpersonal grammatical metaphors and add new functions to the interpersonal and ideational functions already served by more basic forms of modal expression. We have no need for a good evolutionary story about why we should have evolved to have a reliable faculty for "detecting" the relevant modal features or possible worlds.

What we can get instead is a good naturalistic story about why such forms of vocabulary would have evolved as they did, and why they

---

which we might have the very same empirical information, and yet ascribe different modal properties (say, to the statue and the clay).

would have stuck around in our language.[38] And we can tell that story by identifying (as I have begun to do above) the important functions the additional terminology serves for us.

This, of course, is not to deny that we need a good story of some sort about how we *can* come to have modal knowledge of various sorts (acknowledging that somewhat different stories might be required for knowledge of modal claims of different sorts—of metaphysical necessity versus physical necessity, for example). I have myself tried to develop one such story—for knowledge of metaphysical modalities—elsewhere (2020a, ch. 7), arguing that we can come to know basic *metaphysical* modal truths by *mastering* the rules of use for applying and refusing expressions, and learning how to explicitly *convey* those rules and what follows from them in object-language indicatives (2020a, 163–64). (Other, derivative, metaphysical modal truths may also require empirical knowledge.) Accounts for other forms of modal discourse will have to be developed and assessed separately.[39]

But the point here is not to develop positive solutions to the problems of modal epistemology.[40] Instead it is simply this: Once we can see the diversity of functional roles and introduction rules, it begins to seem misguided to think that there is a major *barrier* to giving an account of modal knowledge—a barrier that might appropriately lead us to a form of modal skepticism. The misguided thought that there is an insuperable barrier arises by illegitimately generalizing

---

[38] I begin to develop this story in my (2020a, ch. 7).

[39] Claims about dispositions, empirically grounded counterfactuals, and physical possibilities might be seen as endorsing or prescribing norms of inference about future experience, based on past observations. Ramsey (1929/1978) had suggested that empirical generalizations are "rules for judging." Ryle (likely drawing on Margaret MacDonald's [1937] paper without acknowledgment) suggests a similar line of thought for understanding dispositional claims and claims of scientific laws—treating laws as giving "inference-tickets" that license us "to move from asserting factual statements to asserting other factual statements" (1949, 121). Sellars (1958) treats statements of physical necessities as "expressing our commitment to the goodness of counterfactually robust inferences from necessitating to necessitated conditions" (Brandom 2008, 98), or *endorsing* certain kinds of inference, a view that Brandom (2008) develops more fully and precisely, in arguing that the expressive role of alethic modal vocabulary is "*to make explicit* semantic, conceptual connections and commitments that are already *implicit* in the use of ordinary empirical vocabulary" (2008, 102).

[40] I provide more detailed discussion of these past debates, and their relevance to my earlier normativist view of metaphysical modality, in (2020a, ch. 7).

thoughts about how we can come to know the things tracked by our congruent, observationally acquired, terms, and applying that model to *all discourse whatsoever*. Once the linguistic story is on the table, the challenge for skeptics is to show that their reservations are not just built on a faulty overgeneralization that arises from failing to appreciate the variety of linguistic introduction rules and functions.

All in all, then, sophisticated modal discourse enables speakers to fulfill all three types of metafunction at the same time. Mood and modal systems enter originally to contribute interpersonal functions.[41] But they simultaneously serve *ideational* functions, as they can be expressed in declarative forms that carry propositional content that we can go on to reason with and from in useful ways. Introducing grammatical metaphors to our modal discourse, in turn, enables speakers to serve new functions, including playing key roles in developing sophisticated scientific theories and bureaucracies. Such discourse seems to function perfectly well, and the alleged "metaphysical problems" for modality arise only by imposing on modal discourse a model and presuppositions suitable only for congruent, observationally acquired discourse. By doing the reverse-engineering work that enables us to understand the functions of different forms of modal discourse, and how they come to enter language, we can not only better understand the discourse, but also re-evaluate (and often reject) many old metaphysical debates about modality.

8.4 Re-Evaluating Other Metaphysical Debates

So far, I have aimed to develop a few examples of how we can re-evaluate some long-standing metaphysical debates by doing reverse engineering that enables us to determine the functions and introduction rules of discourse.

The cases I have considered so far—of property talk, number talk, and modal talk—of course, are only examples. It is not hard to see, however, how this work may suggest ways of re-evaluating other

---

[41] In my prior work (2020a), I have been particularly interested in the *regulative* functions, but do not mean to limit them to that.

debates in metaphysics. For it is striking what an enormous portion of the kinds of talk long thought to be "problematic" in metaphysics involve forms of language that we can now see are introduced to add *interpersonal* functions or as *grammatical metaphors*—and so do not follow the paradigm of congruent, observational discourse.

For example, consider talk of events, processes, or states of affairs. These, too, are grammatical metaphors (introduced directly from congruent observational discourse). By reminding ourselves of the functions and entry rules for grammatical metaphors, we might find new reasons for accepting the easy inferences that introduce these noun terms to the language, and new reasons for rejecting arguments that such entities don't meet "general ontological constraints" or lead us into alleged "metaphysical problems." More broadly, we might find new reasons for thinking that ontological debates about whether there "really are such things" are pseudo-problems we'd do well to stop wasting our time on.

Other discourse that derives from the mood and modal systems—which, as we have seen, is introduced to serve interpersonal functions—has also been seen as notoriously metaphysically problematic. For such discourse includes not just alethic modal discourse (as discussed above), but also deontic modal discourse—including talk of normativity, and more specifically of morality.

Normative predicates, like modal predicates, enter via trivial inferences from expressions with (this time deontic) modal verbs, in ways that bring helpful new functions. We can transform deontic modal expressions into declaratives that use normative predicates[42]—for example, shifting from "One mustn't kill" to "Killing *is wrong*," or nouns, shifting to "There is an obligation to refrain from killing." These grammatical metaphors enable us to generalize and reason with normative claims in new ways, so that we can do more than list what one must and mustn't do; we can make generalized claims such as "Those who do wrong actions should be punished."[43] And while we can say,

---

[42] Eggins (2004, 179–81) discusses how modal formulations involving verbs like "should," "must," and the like can be replaced with predicates instead, as we can move from "You must read Henry James" to "You are obliged to read Henry James."

[43] Once we understand all these complex functions of moral discourse, we can see why simple speech-act analyses (say, that the function of "is good" is to commend) were bound to fail. For fully developed moral discourse also permits expression in forms that

"You *should* keep your promises" or "You *mustn't* kill," using auxiliary modal verbs, we can do more sophisticated things by introducing predicates and nouns. For with such predicates and nouns in our vocabulary, we can utter comparatives (e.g., "It is *more* obligatory to refrain from killing than it is to give to charity") and compare the relative *stringency* of various *obligations*. Nominative talk of obligations and permissions also enables us not simply to formulate complex bureaucratic systems, saying (in imperative mode), "Pay taxes," or with modal auxiliaries, "You must pay your taxes," but also to speak of the ways in which property owners in the state of Vermont incur a range of tax *obligations* and can acquire *permissions* for *modifications* to their land, subject to *requirements* for planning *permission* and *environmental stewardship*.[44] We can also quantify and qualify obligations and requirements, saying that students must satisfy *five* requirements to pass Philosophy 80, and that these requirements are *more onerous* than those for Philosophy 1.

Nominalized talk of moral properties and facts also plays a central role in specifically moral *theorizing*—as we ask questions about what, in general, gives some acts the property of *being wrong* (and others of being *morally permissible*), or make general claims such as "The severity of punishments should be proportional to the wrongness of actions." Nominalizations also enable us to generalize about, enumerate, and compare moral requirements, so that we can say things such as "The moral requirements incumbent on any rational being are ...," "Our moral obligations are independent of our desires," "The moral requirement to refrain from murder is more stringent than the requirement to give to charity," and so on. They also enable us to ask

---

serve ideational functions of being used in reasoning (even in embedded contexts). This enables us to see why the infamous Frege-Geach problem (Geach 1965) was bound to arise. The right response to this problem, in my view, is not to give up functionally alternative analyses, but instead to (1) be attentive to the full *range of* functions served by the relevant form of discourse (including ideational functions); (2) carefully distinguish use from function, and further distinguish function (and use) from meaning. I only have space to gesture toward these implications here; fuller discussion will have to be left for elsewhere (but see my 2020a, 77–91, for an approach to resolving the Frege-Geach problem for my normativist analysis of metaphysical modality).

[44] Notice also the other grammatical metaphors involved in this text, and the density of grammatical metaphors in a typical piece of bureaucratic prose.

for and give *justifications* for various *requirements*. Thus, grammatical metaphors like these that are introduced on top of deontic modal discourse play a crucial role in moral theorizing.

This may enable us to re-evaluate some of the metaphysical problems of metaethics, in ways that parallel the re-evaluation of debates about modality I discussed above. Certainly, we can reject some inappropriate reasons for dismissing talk about obligations, requirements, and permissions—such as complaints that such things can't be observed, that we can't be in causal contact with them, or that they won't contribute explanatory power to our theories. And we can say that, *provided we can start from* an uncontroversial moral truth expressed in deontic modal language—such as "One mustn't kill"—we may make trivial inferences to infer that "killing *is wrong*," "killing has the property of being wrong," "it's a fact that killing is wrong," and "we have an obligation not to kill."

There is, however, an additional complication for properly moral talk: For there may be distinctive reasons for controversy about whether there *are* any such distinctively *moral* truths from which we may begin. Such doubts need not be based in metaphysical doubts about truthmakers. Instead, for example, they may arise from the thought that moral judgments are deceptive, say in purporting to give objective, goal-independent reasons for action, which the critic thinks are not available. Eric Campbell, for example, argues that moral claims are a way of "deflecting attention" from our motivations and values (2014, 447), and that many of us would be better off just leaving moral discourse behind and eliminating it from our conceptual repertoire (2014, 448). I will have to leave those complications to the side here—noting only that they are fundamentally not *metaphysical* problems, but rather difficult questions that arise about our first-order moral judgments.[45]

Even problems in philosophy of mind might be re-evaluated given a proper functional analysis of mentalistic language of various sorts. At

---

[45] This is to echo the Quietist's idea that allegedly metaphysical questions may be best addressed at the level of first-order moral discourse, while acknowledging that doubts and complications may also arise there. For discussion of this "internalizing maneuver," see Warren and Thomasson (2023, sec. 1).

least some mentalistic clauses enter as part of the mood system, in ways that modulate proposals, while communicating them in the declarative mood—as in "I'm willing to make you coffee," "I'd like to make you coffee," "I'm determined to make you coffee" (Eggins 2004, 180). Others enter as mood adjuncts that serve to express the speaker's attitude toward a proposition, and enter as grammatical metaphors: for example, "I think the meeting is on Friday," or "I'm sure the meeting is on Friday" (Eggins 2004, 174). Mentalistic terms may also function as expressions of modality, as can be seen, for example, in "I don't believe that pudding ever will be cooked." Here, the "I don't believe" functions as a modal expression, as can be seen from the fact that the appropriate "tag" (when we add on a question seeking confirmation of an assertion) is "Will it?" not "Do I?" (Halliday and Matthiessen 2014, 686–87). The mental clause, on Halliday's analysis, is "a metaphorical realization of probability" (Halliday and Matthiessen 2014, 687). Similarly, for the "I think," in "I think it's going to rain," the appropriate tag is "Isn't it?" not "Don't I?" (Halliday and Mattheissen 2014, 687).[46] This, of course, echoes Sellars's well-known assessment that when the tie salesman Jones says, "The tie looks green to me," he is withholding commitment to the proposition that the tie is green (1956/2000, secs. 16–20). On Brandom's analysis, the function of "looks," "seems," and "appears" talk is "to express the withholding of endorsement from the sentence that appears within the scope of the operator" (Sellars 1956/2000, 142). A fuller reverse-engineering job that considers the functions of different forms of mentalistic talk, the rules by which they are introduced to language, and the implications for traditional problems in philosophy of mind will have to be left for another occasion, or perhaps for others. But it is at the least suggestive that uses of mentalistic terms, similarly, often enter as parts of the mood and modal systems.

---

[46] This is not to imply that this holds for all mental talk. Some mentalistic clauses *do* seem to allow tagging, for example, "You don't believe what she said, do you?"

8.5 Redirecting Metaphysics to More Fruitful Pursuits

I argued in Chapter 6 that we should rethink the project of metaphysics as a project in conceptual engineering—including both reverse engineering and constructive engineering. One aim of this chapter is to demonstrate ways in which reverse engineering enables us to make better decisions in conceptual engineering—particularly regarding whether certain areas of our discourse are to be retained, revised, or rejected.

The forms of discourse discussed above—including talk of abstract objects and modal talk—have long been on the philosophical hit list. Much work has been put into nominalist projects of showing how we can reject noun terms for numbers and other abstract objects, and yet still express our scientific theories. Hartry Field, for example, famously aims to show that the mathematics we need to state our scientific theories "does not include anything which even *prima facie* contains references to (or quantifications over) abstract entities like numbers, functions, or sets," and that where we do have such references, we may adopt a fictionalist stance (2016, 1).[47] And Quine engaged in what Dagfinn Føllesdal refers to as "his long crusade against the modal notions of possibility and necessity" (2013, xxii). Quine repeatedly raised suspicions about modal notions (especially the logical modalities)—in part on grounds connected to his objections to the analytic/synthetic distinction and problems with possible world semantics, but also in part on grounds that the modalities are "ontologically obscure" (Føllesdal 2004, 201). But before taking any eliminative proposals seriously, we need to engage in reverse engineering—to figure out what having such terms does for us.

The reverse-engineering work above enables us to do just that. First, it enables us to see that the alleged metaphysical and epistemological

---

[47] On the other hand, the work done here certainly gives reason to approve of the spirit of Field's view that "mathematical theories are essentially useful calculation devices" (2016, P3). In general, the approach defended here tends to support many fictionalist analyses that suggest that an area of discourse (such as mathematics) may serve other functions than to "pick out" entities in our environment; but disagrees with the assumption that that makes such discourse less than literally true, or means that we should deny that there are such things. For a discussion of the relationship between fictionalism and deflationism (and reasons for preferring the latter), see my (2013).

problems that have motivated eliminativism are pseudo-problems engendered by category mistakes—so we lose these reasons for rejecting the discourse. Moreover, given the extremely useful functions it serves to introduce such grammatical metaphors, we can see that it would be a big mistake to eliminate such terminology from our discourse. Attempts to eliminate such terms from our vocabulary are not only a waste of time (given that they are motivated by mistaken expectations), but positively harmful if they eliminate a range of discourse that is useful for other purposes—for example, centrally useful to our ways of building theories, constructing arguments, developing bureaucracies, etc.[48] The work undertaken by those who aim to reconstruct science without numbers may be clever and valiant, but is ultimately misguided and frankly a bad idea.

Much the same can be said for talk of modality. Quine famously raised suspicion of modal locutions, and of the very idea that there were possible entities, such as the infamous "possible fat man in the doorway," on grounds that we cannot make sense of identity conditions for them (1948/1980, 4). And modal fictionalists are often motivated by finding the status of possible worlds and their contents to be "puzzling, to say the least," with Daniel Nolan citing common reservations such as "What are they? Where, if anywhere, are they supposed to be? How are we supposed to discover facts about them?" (2022, sec. 0).

But once we can reverse-engineer modal discourse and properly understand the functions it serves and the ways in which it enters language, we can again see that the main metaphysical and epistemological qualms raised against it are bogus problems engendered by falsely assimilating this to congruent observational discourse. And we can see why it would be a terrible mistake to eliminate modal discourse from our language, given the crucial functions it adds to the language, which I have outlined above. Finally, we can see that, given the appropriate introduction of the discourse, we have no need for fictionalism, for we

---

[48] Of course, whenever terms are introduced there is some risk of introducing problematic rules that can lead to contradictions or other difficulties. This is what raises the "bad company" problem, and purported cases of contradiction must be addressed on a case-by-case basis. For discussion of the bad company problem, see my (2015a, ch. 8).

are entitled to simply say that there *are* such things as possibilities and even possible worlds—in the only sense these terms have.

In any case, knowledge of linguistic functions can give *grounds for assessing* various proposals in conceptual engineering—such as proposals to eliminate a given area of discourse. And by revealing these functions, we also can open a second level of assessment: assessing the functions themselves, and whether they are ones we *should* (continue to) serve at all. Thus, the appeal to functions, and our prior work on identifying linguistic functions, enables us to make better reverse-engineering assessments of when a part of language should be eliminated or revised, and when it should be retained. And that remains important and valuable work—work far more worth spending our time and attention on than pseudo-problems of metaphysics that are provoked by category mistakes that arise from tacitly assuming a kind of functional monism about language.

In all these ways, reverse engineering, built on a detailed understanding of functions, can be useful. Metaphysics has long been mired in pseudo-problems provoked by failing to grasp the varieties of functions served by parts of our language, and falsely assimilating of all discourse to congruent, observational talk. In rethinking metaphysics, we begin by taking a step back to ask about the functions of the relevant parts of language, before we determine whether various metaphysical questions and problems are legitimate or arise from confusions and category mistakes. And in so doing, we can free ourselves from many "metaphysical" problems, some of which reach back over two thousand years in the Western tradition, diagnosing them as either easily answerable or as pseudo-problems.

But I have also been arguing that there remains something important and transparent for metaphysics to do if we reconceive it as conceptual engineering. The functional analysis of language is also central to this project—for functional analyses can also help us make better decisions in conceptual engineering. As we have seen, the reverse-engineering work outlined here can help us better assess which terms we should retain (as they are downright handy, and don't lead to "insuperable metaphysical problems") and which require revision or rejection. And the work on linguistic function can also help us in constructive and reconstructive projects in conceptual engineering, enabling us to engage in that work in a non-arbitrary and non-mysterious way. I turn to that part of the project next.

9
Pragmatic Conceptual Engineering

I have aimed to dispel the illusion that metaphysics is in the business of discovering deep worldly truths. Instead, I have argued, we should think of those problems that are worth pursuing in metaphysics—as well as many of those elsewhere in philosophy—as problems in conceptual engineering.

But here a puzzle arises. For many would say that if we give up serious metaphysics, then we have no way of making the sorts of decisions we need for conceptual engineering. For (they may say) if we aim to answer the question of what concepts we should have, say, of species, or of freedom, or of gender, the answer is that our concepts should accurately *carve the world at its joints* or *correspond to* what species, freedom, and gender *really are*.[1] If we give up the idea that we can just discover such essences in the world, then (some would say) we also leave ourselves without standards for conceptual engineering—with no non-arbitrary way to choose among a range of possible or proposed concepts. And that threatens to turn conceptual engineering into just a power game, where those in power can simply impose the concepts they choose on the masses, without anyone having grounds on which to critique their choices.

Given the earlier work on function, however, we can see that such concerns arise from a misguided functional monist assumption. For only where terms are *supposed to be* structural and world-tracking is it appropriate to think that the proper standard for evaluating them is *how well they track the structure of the world*. And we should think the proper standard for evaluating a term or concept F is *how accurately*

---

[1] Peter van Inwagen (2020, 17) suggests something like the view that the metaphysician's conceptual choices ought to be driven by facts about what exists, while Theodore Sider (2011) develops and defends the view that (at least when doing fundamental metaphysics) our conceptual choices should be held to the standard of carving the world at its joints or mapping "structure."

it picks out the Fs only if it is a term that is *supposed to serve* the function of tracking and picking out the Fs. But to assume that *all* of our terms (including all of those of interest in metaphysics) have structure-mapping or world-tracking functions is to make the functional monist mistake.

In this chapter I aim to show how we can develop a *pragmatic* approach to conceptual engineering that enables us to evaluate proposals in conceptual engineering in a way that is not at all arbitrary and that can give us grounds for critiquing extant concepts or new proposals without appealing to deep "metaphysical facts" to guide our decisions and justify our evaluations. The key here again is to appeal to functions.[2] For the appeal to functions gives us a way in which decisions in conceptual engineering can be well justified. It can also enable us to make new progress on old debates in areas from metaphysics to philosophy of science to applied ethics.

9.1 Reverse Engineering via Assessing Functions

At this stage in human history, we are always already working from within a conceptual scheme, using one in our lives and in our theorizing. Accordingly, making decisions in conceptual engineering is a matter of deciding what to do with our old conceptual and linguistic system: Should various parts of it be retained, rejected, or revised? Should new parts be added?

But before removing a piece of a car engine, lines in a software program, or an organ from the body, it is always a good idea to begin with reverse engineering: working out what the part does for the engine, program, or organism as a whole. Similarly, in conceptual engineering,

---

[2] Simion and Kelp (2020) also propose a way of evaluating conceptual-engineering projects by appealing to functions, though their focus is on evaluating proposed *conceptual innovations* in terms of whether the "designed functions" (functions intended by the designer) end up succeeding, in such a way that they fulfill the function(s) they were designed for well enough that that becomes an etiological function (such that fulfilling that function helps explain why the concept persists). This seems fine for cases of conceptual innovation, though I am aiming here for a broader view of conceptual engineering that also enables us to evaluate our extant conceptual scheme as a step prior to proposing changes.

we must begin with "reverse engineering"³ that aims to identify the functions that the relevant parts of our conceptual and linguistic scheme serve and have served—either in general or perhaps for particular (groups of) people, with particular concerns and skill sets, in particular social, historical, technological, and environmental contexts.

How are we to identify these functions? I began to address that question in Chapter 7, building on the work of systemic functional linguistics. And I have shown (in Chapter 8) how identifying linguistic functions enables us to unravel a number of old metaphysical problems—for example, by identifying the functional roles served by modal vocabulary (and across various grammatical developments from there), or the roles that grammatical metaphors play in enabling us to generalize and to construct complex theories and bureaucracies.

But taken alone, this approach is incomplete. For while it gives us answers to questions about the kinds of functions generally served by certain forms of language (say, by modal language or by introducing nominalizations), that on its own does not enable us to distinguish the functions of different "flavors" of modal expressions or of different nominalizations. For example, we might go on to ask how the *moral* "must" ("You must not kill") differs from the *metaphysical* modal "must" ("Squares must have four sides") and from the *epistemic* modal "must" ("That must be Alex at the door"). Similarly, while we can gain insight from noting that such philosophically central terms as "truth," "knowledge," "justice," "causation," and "probability" are all grammatical metaphors (and so are likely to play a role in forming generalizations that aid in constructing theories and/or bureaucracies), we have not yet tracked what *differences* there are in functions and rules *across* these different grammatical metaphors.

Matthieu Queloz (2021b) has developed what he calls a "pragmatic" approach to conceptual genealogy, addressing questions such as "why did we come to think in terms of truth, knowledge, justice . . . ?" by aiming to show how these concepts are "rooted in practical needs and concerns generated by certain facts about us and our situation" (2021b, 2).⁴ He goes on to develop this further into a "needs-based"

---

³ I am indebted to David Sanford for first suggesting this point to me.
⁴ The method of pragmatic genealogy, as Queloz argues, can be seen in work in the history of philosophy, from Hume's analysis of the roles of our concepts of justice or

framework for evaluating our concepts, assuming that needs for certain concepts result rom the conjunction of our "concerns, capacities, and circumstances" (2025, 22). In this way, we can ask what we can do with a concept of truth, knowledge, or justice, by "reconstructing the practical problems that these ideas offer practical solutions to . . . reverse-engineering the points of ideas, tracing them to their practical origins, and revealing what they do for us when they function well" (Queloz 2021b, 3). So understood, this approach need not involve determining the *actual* historical development of a term or concept.[5] Instead, it can begin from counterfactual "state of nature" situations, to assess what needs (and desires) would drive creatures like us to develop the concept, and what would be lost if it were abandoned—taking into account both generic human needs and those local to a time, place, situation, or subgroup. Yet it can be combined with rich and detailed historical analyses, also taking into account historical information about the needs, desires, and contextual factors that may have influenced the development of the concept over time. Such work in reverse engineering can then enable us to make better assessments going forward, as we can ask whether we (still) have and endorse the same needs given our (current) concerns, capacities, and circumstances, and so whether it is worth continuing to use and cultivate the concept (Queloz 2021b, 6).

This anthropological, pragmatic approach is parallel to the approach used in reaching the results in systemic functional linguistics I discussed in Chapter 7. For work in systemic functional linguistics begins from asking such questions as these: What human needs does it serve to have a language? What human needs are served by having a *grammar* in a language, in a way that takes us beyond the concerns that could be served by the toddler's simpler protolanguage? What additional concerns are served by including a mood or modal system, or by having a capacity for introducing grammatical metaphors? One thing

---

property, to Nietzsche's account of justice or truthfulness, to Bernard Williams's genealogy of truth and truthfulness and Miranda Fricker's account of testimonial justice. It also has played a prominent role in work in the (neo-)pragmatist tradition.

[5] For work in conceptual genealogy that traces actual historical development, see Catarina Dutilh Novaes (2015 and 2020).

the work in linguistics can add to the useful work Queloz has done is to remind us that such questions needn't always be answered by merely *counterfactual* questions about what we *would be* lacking without the relevant terms or concepts; we can also make use of *developmental* data to see what capacities a child is lacking who hasn't reached each of the relevant stages of language development.[6] For where we can see children who have not (yet) developed certain concepts and/or linguistic abilities, we can take a more direct look at what they may be missing, though they are clearly not in a "state of nature" situation. We can even, in some cases, see what capacities an adult is lacking who has not acquired a first language or has not been through all the standard stages of language development.[7] It can also add a systematic angle, as we can ask not just about individual concepts in isolation, but examine what, on the whole, certain types of grammatical formation do for us in the context of a fully developed language. Nonetheless, there are some functional questions not so easily addressed by the developmental approach: For the developmental approach can make evident what *individuals* would lack if they lacked certain linguistic/conceptual resources, but not what an *entire community* would lack if their language or conceptual scheme completely lacked these resources—for these, a counterfactual approach may be our best hope.[8]

The work on linguistic functions and Queloz's "need-based" framework for evaluating concepts are not merely parallel in approach, however—they are also complementary in the work they do. For we can ask for two different kinds of contrastive explanation. We can ask formal, grammatical contrastive questions: Why (for example) do we have not just basic modal verbs (it *might* rain) but also more sophisticated grammatical forms of modal terminology (rain *is possible*; there

---

[6] The role of clarifying what is functionally added through each stage in linguistic development makes work in systemic functional linguistics particularly important in education—and it is in education departments, at least in the United States, where it has had the greatest impact.

[7] For a fascinating case study of a congenitally deaf man who did not learn a language until he was exposed to sign language in his late twenties, see Schaller (1991) (with thanks to Joshua Gert for pointing this out to me). Schaller also makes it clear that such cases are far more common than has been generally recognized, and that they are importantly different from previously acknowledged cases of "wild" children who grew up not only without language but without substantial human contact.

[8] Thanks to Matthieu Queloz (personal communication) for this important point.

is a *possibility of* rain)? Why not just say some one *knows* something or that a sentence is *true*, but go on to introduce noun forms to talk about *knowledge* and *truth*? Or we can ask what we might call *material* contrastive questions: Why do we need concepts not just of visible attributes such as being tall or being red but also of *knowing* or of being *true*? Taking both the formal and material dimensions into account may enable us to develop a fuller, and more fine-grained, story of the functions served by a given form of language. Accordingly, conceptual engineers interested in a more complete account of linguistic functions must take at least two dimensions of functional assessment into account.[9] We might call the first a "formal" assessment of function (as it assesses functions based in the formal-grammatical forms employed), and the second a "material" assessment of function. So far, using the tools of systemic functional linguistics, I have focused on the "formal," grammatical dimensions of function. We can still ask further questions about what we might call the "material" dimension of function.

That is, for example, we can identify talk of *numbers* and of *truth* as both involving grammatical metaphors, where grammatical metaphors typically add new functions, as I have described in section 7.5. But we can go on from there to also ask about the *differences* between the functions added by nominative *number* talk versus by nominative *truth* talk. One way to combine the two forms of analysis might be (where possible) to begin by identifying the "base form" of the expression, which is transformed to introduce the grammatical metaphor. We can then examine what needs and/or desires the base form ("is true," "must") serves that would not be so well served without it. This may give us insight to the *material* functions served. From there we can go on (step by step) to examine what functional capabilities

---

[9] We may even, as Queloz later points out (2022) need to have somewhat different conceptions of (material) function to draw on for our reverse-engineering work, versus in constructive-engineering work. For in making the assessments we need for reverse engineering, we need to understand what needs would drive introducing a concept like that; but in assessing forward-looking proposals in conceptual engineering, we might need to appeal to what he calls a "concern-satisfaction" account that focuses on the question of which concerns we currently have, such that using the concept would tend to satisfy those concerns (Queloz 2022, 15).

are *added* at each later stage of formal/grammatical transformation.[10] This is an approach I have aimed to apply to modal concepts elsewhere (2023b), distinguishing the functions of modal auxiliary verbs (such as "should," "can," "must") and semi-auxiliary verbs ("has to") from modal predicates ("is possible") and modal nouns ("possibility" and eventually "possible world"), noting the extended range of functions in each case.[11]

Making use of a pragmatic functional analysis has important benefits. First, it is quite distinct from the notion of *intended* function, in a way that is particularly useful here: For we needn't think that much of our linguistic or conceptual scheme was *intentionally* produced to serve various purposes at all, to think that it has functions that we can usefully identify and assess. Second, this pragmatic notion of function also enables us to see that the functions of various parts of our linguistic or conceptual scheme may be *opaque* to us and require uncovering, in a way that can involve a critique and/or re-evaluation of long-familiar concepts and the functions they have served.[12] Third, it enables us to see that these functions may be quite general and enduring or may be very local and contingent. As Queloz emphasizes, we needn't assume that there is a single "best" set of concepts for all times and places, but instead can ask questions about what functions they have served, for whom, in what contexts—in ways that can reveal that even concepts that worked well for us can also cease to do so, and may require renovation or re-evaluation.

---

[10] Where the relevant linguistic forms plausibly derive from prior nonverbal concepts or reactive dispositions, we can press the questions back still further. So, for example, rather than asking simply what we can do with color concepts, we can address stepwise a series of distinct questions: Why would it be useful to have differential responsive dispositions to things of different colors? Why would it be useful to have a linguistic *predicate* for "is red," "is green," or other colors, in a public language? Why would it be useful to be able to transform such predicates into noun form, so that we can speak of the "property of redness"? But we should not assume that we can always begin from reliable responsive dispositions (e.g., this does not seem to be the case for modal discourse); instead it seems distinctive of the forms of discourse Price (2011) labels "e-representational." To assume that all forms of discourse begin this way would be again to make a functional monist mistake.

[11] For the start of a similar approach to moral discourse, see Warren and Thomasson (2023, sec. 4), and my (in progress).

[12] As Queloz puts it, conceptual *needs* can be had "unwittingly and unwillingly" (2025, 249).

By identifying the relevant functions served by our language or concepts (and attending to both the formal and material dimensions), we can make better decisions in conceptual engineering, in ways that can help us with a range of philosophical problems. For we can then evaluate the relevant language or concepts at two levels. First, once we have identified the functions, we can evaluate them—asking if these are functions we (continue to) endorse, would endorse on reflection, or should endorse. If not, critique, and rejection or revision are called for. Second, where we do (currently) endorse the functions, we can ask whether the relevant terms or concepts are continuing to serve the functions *well*—perhaps in spite of changes in our knowledge, or in the social, historical, technological or natural environment, or in spite of developments in our total package of overall concerns. It is time now to consider some illustrative cases, to see how these evaluations may go and how they may help us in philosophical debates covering areas ranging from metaphysics, to philosophy of science, to applied ethics.

9.2 Making Decisions in Pragmatic Conceptual Engineering

If we begin our work in conceptual engineering by a reverse-engineering process that aims to determine what functions are served by an area of discourse (before evaluating whether we should retain, revise, or reject it) we can make better decisions in conceptual engineering—and decisions that do not rely on discovering "metaphysical facts" about the world or essences, but that are nonetheless not *arbitrary*.

We have already seen this approach at work in Chapter 8. For there I argued that, once we can more fully see the functions of nominative talk for numbers, and of talk of possibilities, possible worlds, and the like, we can see that it's downright helpful. And we can see, moreover, that the many functions of number terms and modal nouns are unobjectionable and serve a wide range of human interests across places and times. They become even more helpful and may demand new quantified forms (introducing talk for quantified probability, and additional forms of numerical talk including negative numbers, imaginary numbers, etc.) as a society develops sophisticated scientific theories. We can also see that the problems that were supposed to plague those who accept numbers, possibilities, or possible worlds tend to arise from mistakenly generalized assumptions about language. As a result, it would be not only a waste of time, but a costly mistake, to eliminate such discourse.

The examples studied so far (modal language and mathematical and property language) might make it seem that we should expect such reverse-engineering projects to typically *vindicate* use of a certain area of discourse, in ways that give us reason to retain it. But that needn't be the case. While in the above cases our work in reverse engineering may give us grounds for *retaining* extant concepts (and putting aside the "ontological qualms"), in other cases, work in reverse engineering may contribute to an argument for *rejecting* or *revising* our concepts and language.[13]

9.2.1 Revisions When We Reject the Functions

In some cases, as we do our reverse engineering, we may find that the relevant functions served aren't so helpful—perhaps even that they aren't innocuous. In some cases, combining formal and material dimensions of reverse engineering can reveal a need for change. Consider noun terms for genders and races. A formal reverse-engineering analysis (like that developed from the work in linguistics discussed in Chapter 7) will give us some clues about their functions. For we have already seen that nominalizations enable us to formulate generalizing inferences and predictions in scientific theories, and also serve in developing bureaucracies with their often ornate and layered systems of norms, permissions, and requirements. But then, to do the evaluative work, we must also go on to ask the material reverse-engineering questions: Why would we want *these terms* to figure in our theories—why *should* we theorize in *these terms*? A vindicatory response for theoretic terms is generally pragmatic: because

---

[13] In Queloz's terminology, such reverse-engineering projects may be *subversive* rather than *vindicatory*.

it works—because it enables us to form successful predictions and generalizations across a range of counterfactual circumstances. Using nominative terms for "races," taken as theoretic terms, encourages us to think that these are terms suitable for theorizing with, and might encourage us to use them in a range of inferences, thinking of them as picking out some essence that is suitable to predict and explain a wide range of features of the individuals picked out—as Anthony Appiah argues that Thomas Jefferson and Matthew Arnold assumed that racial classifications enabled us to infer the moral, intellectual, and cultural characteristics of those so classified.[14] But Appiah argues (1994, 94–99) that this kind of vindication is not available, since we have good empirical evidence that standard racial terms are *not* suitable for drawing these kinds of generalizations and inferences. So, if nominalized race terms are supposed to serve *theoretical* functions of these kinds, we have good reason to reject them from our theories.[15]

On the other hand, analyzing the functions of grammatical metaphors can also give us a clue about what other roles such terms play, which may account for their persistence. For as we have seen, grammatical metaphors serve central roles not only in scientific *theorizing*, but also in *bureaucracies*—systems that aim not to *predict and explain* but to construct a web of interlocking *norms and requirements*. Race terms may then *purport to* or *be taken to* function as suitable for scientific theorizing,[16] and yet turn out to not serve well in those roles. In fact, they have played a more central role in embedding the individuals referred to into a web of social norms and even legal requirements. As Appiah puts it, "race is taken by so many more people to be the basis for treating people differentially" (1994, 109). Now we must ask again the material reverse-engineering question: What interests, and whose interests, desires, and needs, would it serve (and

---

[14] Along these lines, see also Ritchie (2021), who identifies important differences between adjectives like "is female" and predicate nominals like "is *a* female."

[15] On the other hand, as Quayshawn Spencer (2019) argues, some race terms may play a useful role in picking out population groups in ways that are helpful in medical genetics. Spencer is careful to note (2019, 105), however, that this does not conflict with Appiah's conclusions.

[16] As Appiah argues, the 19th-century intellectual and political elites of the United States and United Kingdom tended to regard race terms as scientific terms, so ordinary individuals could defer to the scientists as experts on their use (1994, 65).

has it served) to bureaucratize in *these* terms rather than others—to bureaucratize in racial terms? Once the question is raised, we needn't look far to see that structuring norms, permissions, and requirements (whether formal or informal) on "racial" lines has primarily served the (perceived) interests of colonial and postcolonial white Europeans and their descendants, at the expense of other groups. And once we see both the formal and material sides of the functional story, it becomes quite clear that we have good grounds to revise or reject this terminology. In fact, once we are transparent about the functions such terminology tends to serve, it is hard to imagine any remotely plausible, publicly acceptable, justification for structuring large webs of social or legal norms around these alleged "racial categories"—and (to all but the most unabashed white supremacist) it is clear that we should not continue to endorse these functions.

Of course, this doesn't yet tell us precisely what we *should* do *now*, in our current complex social and historical context. For as Sally Haslanger's work makes clear, having *something in the vicinity of* race terms is needed to "help us identify and critique broad patterns of racial . . . oppression" that were facilitated by the original terminology (2012, 240). For without something like race terms, we also can't make institutional interventions to try to track and remedy problems caused by racism, making difficult to address questions about the consequences being Black, say, has on one's job opportunities, educational, economic, and housing prospects, treatment by the police, and so on—and thus hard to identify, and aim to fight against, racism.

This leads to the very real practical problem for conceptual engineering: What should we do *now* (given our current scientific knowledge and our social and historical situation)? I won't pronounce on that here.

But one thing is clear: Reverse engineering can help reveal why our traditional race terms are problematic. For, to the extent that their function was to serve in theoretic generalizations of the sort Jefferson and Arnold sought, they are failures. And to the extent that they have functioned as ways of structuring (formal and informal) social and bureaucratic norms around how people appear or where their ancestors (are presumed to) come from, those are deeply objectionable functions that we should now reject. In this way, it can make clear why some form of conceptual revision is urgently called for—and why, given the *functions* of the terms, the *functions* we endorse, and given what we know empirically, it is not at all arbitrary to decide that revision is called for.

9.2.2 Revisions Prompted by Technological or Social Change

In other cases, reverse engineering may reveal not that the relevant functions served are problematic and to be rejected (as the bureaucratic functions of race terms are), but rather that an acceptable or even desirable function is not being served—or not served *well* anymore, given a new social or technological context. In such cases, too, we may have entirely non-arbitrary reasons for conceptual change and revision—without relying on purported metaphysical "discoveries." Nonetheless, conceptual revisions certainly may be, and often are, prompted by *empirical* discoveries and changes in our empirical situation.

In these cases as well, the pragmatic approach can ensure that our choices in conceptual engineering are not merely arbitrary or subjective. For such conceptual choices also must be responsive to the combination of worldly factors, and the functions at stake.

Consider the concept of death, as examined by Bernard Gert, Charles Culver, and K. Danner Clouser (2006). Even though death seems like a biological concept, it serves many functions *beyond* serving in biological theories. As Gert, Culver, and Clouser argue, the concept of death serves a variety of functions. Without a concept of death, we not only couldn't track crucial changes in the world, but also couldn't make relevant practical decisions, such as determining when medical care should cease, funeral preparations should begin, survivors' benefits put into effect, and so on. Yet (they argue) there is no precise joint in nature marked by the concept of death, but rather a continuum of changes that go on in the process.

A vague concept of death (that specified the day of death) may have served us well two centuries ago, when most people died at home, without the availability of modern medical interventions (Gert et al.

2006, 284). But changes in the technological and practical context may give us non-arbitrary reasons for revising the concept of death as circumstances change. Changes in technology might place new pressure on our old concept. First, the old way of treating cessation of spontaneous breathing and circulation as a criterion for death comes into question with the technology of artificial ventilation, which in turn puts pressure on finding new ways of identifying criteria for death. At the same time, the use of new and increasingly expensive medical treatments, and new technological abilities to transplant organs (which must be done quickly), puts new pressure on determining the *time* of death more precisely than before. For there is pressure to know more *precisely* when expensive treatments can be stopped and when organs can be harvested (to have a greater chance of success for the recipient). Such empirical and technological factors give reasons for at least precisifying the concept of death and altering the criteria typically used in applying it, so that it may continue to serve its functions.

Other concepts similarly may need to be revised in a new technological context—and our technological context is changing in strikingly rapid ways. For example, we have needed to change our concept of *privacy*, from a version that served adequately when the main risk was someone peering in our windows, listening to our conversations, or looking at our physical documents, to determine how we should extend the concept to include personal data stored electronically.[17] The concepts of responsibility, bias, intelligence, cheating, etc. all have to be altered in a context where artificial intelligence systems are driving cars, making hiring decisions, writing essays, and more. These are all changes we urgently need to think through in the present context. In doing so, we will do well to start by stepping back to consider what functions these concepts have served, which (and whose) concerns they were responsive to, and which (if any) among those we endorse going forward, in order to better evaluate which changes to make in the new technological context. But we will be able to do this task better if we can begin by explicitly reverse engineering the functions

---

[17] Anita Allen (e.g., 2011) has done a great deal of important recent philosophical work on various aspects of privacy.

that these concepts serve, to determine transparently which we should continue to serve going forward, and how we can best do so.

Social changes may also bring about the need to change our concepts, if they are to serve their functions well. Consider the concept of marriage, and ask why it is useful to have a concept like *marriage*: What role(s) might it play (perhaps along with other social concepts) in our overall conceptual system, and what would we be missing if we lacked such a concept? Again, we can see that it is a nominalization from the verb "marry," itself introduced not as a way of tracking observed worldly features, but rather as a bureaucratic innovation that endows couples with a certain legal and institutional status. What would we be missing if we lacked such a bureaucratic function? In the current social and legal context, the concept of marriage enables us to endow a range of close relationships (typically involving long-term cohabitation, often involving childrearing, and the intertwining of life commitments, as well as emotional ties) with a special legal and social status (the status is tied up with some 3,000 relevant legal obligations and entitlements in the United States).[18]

But if that is the function of the concept of marriage that we endorse, then one can see that function as served *better* by extending the criteria to include same-sex relationships that otherwise are similar in character to those previously included in the extension. Moreover, as same-sex couples become more socially accepted, and more visible and known, and perhaps also more common and public, we have developed clear and evident reasons to change the concept by broadening the criteria. In that way, we can see the change in the concept of marriage as a conceptual improvement, and an entirely non-arbitrary one, given the social situation and the functions of the concept that we continue to endorse.

---

[18] The concept of marriage also provides an interesting case in which the *historical* genealogy of the concept and the functions it *has been used to serve historically* may come apart from those we endorse going forward, and would use in supporting conceptual innovations. In earlier times, the concept in part served to make women legally *subject to* their husbands in ways many of us would not endorse. In re-engineering the concept, we may look for a way to preserve the functions we see as beneficial while rejecting those we see as harmful.

In sum, the pragmatic approach to normative conceptual work is certainly worldly in that, to do it well, one must be responsive to worldly constraints and new empirical, technological, and social situations. In conceptual engineering no less than civil engineering, the question of which design (of concept or bridge) will best fulfill the relevant functions, given the requirements, does not leave room for a merely "arbitrary" or power-driven answer, and must be addressed while being sensitive to a variety of worldly factors.[19]

9.2.3 Revisions as Concerns Evolve

Conceptual re-engineering may also be needed when our concerns evolve in new ways. Changes in the concept of "fish" may be seen as responses both to empirical discoveries, and to changes in what we ask the concept to do for us. The concept of "fish" has, no doubt, served many functions in our practices historically, in interacting with our environment in ways that enabled us to track and identify (and sometimes capture and eat) swimming creatures in the sea, and to communicate with others about how to find them. But as biology developed, so did the functions that our animal concepts were asked to serve—as we needed them not just to track things we could catch and eat but to serve in theoretical generalizations and predictions. Once we see these additional functions come into play for (what are to be) biological kind concepts, and combine that with empirical discoveries, we can see that changes in the use of the term "fish" were not at all arbitrary, and that further changes may be in order. Carnap (1950/1962) discusses this case. As he puts it, one thing we centrally want in formulating general predictive and explanatory biological theories is for the relevant concepts to be "fruitful"—where a concept is more fruitful "the more

---

[19] This is not to say, however, that there will always be a uniquely best answer. While there may be some bridge designs that are far better than others, there nonetheless may be two or more that do the work (of traversing the chasm, safely supporting the intended vehicles, and staying within budget) equally well. So similarly, we should allow the possibility that two or more different conceptual choices may (like different axiomatizations of geometry, or choices of different logical constants) serve equally well, without assuming there must be a "worldly" fact to determine which of these "carves at the metaphysical joints."

it can be used for the formulation of laws" (1950/1962, 6). Given that function, we can easily see why the change from using a term that applied to "animal living in water" (Carnap 1950/1962, 6)—including seals and whales—to a term that applied only to "animals which live in water, are cold-blooded vertebrates, and have gills throughout life" was entirely non-arbitrary, and a clear improvement at fulfilling the function of enabling law-like generalizations. For, as we came to discover empirically (not through metaphysics), far more generalizations hold, and inferences can be made, about the inner structure, reproductive capacities, etc., of animals in the latter category than about all those in the former.

Nonetheless, we can also see why, in the current context of biological theory, controversy has arisen again about what we should do with the concept "fish," and if (rather than simply narrowing it) we should remove it from biological theories. For there remains enormous variation across different groups of so-called fish, from the ray-finned fish (including tuna, cod, and seahorses) to the lobe-finned fish (including lungfish and coelacanths), to the cartilaginous fish (including sharks, skates, and rays)—inhibiting our ability to generalize. Moreover, these groups have distinct evolutionary lineages, and there are much closer evolutionary connections between lobe-finned fish and land creatures including amphibians, reptiles, and mammals. Thus phylogenetic systematic classifications of creatures in terms of common ancestry tend to reject the category of fish altogether. The decisions we make may vary depending on whether the functions we aim to serve, going forward, are angling, or engaging in biological theorizing of various sorts—but in each case they are practical decisions based on the total set of concerns we endorse, and the known facts on the ground. There is no need for them to be arbitrary, even if we reject the idea that they must be made in response to "metaphysical" discoveries.

9.3 The Role of Site Constraints and Human Factors

This is not the only way, however, in which our conceptual-engineering work is subject to constraints that make our choices in conceptual engineering non-arbitrary. Civil engineering projects must take into account not only the functions to be served by the project, but also the constraints of the site: what the relevant land and geography are like, what the constraints are on surrounding extant structures and geographic features, etc. Similarly, when we engage in conceptual engineering, we must engage in descriptive conceptual work so that we can analyze, assess, and go on to be mindful of the multiple inferential connections our concepts bear to other concepts and practices.[20] Conceptual engineering is more like rebuilding part of a crowded and complex city like Rome than it is like designing new structures to be built on an untouched plain.

Gert et al. (2006) again emphasize this point for the concept of death, appealing to the conceptual connections between death and a wide range of other social and personal (not merely medical) concepts as a way of criticizing the conceptual revisionism of certain medical doctors, who aimed to (re)define death in such a way that they would be permitted to harvest organs sooner, when they would have a greater chance of success with transplantation. Such physicians, they argue, make the mistake of noticing only the connections between "death" and other *medical* terms and practices, not the wider system of concepts and social practices in which "death" plays a central role. Gert et al. use this example as part of a generalized argument for conservatism in conceptual change: New circumstances (such as new medical technologies in keeping patients alive using artificial respiration, and in enabling organ transplantation) may require new precisifications of terms like "death," Gert et al. argue.

> When a term plays an important part in social and legal practices, as "death" does, then the greater the change in the meaning of the term, the greater the likelihood that there will be significant social and legal problems. (2006, 284)

Given the dangers of introducing confusion, distrust, and other social and legal problems in changing a common term, they defend a strong principle of conservativism regarding meaning change:

---

[20] I suspect that this is related to the point Eklund makes as he argues that one cannot "selectively" engineer the quantifier (or, presumably, other concepts) (2015, 380).

It is almost impossible to describe a situation in which it is appropriate to redefine a term with widespread ordinary use in order to change any particular medical (or even social or legal) practice, in which that term plays a significant role. (2006, 285)

I think it is an underappreciated point that conceptual engineering, no less than civil, does not take place in a vacuum, and that it is extremely important to note and be responsive to the inferential connections between the term in question (which we are considering revising or eliminating) and our other terms and broader practices.

Nonetheless, I think this is better taken as a caution than as an argument for a general principle of conservativeness in conceptual engineering. In civil engineering it may be a good—but defeasible—principle in constructing your new bridge or building to interfere as little as possible with surrounding roads and structures. But when problems get bad enough, or there are overriding social or moral purposes at stake, there are times for a more complete ground-clearing. So similarly, though "marriage" is connected to a wide range of social practices, those who value equality and happiness had good reason to change the legal definition to not precisify but rather expand the applicability of the term to same-sex partnerships, just as those who do not endorse racism had reasons to bulldoze the whole network of race concepts such as "octaroon," "quadroon," and "mulatto" that played an influential bureaucratic, social, and legal role in former slaveholding and colonial societies. (As Burgess and Plunkett note, one question in conceptual ethics is "whether we ought to be using a given concept *at all*" [2013a, 1095].)

There is also an analog of the "human factors" that must be considered in civil engineering. Even a (otherwise) great new car design is not going to take off if it is impossible for most people to reach both the brake and the steering wheel. Similarly, conceptual-engineering tasks are constrained by *usability*. Again, this is a point Matthieu Queloz makes, noting (following Edward Craig) that the concept of *knowledge* comes with certain imperfect and fallible "indicator properties" such as standing in the right causal relation to the state of affairs, or being able to justify the claim, or having a good track record on this kind of question (2025, 245-48). But the imperfect nature of these conditions, he argues, is necessary to make the concept *usable* at all. Since the relevant conceptual need is to identify good informants, a concept that is flexible and usable is more valuable than one that would offer necessary and sufficient conditions but be unusable. As Queloz puts it, "The need matrix thereby casts doubt on definitions of knowledge in terms of necessary and sufficient conditions. It presents the concept we need as being more flexible and less reliable for good reason" (2025, 248).

The same can be said of many of the everyday concepts criticized by metaphysicians for vagueness. Ordinary object concepts such as "table" and "chair" may be vague in ways that open them to sorites arguments. But the more precise substitute concepts, of a certain mereological sum of particles maintained in a certain arrangement, are disastrous from the point of view of human usability. For we use such concepts to seat our guests and have no access to, and little everyday use for, concepts of "particles," however useful cognate concepts may be in physical theory. This can again enable us to reassess metaphysical debates about whether there "really are" tables and chairs. As I have argued in previous work (2007, 2015a), if the question is interpreted "factually" (as what Carnap would call an "internal question"), the answer is: yes, obviously. If, instead, the question is interpreted as one of conceptual engineering, asking (the "external question") whether these and other (vague) everyday concepts should be retained, the answer is again: yes, obviously.

9.4 Conclusions

Like civil engineering, conceptual engineering is not a matter for discovery but for invention. But also like civil engineering, that does not mean that the choices we make are arbitrary, unconstrained, merely subject to our will, or "subjective." It may often be an objective matter, once all constraints are in, which boat, or development of a concept, will work best *given the functions we (continue to) endorse, our knowledge, and our social, environmental and technological situation*, while taking into account the surrounding conceptual environment and human limitations. Of course, this doesn't mean that there will always be a *uniquely best* solution to a problem in civil or conceptual engineering. But that is no embarrassment—instead, we may recognize the value in developing a plurality of concepts to serve a plurality of functions, as well as the possibility that two or more concepts could (like different bridge designs) serve a desirable function equally well.

The crucial point here is that, once we understand the approach better, we can easily see that the problems thought to plague the pragmatic approach to conceptual engineering are avoidable. Making practical choices like these is an undeniably complex and often difficult matter. It is difficult to work out how to balance the different concerns of one person (or group of people), and (where we must share a conceptual system), it is still more difficult to work out how to balance the different concerns of different individuals or groups. It is also difficult to know what changes are needed to continue to serve certain needs in constantly changing technological, social, and environmental contexts, and which will serve us well, given the constraints of the surrounding conceptual system and of (current local, as well as enduring) human abilities and limitations. Nonetheless, these are the honest difficulties we face when we confront challenging practical problems, not the mysterious difficulties of discerning the "metaphysical facts of the world" or its metaphysical "structure." Thinking of the task in metaphysical terms only distracts and misleads us.

Taking a pragmatic approach to conceptual engineering enables us to make the functions served by our terms and concepts *visible*, and so enables us to make better informed and more transparent conceptual decisions. Once all the relevant factors are on the table, these practical decisions need not be at all arbitrary, and we can also show paths for critique of problematic concepts. Most importantly, we can make new progress on old philosophical (and practical, scientific, and political) debates, in projects ranging from metaphysics (modality, numbers, ordinary objects), to philosophy of science (fish, gene, species, time), to applied ethics (privacy, death, responsibility).

10
The Perennial Philosophical Project

Throughout this book, I have been arguing that we should give up the traditional view of metaphysics as aiming to discover "deep facts about reality."[1] For such a view leads to a rivalry with the sciences, epistemological mystery, and skepticism. I have also aimed to diagnose where various views of metaphysics go wrong: in attempting to address *all areas of discourse* while assuming that they all serve the function of tracking or describing "features of reality." Instead, I have argued, we should step back to first examine questions about the functions different aspects of language serve, and the rules by which they fulfill those functions. Doing so enables us to see that some "ontological problems" (e.g., about the existence of numbers, properties, or ordinary objects) are easily answered—and don't require extensive metaphysical debates. It also enables us to see that many other "metaphysical problems" thought to arise for numbers, properties, modality, or morality are pseudo-problems based on category mistakes that arise from misguided presuppositions about how the relevant areas of language work and what functions they serve. Taking these views on board will involve rejecting much of the work that goes under the heading of "metaphysics" today, or at the least subjecting it to a kind of therapy.

Questions that naturally arise at this stage, then, are these: Is the work that remains still worth doing? And does it still deserve to be called "metaphysics"? I will address these in reverse order. On the latter, I am admittedly unsure. But for the former I will give an emphatic yes: The work that remains is important and worth doing, whatever we call it.

---

[1] Portions of this chapter are adapted from my (2021).

10.1 Should We Still Call It "Metaphysics"?

As I have been presenting this work throughout its development, I have heard a lot of pushback on this question, from both sides. From the serious metaphysicians, I have heard that it doesn't capture what they wanted out of metaphysics—a deep worldly reckoning of what there is, how the world is structured, or what grounds what. From many pragmatists and skeptics, on the other hand, I have similarly gotten pushback, to the effect that it's not worth preserving the title "metaphysics," that we would do better to, like the positivists, use the term "metaphysics" only as a term of derision for an outmoded area of inquiry we should reject.

The question of whether to retain the term "metaphysics," of course, is itself a conceptual-engineering question: *What should we do with that old term, now?*

I have mixed feelings about that myself—and have intentionally made the title of the book readable in either way: as rethinking *how* we should do metaphysics, or *whether* we should do metaphysics.

As will be clear to those who have read this far, I am somewhat inclined to keep the term. Why? Metaphysics, of course, is a tradition that reaches back far before the 1950s. Many of the mistakes I have aimed to identify—in particular, the focus on ontological questions on a scientific model, as well as ways of thinking of metaphysics on an explanatory, structural, truthmaking, or grounding model—have originated only after the post-Quinean "revival" of metaphysics.

But there is of course a much longer tradition of work classified as "historical metaphysics"—including Hume on causation, liberty, and necessity, Berkeley on matter, Locke on persons, Kant on the phenomenal world, and far more. Much of that work remains relevant and valuable on this conception, along with many recent debates about free will (especially those between compatibilists and incompatibilists), the nature of art, social ontology, etc. Classic puzzles and paradoxes long discussed in metaphysics remain relevant, too—though this approach will tend to treat them as relevant to showing features of how our language or conceptual scheme works (much as study of disorders can show us things about how our brains work).

So, suppose we aim to conceptually re-engineer the term "metaphysics." As always, it is useful to begin from some reverse engineering, and that will proceed not by asking contemporary practitioners how they think of metaphysics (in which case the majority today will give one of those views examined and rejected in Part I), but by asking what this term has done for us, and what could not be done (or not be done so easily) without it. General terms such as "metaphysics" enable us to collect together areas of literature that speak to each other and that address related problems. We use the term "metaphysics" in compiling anthologies and histories, in arranging course catalogs and syllabi, and similar activities. We also use the term to organize conferences, gather together people whose work speaks to each other, and figure out whom to hire to teach the relevant courses.

What should we do now? Should we exclude (from such anthologies, courses, and conferences) critics of the problems that others are working on? That would seem to be a mistake—leading the practitioners to just ignore questions about whether the problems they spend their time on are pseudo-problems. Should we use the term as a term of derision, and (with the positivists) seek to eliminate metaphysics? If I am right, that, too, would be a mistake. For there is much of value that is and has been done in metaphysics, even if some of the value will be in disentangling old puzzles, and even if seeing the value will often require reinterpreting what much of the past work is good for. (I will aim to do that below.)

In conceptually re-engineering "metaphysics," if we are to retain the term, one reasonable set of goals is to retain historical continuity with that prior tradition of work while also articulating a clear and worthwhile project to undertake going forward. If we take that route, then we may have reason to retain the term, emphasizing the connections to the valuable parts of the tradition while describing its work in ways that make sense in the context of our current state of inquiry and knowledge, and that show what it can contribute that is valuable and transparent.

As I have tried to make clear, a great deal of past work in metaphysics can be seen as contributing to the project of descriptive and normative conceptual engineering. For large portions of many past debates—including debates about free will and determinism, debates in philosophy of mind, debates about matter and ordinary objects, debates about what art is, etc.—can be seen as implicitly engaged in either understanding how our conceptual scheme works or pressing for views about how it *should* work. Work undertaken in understanding how our conceptual scheme or language works—whether by phenomenology, by ordinary language philosophy, or by other approaches to conceptual analysis—is easily included here, as part of the work I have here presented as "reverse engineering."[2]

"But wait," some might say, "many of the classic philosophers don't present what they're doing as just aiming to understand, evaluate, or re-shape our terms or concepts—they talk about the *world*." Plato talks about *what justice is*, John Locke about what *makes a person the same over time*, David Hume about *what freedom is*, Clive Bell and Arthur Danto about *what art is*, and so on.

It is certainly true that many philosophers simply *use* the relevant words in their discussions of what justice, persons, freedom, or art are. But often, even in our daily lives—in our political conversations, arguments with our friends, pub discussions—we use words not as a way of expressing disagreements about empirical facts of the world but rather as ways of pressing for views about how we *should* use our terms.[3]

Think of the debates that inevitably ensue with the Olympics, about whether air pistol or synchronized swimming is really a sport. Or think of more serious debates about whether the Oklahoma City bombing was terrorism, or whether waterboarding is torture. These are cases of what David Plunkett and Tim Sundell (2013) call "metalinguistic negotiation": where we *use* words in certain ways as a way to implicitly negotiate for how (or whether) these terms *ought to be* used. Such debates needn't arise from different beliefs about other facts (say about the skills or training of air pistol competitors), and there's no sense that further "discoveries" would resolve the debate. Nor are such debates resolved just by seeing how the relevant words ("sport," for example)

---

[2] For discussion of the relation between phenomenology and ordinary language philosophy, see my (2007b).
[3] For a fuller discussion of ways in which we can see many debates as engaged implicitly in metalinguistic negotiation, see my (2016b) and my (2020a, 201–6). See also Plunkett (2015).

are *actually* used or by acknowledging that the disputants are using a key word in different ways. For at bottom these disputes are not about what the *world is like* or about how words *are used* but rather about how they *should be used.*

We can see metalinguistic negotiation at work in many historical debates within metaphysics as well. When John Locke (1690) argues that preserving a continuity of consciousness (not just of body) is essential to the same person continuing to exist over time, he acknowledges that this doesn't match the standard practices of the time. But he argues that this is how we *should* come to think of persons, since person is "a forensic term, appropriating actions and their merit," and it is only right and just to reward and punish one who shares a continuous consciousness with the person who committed the act.[4] George Berkeley's (1713) arguments that there is no such thing as material substance proceed by showing that the Lockean concept of "material substance" is confused and nonsensical, and tends to lead to skepticism—so that we are better off ridding ourselves of that concept. David Hume's (1748) arguments that liberty and necessity are compatible are based on arguments that "necessity" *can't* mean a kind of necessary force in the world (for no such thing is ever observed), and that the only sense of "liberty" relevant to morality is the sense in which someone acts from their own will and motivations. More recent debates between compatibilists and incompatibilists rely on questions about how we *should* come to use the relevant concepts. For example, when Paul Edwards (1961) argues that there is no free will, he is not concerned with the fact (noted by Hume) that we typically call an action "free" if someone is doing what they want to do, without external constraint. He argues instead that taking people to be *free* means holding them *responsible*. But, he argues, we *shouldn't* treat anyone as responsible unless they originally *chose* their own character, and he argues that this condition is never met.

What such philosophers are doing can often be seen as pressing for views about how we *should* think of persons or of freedom—as engaged in metalinguistic negotiation. It's also important to note

---

[4] See Locke, *An Essay Concerning Human Understanding*, Chapter XXVII.

that such debates aren't just "about words." They matter for who we blame, punish, give property and other rights to, for how we raise our children and treat our friends and our debtors, and for our own feelings of guilt. And in this way this past work in metaphysics often can be seen as contributing to the project of conceptual engineering—broadly construed. By including both a kind of (descriptive) reverse-engineering work and (normative) constructive conceptual engineering, asking what concepts we should retain, reject, or revise, we can retain continuity with much of the most interesting and valuable work in historical metaphysics. If we undertake this task, we may provide therapy for some classic "metaphysical problems" or reassess some recent work in metaphysics, while also providing a new way of characterizing the clear and valuable work that metaphysics can do, going forward.

Those are my reasons for continuing to use the title "metaphysics," retaining the connection to the historical work that precedes this, while rethinking what it can do, and how we can do it. I don't want to insist on the title, however. What I do want to insist on is that, whatever we call it, this work *matters*, and provides an important and perennial project for philosophy. I will turn to make that case now.

10.2 What Should We Do?

On my view, the most basic and enduring question of philosophy is "What should we do?"[5] Or perhaps better, "What should we do *now*?"—given our current state of history and our current situation of knowledge, technology, environment, preferences and needs. Seeing philosophy in this practical, normative light fits quite naturally with work in other areas of philosophy: work in ethics, of course, addresses questions of how we should live and act, work in political philosophy addresses questions of what form of government, what voting system, what distribution of goods, etc. we should have. Questions of epistemology and logic are easily brought under this heading, too, as asking

---

[5] For development of the idea that philosophical work should be seen as fundamentally *normative* work, see my (2015b).

how we should work to acquire knowledge and how we should reason (perhaps allowing differences in various domains of inquiry).

The questions of metaphysics are the hardest to bring under this banner, since they superficially appear to be asking questions about what exists, or what the "natures" of various sorts of thing are. But I have been arguing that we can bring much of the valuable work of metaphysics in here, too, by reconceiving of it as engaged in conceptual engineering—ultimately asking what concepts and language we should use going forward, in ways that require a clear understanding of how our extant scheme works, before we consider questions about which elements of it should be retained, revised, or rejected. I have argued that better reverse-engineering work that includes an understanding of linguistic functions enables us to diagnose and disentangle ourselves from a morass of old "metaphysical problems." And this frees us up to turn to more fruitful work, including constructively (re-)engineering the concepts we need, whether for improving government, science, art, education, or the very structure of society.

An important consequence of this change in how we think of the work of metaphysics—thinking of it as conceptual engineering rather than as world-discovery—is that we can then see that it is not a second-rate rival to the empirical work of the sciences. Yet we can nonetheless see how it can be relevant, even world-changing, and we can also see why it is a never-ending, perennial project.

Historically, philosophy has often focused on highly *general* concepts that have long been central to human life: concepts like *person, freedom, right, art, knowledge, mind,* and *justice*. Consider to what a great extent our lives are shaped by what sort of action counts as *free*; by what sort of political *freedom* a state should guarantee; by what should count as a *human right*; by who counts as having *knowledge*; by what counts as *justice*. Consider also the impact of our conceptions of what qualifies as a work of *art* worthy of exhibition, study, interpretation and veneration; and of the impact of our concept of mind on how we think about and treat nonhuman animals, and how we respond to and build policies around artificial intelligence. Understanding, assessing, and re-engineering these concepts has always played a central role in philosophical work; and shaping our understanding and use of these concepts has had and can have an enormous impact on human life.

Rethinking the work of metaphysics as work in conceptual engineering helps erode the boundary between metaphysics and other areas of philosophy as well. Whether the concepts are highly general or more specific, they are interconnected in important ways, and changes in our conceptual scheme can lead to changes in the world. Some of these changes are social changes—in our laws, governments, and the ways we live together. Think of the roles that philosophical conceptions of liberty, responsibility, and property played in shaping the system of government, laws, and practices of the United States and elsewhere.[6]

The great social movements of the last century have been tied up with revolutions in the language and concepts we use. Our social concepts are typically tied not simply to "picking out" some group in the world, but to imposing certain norms for how they are to be treated and regarded.[7] Pejoratives (say for race or national origin) do not simply pick out a group of people but derogate members of that group. Even terms that are not pejoratives may impose norms of treatment—think of why feminists have long emphasized the need to stop calling grown women "girls."

Sometimes terms and concepts enable the formation of whole systems of laws—consider the old "racial" terms such as "quadroon" and "octoroon," used in imposing fine-grained discriminatory legal practices. Drop the concepts, and it is no longer possible to develop or enforce such systems of laws and the fine-grained racial hierarchies they supported.

Sometimes changes of concepts go hand in hand with changes in laws or in how laws are applied. As the criteria for marriage were reformed in many places, the concept was changed—and with it, our social reality changed. For while we dropped the inferential connections that entitled us to infer that one man and one woman were involved

---

[6] Of course, I don't mean to imply that these were all *positive* changes, or that none need(ed) rethinking—only that the concepts we use, philosophically articulated and fought out, have enormous impact.
[7] For more on the idea that social group terms impose norms, see my (2016a).

in any marriage, the connections to thousands of legal rights and entitlements tied to marriage remained the same, as did the more informal connections to gaining public social recognition of a life-shaping relationship. Similarly, the ways we formulate our concepts of disability also have immediate legal consequences—for what sorts of accommodation are required in schools, what sorts of discrimination are protected against, what sorts of treatment are paid for by insurance, and even for who is permitted to immigrate to some countries.

Conceptual innovation also plays a central role in social and moral change. As Michele Moody-Adams has argued (2017), moral progress requires conceptual progress—where this includes not only progress in developing new moral concepts, but also in introducing new categories for describing and interpreting our experience—for example, consider the introduction of terms for "genocide" and "crimes against humanity." As she writes, "effective social movements often rely on moral pioneers to be linguistic visionaries who can recognize when some way of describing the world is an obstacle to revealing, and eventually correcting, deficiencies in our moral beliefs and practices" (2017, 161). Introducing words (and concepts) like "sexual harassment" (coined by activists at Cornell University in 1975) and "hostile environment" was the key to getting certain patterns of behavior identified, acknowledged as problematic, and as suitable for prohibition and prosecution. Introducing the term and concept of "genocidal rape" was crucial to the developing international laws for its prosecution (philosophers Asja Armanda, and philosophers/lawyers Natalie Nenadic and Catherine McKinnon were central in working to bring about this change). Changes in how we understand "consent," "rape," "bodily autonomy," and "misogyny" are also central to work in feminist philosophy.

Nor are the changes wrought by our concepts limited to legal, social, or moral changes. Changes in our concepts also go along with changes in our practices of investigation and treatment. Think of the changes in our terminology for emotional, behavioral, and cognitive differences, as we moved using from terms like "madman" or "lunatic" to speaking of people with "mental illness," and as authors of the Diagnostic and Statistical Manuals introduced an enormous (and ever-changing) number of new classifications. Think of the difference between whether our psychological terms reflect a supernatural, medical, or social model of cognitive and behavioral differences—and of the differences these lead to in whether we engage in an attempted religious, biochemical, behavioral, or contextual approach to dealing with these differences.

As Thomas Kuhn emphasized, conceptual change has also been central to scientific revolutions. Think of the conceptual changes in the meaning of "gene" that were crucial to the development of biology. Moreover, the ways we understand what should count as the same, or a different, species, makes an enormous difference to how we investigate and report on biodiversity, how we identify and count endangered species, and how we make plans for environmental protection or remediation. In physics, changes in how we understand space, time, and their relationship were essential to developing the theory of relativity.

Conceptual innovation and change may also lead to changes in other practices—such as journalism, or the management of social media. New work in philosophy of language such as Jennifer Saul's (2024) introduction of the term "figleaf" to identify under a single heading some insidious ways that racist or other problematic discourse can become "accepted" by a wider audience, for example, may enable us to do more to both identify the phenomenon and to fight it on social media.

The concepts we use and have available to us also play a central role in our self-conception and action. As Anthony Appiah puts it, "what people can do depends on what concepts they have available to them; and among the concepts that may shape one's action is the concept of a certain kind of person and the behavior appropriate to that kind" (1994, 106).

In all these ways, change in the world comes about with changes in our concepts. And that is because our terms and concepts aren't just a way of pointing to individuals or transparently discovering how the world is. Our terms come with *norms*—including implicit rules for what we can infer from them. And these may be inferences about how individuals of different groups should be treated, what rights and obligations they have, or how conditions of various kinds are to be investigated and treated. Change the concepts, and you can change the inferences, and in turn you can change the social, legal, and even scientific practices.

To say that changes in our conceptual scheme can have worldly importance in this way is not to embrace a kind of idealist philosophical view that our minds "create reality." It is merely to acknowledge the ways in which our concepts are tied to all kinds of *norms* for how we think and live—and to acknowledge the enormous difference this may make for how we act and think of ourselves, how we treat each other, how we run our social institutions, and how we conduct our scientific investigations.

10.3 The Perennial Project

Conceptual engineering provides a promising and interesting route for reconceptualizing central areas of philosophy—in a way that both avoids the threat of a rivalry with science and also avoids the feeling that philosophical work is trivial or uninteresting.[8] This conceptual work can both make sense of much of what philosophy *has done* and of what philosophy *can do*, as well as why it matters. In engaging in conceptual engineering, it is also crucial to make the *reasons* for these conceptual and linguistic choices explicit and open for examination. And that will require bringing up front the reasons for these conceptual choices, rather than thinking of ourselves as like scientists but making our own (metaphysical) "discoveries." It will require being transparent about what we are doing and abandoning the quasi-scientific "discovery" model of philosophy in general, as well as the versions of that model that have played such a central role in metaphysics.

An interesting, and to my mind positive, consequence of this is that it also makes clear why philosophy should be a *perennial* project. On this view, philosophy is not in the business of looking for eternal answers to deep worldly questions. Instead, we must constantly *rethink* what concepts and language we *should* use, in new contexts. Mary Midgley recognized this need to constantly revise and rethink

---

[8] Other parts of philosophy, such as ethics, may not need any such reconceptualization to avoid these problems.

the ideas we live by, insisting that conceptual schemes are partial and limited: "This provisionalness, in fact, is a regular feature of conceptual schemes. None of them is isolated; none of them is safe from the possibility of clashing with others" (1992, 144). As a result, she insisted that this is work that is never complete or finished, writing, "Thought ... ought to be conceived dynamically, as something that we do, and must constantly keep doing" (1992, 149).

Since this reconception involves turning philosophy into a *practical* project, it perhaps isn't surprising that this conclusion coincides with that of some persuasive approaches to moral philosophy, such as that of Moody-Adams, who sees moral questions as not being susceptible to final, permanent solutions, but as requiring continual reassessment over varying times and places (2017, 162), and yet argues that this does not undermine the idea that we can nonetheless make moral progress: "When we appropriately tailor our expectations to the moral domain, we will stop expecting progress in moral inquiry to involve convergence on permanent resolutions of moral problems" (2017, 163).

There are many types of case in which we will have reason to rethink, and aim to improve, our conceptual scheme. With changes in the environmental context, wrought by climate change, we must rethink our concepts of the natural and the artificial, as well as rethinking our concepts of moral obligation and responsibility. With changes in the social context, and in empirical knowledge (for example, ushered in by the Kinsey report and Edward Laumann's later work)[9] we have come to rethink our concepts of marriage, family, sexual orientation, and gender. Our concepts and language must also constantly be rethought in the context of new background beliefs, new knowledge, and new technology. For background beliefs, consider, for example, the massive ways in which Western European concepts of person, freedom, life, mind, function, and morality have shifted and required re-evaluation as the dominance of religion has waned. Such needs have fueled a large portion of post-Enlightenment philosophical work. For knowledge, consider the ways in which discoveries about

---

[9] For a very brief introductory overview, see https://slate.com/human-interest/2007/09/fifty-years-after-alfred-kinsey-what-more-do-we-know.html.

the varieties of sea creatures and of evolution have forced biologists to rethink the concept of "fish," or the ways discoveries about animal behavior and communities are leading many to rethink concepts of intelligence, mind, and morality. New technology is visibly shaking our current conceptual scheme as I write this, as advances in technology and artificial intelligence lead us to rethink concepts of plagiarism, bias, privacy, mind, and intelligence.

10.4 Conclusion

I have aimed to show that doing work in conceptual engineering, understanding, evaluating and altering our conceptual scheme, is not merely shallow or trivial. For changing our concepts and language can have great worldly importance: importance for how we treat each other, for how we live, for how we run our social and legal institutions and conduct our scientific investigations. Once we can see that, we can see that rethinking metaphysics, to see it as engaged in conceptual work rather than as "investigating the world," needn't leave its work superficial or uninteresting.

On this reconception, then, we can see philosophy not as a deep inquiry into "the nature of reality" or "what exists" that is a second-rate rival to the natural sciences. Nor is it merely concerned with how we "happen to" think and talk. Nor is it a project that, for thousands of years, has been *failing* to find the answers to the deep questions about the world and human life. Instead, we can see philosophy as a project of trying to figure out, and reason about, how we *should* think and talk—a project that is centrally important, always changing, and never completed.[10]

Thinking of metaphysics as conceptual engineering rather than as worldly discovery also enables us to avoid the feeling that the answers

---

[10] In this way, it becomes a project of *practical* philosophy. This reconception of philosophical work as work in practical philosophy (and the insistence that its methods are very different from those of the natural sciences) then fits nicely with Michele Moody-Adams's (1990) view that it is a mistake to compare the methods of ethics and the methods of science (and to think that ethics is problematic because it can't meet the scientific standard).

to philosophical questions are unknowable, so we should just give up trying. We must go on using some conceptual system. The worst thing we could do would be to let skepticism about our ability to find "the true answers" convince us to give up on thinking seriously about which concepts we should use and how we should use them. For how we think of and speak about ourselves, each other, and our world really matters.

Bibliography

Ajdukiewicz, Kazimierz. (1934/1978). "Language and Meaning." In Jerzy Giedymin, ed., *The Scientific World-Perspective and Other Essays, 1931–1963*. Dordrecht: D. Reidel, 35–66.
Allen, Anita. (2011). *Unpopular Privacy: What Must We Hide?* New York: Oxford University Press.
Alston, William P. (1958). "Ontological Commitments." *Philosophical Studies* 9 (1–2): 8–17.
Ambrose, Alice. (1952). "Linguistic Approaches to Philosophical Problems." *Journal of Philosophy* 49 (9): 289–301.
Appiah, Anthony. (1994). "Race, Culture, Identity: Misunderstood Connections." Tanner Lectures on Human Values.
Armstrong, David M. (1978). *A Theory of Universals: Universals and Scientific Realism*. Cambridge: Cambridge University Press.
Armstrong, David M. (1997). *A World of States of Affairs*. Cambridge: Cambridge University Press.
Armstrong, David M. (2004). *Truth and Truthmakers*. Cambridge: Cambridge University Press.
Audi, Paul. (2012). "Grounding: Toward a Theory of the In-Virtue-Of Relation." *Journal of Philosophy* 109 (12): 685–711.
Aurora, Simone. (2015). "A Forgotten Source in the History of Linguistics: Husserl's Logical Investigations." *Bulletin d'Analyse Phénoménologique* 11 (5): 1–19.
Austin, J. L. (1961). "Performative Utterances." In J. O. Urmson and G. J. Warnock, eds., *Philosophical Papers*. Oxford: Clarendon Press, 233–52.
Ayer, A. J. (1936/1952). *Language, Truth and Logic*. New York: Dover.
Barnes, Elizabeth. (2014). "Going Beyond the Fundamental: Feminism in Contemporary Metaphysics." *Proceedings of the Aristotelian Society* 114 (3): 335–51.
Baron, Sam, and James Norton. (2021). "Metaphysical Explanation: The Kitcher Picture." *Erkenntnis* 86: 187–207.
Bartlett, Tom, and Gerard O'Grady, eds. (2017). *The Routledge Handbook of Systemic Functional Linguistics*. London: Routledge.
Bateman, John A. (2017). "The Place of Systemic Functional Linguistics as a Linguistic Theory in the Twenty-First Century." In Tom Bartlett and Gerard O'Grady, eds., *The Routledge Handbook of Systemic Functional Linguistics*. New York: Routledge, 11–26.
Bavali, Mohammed, and Firooz Sadighi. (2008). "Chomsky's Universal Grammar and Halliday's Systemic Functional Linguistics: An Appraisal and a Compromise." *Journal of Pan-Pacific Association of Applied Linguistics* 12 (1): 11–28.

Beebee, Helen, and Julian Dodd, eds. (2005). *Truthmakers: The Contemporary Debate.* Oxford: Clarendon Press.
Bennett, Karen. (2004). "Spatio-Temporal Coincidence and the Grounding Problem." *Philosophical Studies* 118: 339–71.
Bennett, Karen. (2009). "Composition, Colocation, and Metaontology." In David Chalmers, David Manley, and Ryan Wasserman, eds., *Metametaphysics: New Essays on the Foundations of Ontology.* Oxford: Oxford University Press, 38–76.
Bennett, Karen. (2017). *Making Things Up.* Oxford: Oxford University Press.
Berkeley, George. (1713/1979). *Three Dialogues Between Hylas and Philonous.* Indianapolis, IN: Hackett.
Bicchieri, Cristina, and Hugo Mercier. (2014). "Norms and Beliefs: How Change Occurs." *Iyyun: Jerusalem Philosophical Quarterly* 63: 60–82.
Black, Max. (1949). *Language and Philosophy: Studies in Method.* Ithaca: Cornell University Press.
Blackburn, Simon. (1993). *Essays in Quasi-Realism.* New York: Oxford University Press.
Blackburn, Simon. (2005). "Quasi-Realism no Fictionalism." In Mark Eli Kalderon, ed., *Fictionalism in Metaphysics.* New York: Oxford University Press, 322–38.
Bliss, Ricki, and Kelly Trogdon. (2021). "Metaphysical Grounding." In Edward N. Zalta, ed., *Stanford Encyclopedia of Philosophy.* Winter 2021 ed. https://plato.stanford.edu/archives/win2021/entries/grounding/.
Braddon-Mitchell, David. (2020). "Reactive Concepts: Engineering the concept CONCEPT." In I. Alexis Burgess, Herman Cappelen, and David Plunkett, eds., *Conceptual Engineering and Conceptual Ethics.* Oxford: Oxford University Press, 79–99.
Brandom, Robert. (1994). *Making It Explicit.* Cambridge, MA: Harvard University Press.
Brandom, Robert. (2000). "Facts, Norms, and Normative Facts: A Reply to Habermas." *European Journal of Philosophy* 8 (3): 356–74.
Brandom, Robert. (2002). *Tales of the Mighty Dead: Historical Essays in the Metaphysics of Intentionality.* Cambridge, MA: Harvard University Press.
Brandom, Robert. (2008). *Between Saying and Doing: Towards an Analytic Pragmatism.* New York: Oxford University Press.
Brenner, Andrew, Anna-Sofia Maurin, Alexander Skiles, Robin Stenwall, and Naomi Thompson. (2021). "Metaphysical Explanation." In Edward N. Zalta, ed., *Stanford Encyclopedia of Philosophy.* Winter 2021 ed. https://plato.stanford.edu/archives/win2021/entries/metaphysical- explanation/.
Bricker, Phillip (2020). *Modal Matters: Essays in Metaphysics.* Oxford: Oxford University Press.
Brigandt, Ingo. (2010). "The Epistemic Goal of a Concept: Accounting for the Rationality of Semantic Change and Variation." *Synthese* 177 (1): 19–40.
Brożek, A., M. Będkowski, A. Chybińska, S. Ivanyk, and D. Traczykowski. (2020). *Anti-Irrationalism: Philosophical Methods in the Lvov-Warsaw School.* Warsaw: Semper Wydawnictwo Naukowe.
Brun, Georg. (2016). "Explication as a Method of Conceptual Re-Engineering." *Erkenntnis* 81: 1211–41.
Brun, Georg. (2020). "Conceptual Re-Engineering: From Explication to Reflective Equilibrium." *Synthese* 197: 925–54.

Bueno, Otavio, and Scott Shalkowski. (2015). "Modalism and Theoretical Virtues: Toward an Epistemology of Modality." *Philosophical Studies* 172: 671–89.
Burgess, Alexis, and David Plunkett. (2013). "Conceptual Ethics I." *Philosophy Compass* 8 (12): 1091–101.
Cameron, Ross. (2008). "Truthmakers and Ontological Commitment: Or How to Deal with Complex Objects and Mathematical Ontology Without Getting into Trouble." *Philosophical Studies* 140: 1–18.
Cameron, Ross. (2010). "How to Have a Radically Minimal Ontology." *Philosophical Studies* 151: 249–64.
Cameron, Ross. (2020). "Easy Ontology, Two-Dimensionalism and Truthmaking." In Karen Bennett and Dean Zimmerman, eds., *Oxford Studies in Metaphysics*, vol. 12. Oxford: Oxford University Press, 35–57.
Cameron, Ross. (2021). "Truthmaking and Metametaphysics." In Ricki Bliss and J. T. M. Miller, eds., *The Routledge Handbook of Metametaphysics*. London: Routledge, 233–44.
Campbell, Eric. (2014). "Breakdown of Moral Judgment." *Ethics* 124: 447–80.
Cantalamessa, Elizabeth. (2021). "Disability Studies, Conceptual Engineering, and Conceptual Activism." *Inquiry* 64 (1–2): 46–75.
Cappelen, Herman. (2018). *Fixing Language: An Essay on Conceptual Engineering*. Oxford: Oxford University Press.
Carey, Susan. (2009). *The Origin of Concepts*. Oxford: Oxford University Press.
Carnap, Rudolf. (1931). "Überwindung der Metaphysik durch logische Analyse der Sprache." *Erkenntnis* 2: 219–41.
Carnap, Rudolf. (1937/2002). *The Logical Syntax of Language*. Trans. Amethe Smeaton. Chicago: Open Court.
Carnap, Rudolf. (1950/1956). "Empiricism, Semantics, and Ontology." In *Meaning and Necessity*. 2nd ed. Chicago: University of Chicago Press.
Carnap, Rudolf. (1950/1962). "On Explication." In *Logical Foundations of Probability*. Chicago: University of Chicago Press.
Chalmers, David, David Manley, and Ryan Wasserman, eds. (2009). *Metametaphysics: New Essays on the Foundations of Ontology*. Oxford: Oxford University Press.
Correia, Fabrice. (2014). "From Grounding to Truth-Making: Some Thoughts." In A. Reboul, ed. *Mind, Values, and Metaphysics: Philosophical Essays in Honor of Kevin Mulligan*, vol. 1. New York: Springer, 85–98.
Cournane, Ailis. (2020). "Learning Modals: A Grammatical Perspective." *Language and Linguistics Compass* 14 (10): 1–22.
Creath, Richard. (1990). Introduction. In Richard Creath, ed., *Dear Carnap, Dear Van: The Quine-Carnap Correspondence and Related Work*. Berkeley: University of California Press, 1–46.
Cummins, Robert. (1975). "Functional Analysis." *Journal of Philosophy* 72: 741–64.
Dąmbska, Izydora. (1958). "On the Notion of Understanding." In A. Brożek and J. Jadacki, eds., *Knowledge, Language and Silence*. Leiden: Brill; Boston: Rodopi, 331–40.
Dasgupta, Shamik. (2017). "Constitutive Explanation." *Philosophical Issues* 27 (1): 74–97.

Dasgupta, Shamik. (2018). "Realism and the Absence of Value." *Philosophical Review* 127 (3): 279–322.
Dembroff, Robin. (2020). "Beyond Binary: Genderqueer as Critical Gender Kind." *Philosophers' Imprint* 20 (9): 1–23.
deRosset, Louis. (2013). "Grounding Explanations." *Philosopher's Imprint* 13 (7): 1–26.
Diaz-Leon, Esa. (2022). "The Meaning of 'Woman' and the Political Turn in Philosophy of Language." In D. Bordonaba, V. Fernández-Castro, and J. R. Torices, eds., *The Political Turn in Analytical Philosophy*. Berlin: de Gruyter, 229–55.
Donaldson, Thomas. (2015). "Reading the Book of the World." *Philosophical Studies* 172 (4): 1051–77.
Donaldson, Thomas. (2020). "David Armstrong on the Metaphysics of Mathematics." *Dialectica* 74 (4): 113–36.
Donnellan, Keith S. (1974). "Speaking of Nothing." *Philosophical Review* 83 (1): 3–31.
Dorr, Cian. (2008). "There Are No Abstract Objects." In Theodore Sider, John Hawthorne, and Dean Zimmerman, eds., *Contemporary Debates in Metaphysics*. Oxford: Blackwell, 32–64.
Dutilh Novaes, Catarina. (2015). "Conceptual Genealogy for Analytic Philosophy." In J. Bell, A. Cutrofello, and P. M. Livingston, eds., *Beyond the Analytic-Continental Divide: Pluralist Philosophy in the Twenty-First Century*. New York: Routledge, 75–108.
Dutilh Novaes, Catarina. (2020). "Carnapian Explication and Ameliorative Analysis: A Systematic Comparison." *Synthese* 197 (3): 1011–34.
Dyke, Heather. (2008). *Metaphysics and the Representational Fallacy*. New York: Routledge.
Edwards, Paul. (1961). "Hard and Soft Determinism." In Sidney Hook, ed., *Determinism and Freedom in the Age of Modern Science*. New York: Collier Books, 117–25.
Eggins, Suzanne. (2004). *An Introduction to Systemic Functional Linguistics*. 2nd ed. London: Continuum.
Eklund, Matti. (2009). "Bad Company and Neo-Fregean Philosophy." *Synthese* 170 (3): 393–414.
Evnine, Simon. (2016). "Much Ado about Something-from-Nothing; or, Problems for Ontological Minimalism." In Stephan Blatti and Sandra Lapointe, eds. *Ontology After Carnap*. Oxford: Oxford University Press, 145–64.
Field, Hartry. (2016). *Science Without Numbers*, 2nd ed. Oxford: Oxford University Press.
Fine, Kit. (1994). "Essence and Modality." *Philosophical Perspectives* 8: 1–16.
Fine, Kit. (1995). "Ontological Dependence." *Proceedings of the Aristotelian Society* 95 (1): 269–90.
Fine, Kit. (2001). "The Question of Realism." *Philosophers' Imprint* 1 (2): 1–30.
Fine, Kit. (2012). "Guide to Ground." In Fabrice Correia and Benjamin Schnieder, eds., *Metaphysical Grounding: Understanding the Structure of Reality*. New York: Cambridge University Press, 37–80.
Firth, J. R. (1962). *Studies in Linguistic Analysis*. Oxford: Blackwell.

Føllesdal, Dagfinn. (2004). "Quine on Modality." In Roger F. Gibson, ed., *The Cambridge Companion to Quine*. Cambridge: Cambridge University Press, 200–213.
Føllesdal, Dagfinn. (2013). Preface. In W. V. O. Quine, *Word and Object*. Cambridge, MA: MIT Press, xv–xxviii.
Frege, Gottlob. (1884). *Grundlagen der Arithmetik*. Breslau: Marcus.
Frege, Gottlob. (1893). *Grundgesetze der Arithmetic: Begriffsschriftlich Abgeleitet*, Vol. 1. Jena: Pohle.
Garson, Justin. (2022). *Madness: A Philosophical Exploration*. Oxford: Oxford University Press.
Geach, Peter. (1965). "Assertion." *Philosophical Review* 74 (4): 449–65.
Geirsson, Heimir, and Michael Losonsky, eds. (1998). *Beginning Metaphysics: An Introductory Text with Readings*. Oxford: Blackwell.
Gert, Bernard, Charles M. Culver, and K. Danner Clouser. (2006). "Death." In *Bioethics: A Systematic Approach*. 2nd ed. Oxford: Oxford University Press, 283–308.
Gert, Joshua. (2021). "Neopragmatist Semantics." *Philosophy and Phenomenological Research* 106 (1): 107–35.
Gert, Joshua, ed. (2023). *Neopragmatism: Interventions in First-Order Philosophy*. Oxford: Oxford University Press.
Gibbard, Allan. (1990). *Wise Choices, Apt Feelings*. Cambridge, MA: Harvard University Press.
Gibbard, Allan. (2003). *Thinking How to Live*. Cambridge, MA: Harvard University Press.
Hacker, P. M. S. (1996). *Wittgenstein's Place in Twentieth-Century Analytic Philosophy*. Oxford: Blackwell.
Halliday, Michael. (1964). "Syntax and the Consumer." In C. I. J. M. Stuart, ed., *Report of the Fifteenth Annual (First International) Round Table Meeting on Linguistics and Language*. Washington, DC: Georgetown University Press, 11–24.
Halliday, Michael. (1973). *Explorations in the Functions of Language*. New York: Elsevier.
Halliday, Michael. (1975). *Learning How to Mean: Explorations in the Development of Language*. New York: Elsevier.
Halliday, Michael. (2009). *The Essential Halliday*. Ed. Jonathan Webster. London: Continuum.
Hallliday, Michael. (2014). *Halliday's Introduction to Functional Grammar*. 4th ed. Revised by Christian M. I. M. Matthiessen. London: Routledge.
Hare, R. M. (1952). *The Language of Morals*. Oxford: Clarendon Press.
Harris, Daniel, Daniel Fogal, and Matt Moss. (2018). "Speech Acts: The Contemporary Theoretical Landscape." In Daniel Fogal, Daniel Harris, and Matt Moss, eds., *New Work on Speech Acts*. Oxford: Oxford University Press, 1–39.
Haslanger, Sally. (2000). "Gender and Race: (What) Are They? (What) Do We Want Them to Be?" *Noûs* 34 (1): 31–55.
Hawking, Stephen, and Leonard Mlodinow. (2012). *The Grand Design*. New York: Bantam Books Trade Paperbacks.
Hawley, Katherine. (2006). "Science as a Guide to Metaphysics?" *Synthese* 149 (3): 451–70.

Heil, John. (2003). *From an Ontological Point of View*. Oxford: Oxford University Press.
Hirsch, Eli. (1997). "Basic Objects: A Reply to Xu." *Mind & Language* 12 (3-4): 406-12.
Hirsch, Eli. (2002a). "Quantifier Variance and Realism." *Philosophical Issues* 12: 51-73.
Hirsch, Eli. (2002b). "Against Revisionary Ontology." *Philosophical Topics* 30: 103-27.
Hofweber, Thomas. (2005a). "A Puzzle About Ontology." *Noûs* 39 (2): 256-83.
Hofweber, Thomas. (2005b). "Number Determiners, Numbers, and Arithmetic." *Philosophical Review* 114 (2): 179-225.
Huemer, Michael. (2009). "When Is Parsimony a Virtue?" *Philosophical Quarterly* 59 (235): 216-36.
Hume, David. (1748/1993). *An Enquiry Concerning Human Understanding*. 2nd ed. Ed. Eric Steinberg. Indianapolis: Hackett.
Husserl, Edmund. (1900/2000). *Logical Investigations*. Trans. J. N. Findlay. New York: Humanity Books.
Ingarden, Roman. (1964b). *Time and Modes of Being*. Trans. Helen R. Michejda. Springfield, IL: Charles C. Thomas.
Irmak, Nurbay. (2019). "An Ontology of Words." *Erkenntnis* 84 (5): 1139-58.
Isaac, Manuel Gustavo. (2021). "Broad-Spectrum Conceptual Engineering." *Ratio* 34 (4): 286-302.
Isaac, Manuel Gustavo. (2023). "Which Concept of Concept for Conceptual Engineering?" *Erkenntnis* 88 (5): 2145-69.
Jackson, Frank. (1998). *From Metaphysics to Ethics: A Defense of Conceptual Analysis*. Oxford: Oxford University Press.
Johnston, Mark. (1992). "Reasons and Reductionism." *Philosophical Review* 101 (3): 589-618.
Joyce, R. (2006). *The Evolution of Morality*. Cambridge, MA: MIT Press.
Kaplan, David. (1990). "Words." *Aristotelian Society Supplementary Volume* 64 (1): 93-119.
Katz, Jerrold J. (1998). *Realistic Rationalism*. Cambridge, MA: Bradford.
Kim, Jaegwon. (1993). *Supervenience and Mind: Selected Philosophical Essays*. Cambridge: Cambridge University Press.
Kim, Jaegwon. (2002). "The Layered Model: Metaphysical Considerations." *Philosophical Explorations* 5 (1): 2-20.
Kim, Jaegwon, Daniel Z. Korman, and Ernest Sosa. (2012). *Metaphysics: An Anthology*. 2nd ed. Oxford: Blackwell.
Kitcher, Philip. (1981). "Explanatory Unification." *Philosophy of Science* 48: 507-31.
Kitcher, Philip. (1993). *The Advancement of Science: Science Without Legend, Objectivity Without Illusions*. Oxford: Oxford University Press.
Kitsik, Eve. (2021). "Attentional Progress by Conceptual Engineering." *Metaphilosophy* 53: 254-66.
Koslicki, Kathrin. (2015). "The Coarse-Grainedness of Grounding." In Karen Bennett and Dean W. Zimmerman, eds., *Oxford Studies in Metaphysics*, vol. 9. Oxford: Oxford University Press, 306-42.
Koslow, Allison. (2022). "Meaning Change and Changing Meaning." *Synthese* 200 (2): 1-26.

Kovacs, David. (2018). "The Deflationary Theory of Ontological Dependence." *Philosophical Quarterly* 68: 481–502.
Kovacs, David. (2020). "Metaphysically Explanatory Unification." *Philosophical Studies* 177: 1659–83.
Kraut, Robert. (2012). "Ontology." *The Monist* 95 (4): 684–710.
Kriegel, Uriah. (2013). "The Epistemological Challenge of Revisionary Metaphysics." *Philosophers' Imprint* 13 (12): 1–30.
Lance, Mark Norris, and John O'Leary-Hawthorne. (1997). *The Grammar of Meaning: Normativity and Semantic Discourse.* Cambridge: Cambridge University Press.
Langton, Rae. (1993). "Speech Acts and Unspeakable Acts." *Philosophy and Public Affairs* 22: 293–330.
Laudan, Larry. (1981). "A Confutation of Convergent Realism." *Philosophy of Science* 48 (1): 19–49. https://doi.org/10.1086/28897.
Lazerowitz, Morris. (1960). "The Hidden Structure of Philosophical Theories." *Massachusetts Review* 1 (4): 723–47.
Lazerowitz, Morris. (1970). "A Note on 'Metaphilosophy.'" *Metaphilosophy* 1 (1): 91.
Leon, Felipe. (2017). "From Modal Skepticism to Modal Empiricism." In Bob Fischer and Felipe Leon, eds., *Modal Epistemology After Rationalism.* New York: Springer, 247–62.
Le Poidevin, Robin. (2009). "General Introduction: What Is Metaphysics?" In Robin Le Poidevin, Peter Simons, Andrew McGonigal, and Ross P. Cameron, eds., *The Routledge Companion to Metaphysics.* New York: Routledge, xviii–xxii.
Lewis, David K. (1973). *Counterfactuals.* Cambridge, MA: Harvard University Press.
Lewis, David K. (1983/1999). "New Work for a Theory of Universals." In *David Lewis: Papers in Metaphysics and Epistemology.* Cambridge: Cambridge University Press, 8–55.
Lewis, David K. (1986). *On the Plurality of Worlds.* Oxford: Blackwell.
Locke, John. (1690). *An Essay Concerning Human Understanding.* London: Thomas Basset.
Locke, Theodore. (2020). "Metaphysical Explanations for Modal Normativists." *Metaphysics* 3 (1): 33–54.
Lowe, E. J. (2002). *A Survey of Metaphysics.* Oxford: Oxford University Press.
Łukasiewicz, Jan. (1905/2022). "Analysis and Construction of the Concept of Cause." In J. J. Jadacki and E. M. Swiderski, eds., *The Concept of Causality in the Lvov-Warsaw School: The Legacy of Jan Łukasiewicz.* Leiden: Brill, 3–64.
Macarthur, David, and Huw Price. (2007). "Pragmatism, Quasi-Realism, and the Global Challenge." In Cheryl Misak, ed., *New Pragmatists.* Oxford: Oxford University Press, 91–121.
MacDonald, Margaret. (1937). "Symposium: Induction and Hypothesis." *Proceedings of the Aristotelian Society* 16: 20–35.
Machery, Édouard. (2017). *Philosophy Within Its Proper Bounds.* Oxford: Oxford University Press.
Mackie, J. L. (1977). *Ethics: Inventing Right and Wrong.* London: Penguin Books.
MacKinnon, Catharine. (1993). *Only Words.* Cambridge, MA: Harvard University Press.

Magidor, Ofra. (2013). *Category Mistakes*. Oxford: Oxford University Press.
Malmkjaer, Kirsten, ed. (1991). *The Linguistics Encyclopedia*. London: Routledge.
Maurin, Anna-Sofia. (2019). "Grounding and Metaphysical Explanation: It's Complicated." *Philosophical Studies* 176 (6): 1573–94.
McFarlane, John. (2000). "What Does It Mean to Say That Logic Is Formal?" Ph.D. Dissertation, University of Pittsburgh.
Merricks, Trenton. (2001). *Objects and Persons*. Oxford: Clarendon.
Merrill, G. H. (1980). "The Model-Theoretic Argument Against Realism." *Philosophy of Science* 47: 69–81.
Midgley, Mary. (1992). "Philosophical Plumbing." *Royal Institute of Philosophy Supplements* 33: 139–51.
Mikkola, Mari. (2017). "On the Apparent Antagonism Between Feminist and Mainstream Metaphysics." *Philosophical Studies* 174: 2435–48.
Miller, Kristie, and James Norton. (2017). "Grounding: It's (Probably) All in the Head." *Philosophical Studies* 174: 3059–81.
Millikan, Ruth. (1984). *Language, Thought, and Other Biological Categories*. Cambridge, MA: MIT Press.
Misak, Cheryl. (2016). *Cambridge Pragmatism: From Peirce and James to Ramsey and Wittgenstein*. Oxford: Oxford University Press.
Misak, Cheryl. (2020). *Frank Ramsey: A Sheer Excess of Powers*. Oxford: Oxford University Press.
Misak, Cheryl. (2024). "Ryle's Debt to Pragmatism and to Margaret Macdonald." *Journal of the History of Philosophy* 62 (4): 639–56.
Moltmann, Friederike. (2022). "Natural Language Ontology." In Edward N. Zalta and Uri Nodelman, eds., *The Stanford Encyclopedia of Philosophy*. Winter 2022 ed. https://plato.stanford.edu/archives/win2022/entries/natural-language-ontology/.
Moody-Adams, Michele. (1990). "On the Alleged Methodological Infirmity of Ethics." *American Philosophical Quarterly* 27 (3): 225–35.
Moody-Adams, Michele. (2017). "Moral Progress and Human Agency." *Ethical Theory and Moral Practice* 20 (1): 153–68.
Mulligan, Kevin, Peter Simons, and Barry Smith. (1984). "Truth-Makers." *Philosophy and Phenomenological Research* 44 (3): 287–321.
Neander, Karen. (1995). "Misrepresenting and Malfunctioning." *Philosophical Studies* 79 (2): 109–41.
Nolan, Daniel. "Modal Fictionalism." In Edward N. Zalta and Uri Nodelman, eds., *Stanford Encyclopedia of Philosophy*. Winter 2022 ed. https://plato.stanford.edu/archives/win2022/entries/fictionalism-modal/.
Nozick, Robert. (2001). *Invariances: The Structure of the Objective World*. Cambridge, MA: Harvard University Press.
O'Leary-Hawthorne, John, and Huw Price. (1996). "How to Stand Up for Non-Cognitivists." *Australasian Journal of Philosophy* 74: 275–92.
Oppenheim, Paul, and Hilary Putnam. (1958). "Unity of Science as a Working Hypothesis." In Herbert Feigl, Michael Scriven, and Grover Maxwell, eds., *Minnesota Studies in the Philosophy of Science*, vol. 2: *Concepts, Theories and the Mind-Body Problem*. Minneapolis: University of Minnesota Press, 3–36.
Ossowska, Maria. (1931/1983). "Słowa i myśli." In *O człowieku, moralności i nauce*. Miscellanea. Warsaw: PWN, 183–225.

Papafragou, Anna. (1998). "The Acquisition of Modality: Implications for Theories of Semantic Representation." *Mind and Language* 13 (3): 370–99.
Papineau, David. (2019). "Knowledge Is Crude." *Aeon*. https://aeon.co/essays/knowledge-is-a- stone-age-concept-were-better-off-without-it. Accessed November 12, 2024.
Parfit, Derek. (1971). "Personal Identity." *Philosophical Review* 80 (1): 3–27.
Paul, L. A. (2012). "Metaphysics as Modeling: The Handmaiden's Tale." *Philosophical Studies* 160 (1): 1–29.
Perez Carballo, Alejandro. (2016). "Structuring Logical Space." *Philosophy and Phenomenological Research* 92 (2): 460–91.
Plunkett, David, and Tim Sundell. (2013). "Disagreement and the Semantics of Normative and Evaluative Terms." *Philosophers' Imprint* 13 (23): 1–37.
Plunkett, David. (2015). "Which Concepts Should We Use? Metalinguistic Negotiations and the Methodology of Philosophy." *Inquiry* 58 (7–8): 828–74.
Povich, Mark. (2024). *Rules to Infinity: The Normative Role of Mathematics in Scientific Explanation*. Oxford: Oxford University Press.
Price, Huw. (2009). "Metaphysics After Carnap: The Ghost Who Walks?" In David Chalmers, David Manley, and Ryan Wasserman, eds., *Metametaphysics: New Essays on the Foundations of Ontology*. Oxford: Oxford University Press, 320–46.
Price, Huw. (2011). *Naturalism Without Mirrors*. Oxford: Oxford University Press.
Price, Huw. (2013). *Expressivism, Pragmatism and Representationalism*. Cambridge: Cambridge University Press.
Psillos, Stathis. (1999). *Scientific Realism: How Science Tracks Truth*. London: Routledge.
Putnam, Hilary. (2004). *Ethics Without Ontology*. Cambridge, MA: Harvard University Press.
Queloz, Matthieu. (2021a). "Tracing Concepts to Needs." *The Philosopher* 109 (3): 34–39.
Queloz, Matthieu. (2021b). *The Practical Origins of Ideas*. Oxford: Oxford University Press.
Queloz, Matthieu. (2022). "Function-Based Conceptual Engineering and the Authority Problem." *Mind* 131 (524): 1247–78.
Queloz, Matthieu. (2025). *The Ethics of Conceptualization: Tailoring Thought and Language to Need*. Oxford: Oxford University Press.
Quine, W. V. O. (1948/1980). "On What There Is." In *From a Logical Point of View*. 2nd ed. Cambridge, MA: Harvard University Press, 1–19, 20–46.
Quine, W. V. O. (1951/1953). "Two Dogmas of Empiricism." In *From a Logical Point of View*. Cambridge, MA: Harvard University Press, 20–46
Quine, W. V. O. (1960). *Word and Object*. Cambridge, MA: MIT Press.
Quine, W. V. O. (1976). "Carnap and Logical Truth," reprinted in *The Ways of Paradox and Other Essays*, Revised edition. Cambridge, MA: Harvard University Press, 107–32.
Quine, W. V. O. (1981). *Theories and Things*. Cambridge, MA: Harvard University Press.
Quinn, Aleta. (2017). "When Is a Cladist Not a Cladist?" *Biology and Philosophy* 32 (4): 581–98.
Ramsey, Frank P. (1925). "Universals." *Mind* 34 (136): 401–17.

Ramsey, Frank P. (1929/1978). "General Propositions and Causation." In *Foundations: Essays in Philosophy, Logic, Mathematics and Economics*. Atlantic Highlands, NJ: Humanities Press, 133–51.

Rayo, Agustin. (2009). "Towards a Trivialist Account of Mathematics." In Otávio Bueno and Øystein Linnebo, eds., *New Waves in Philosophy of Mathematics*. New York: Palgrave Macmillan, 239–62.

Renfrew, Colin, and Paul Bahn. (2016). *Archeology: Theories, Methods, and Practice*. London: Thames and Hudson.

Restall, Greg. (2012). "A Cut-Free Sequent System for Two-Dimensional Modal Logic, and Why It Matters." *Annals of Pure and Applied Logic* 163 (11): 1611–23.

Rettler, Bradley. (2016). "The General Truthmaker View of Ontological Commitment." *Philosophical Studies* 173 (5): 1405–25.

Ritchie, Katherine. (2015). "The Metaphysics of Social Groups." *Philosophy Compass* 10 (5): 310–21.

Ritchie, Katherine. (2021). "Essentializing Language and the Prospects for Ameliorative Projects." *Ethics* 131 (3): 460–88.

Roca-Royes, Sonia. (2017). "Similarity and Possibility: An Epistemology of *de re* Possibility for Concrete Entities." In B. Fischer and F. Leon, eds., *Modal Epistemology After Rationalism*. New York: Springer, 221–46.

Rosen, Gideon. (2010). "Metaphysical Dependence: Grounding and Reduction." In Bob Hale and Aviv Hoffman, eds., *Modality: Metaphysics, Logic, and Epistemology*. Oxford: Oxford University Press, 109–36.

Ryle, Gilbert. (1949). *The Concept of Mind*. London: Hutchinson.

Ryle, Gilbert. (1950/1971). "'If,' 'So,' and 'Because.'" In *Collected Papers*, vol. 2. London: Hutchison, 234–49.

Ryle, Gilbert. (1970). "Autobiographical." In Oscar Wood and George Pitcher, eds., *Ryle*. New York: Doubleday, 1–15.

Saatsi, Juha. (2017). "Explanation and Explanationism in Science and Metaphysics." In Matthew Slater and Zanja Yudell, eds., *Metaphysics and the Philosophy of Science: New Essays*. Oxford: Oxford University Press, 163–93.

Saatsi, Juha. (Forthcoming). "Explanatory Power: Factive vs. Pragmatic Dimensions." In Insa Lawler, Kareem Khalifa, and Elay Shech, eds., *Scientific Understanding and Representation: Modeling in the Physical Sciences*. New York: Routledge.

Saul, Jennifer. (2024). *Dogwhistles and Figleaves: How Manipulative Language Spreads Racism and Falsehood*. New York: Oxford University Press.

Sawyer, Sarah. (2020). "Talk and Thought." In Alexis Burgess, Herman Cappelen, and David Plunkett, eds., *Conceptual Engineering and Conceptual Ethics*. Oxford: Oxford University Press, 379–95.

Schaffer, Jonathan. (2008). "Truthmaker Commitments." *Philosophical Studies* 141: 7–19.

Schaffer, Jonathan. (2009). "On What Grounds What." In David Chalmers, David Manley, and Ryan Wasserman, eds., *Metametaphysics: New Essays on the Foundations of Ontology*. Oxford: Oxford University Press, 347–83.

Schaffer, Jonathan. (2010a). "The Least Discerning and Most Promiscuous Truthmaker." *Philosophical Quarterly* 60 (239): 307–24.

Schaffer, Jonathan. (2010b). "Monism: The Priority of the Whole." *Philosophical Review* 119 (1): 31–76.

Schaffer, Jonathan. (2012). "Grounding, Transitivity and Contrastivity." In Fabrice Correia and Benjamin Schnieder, eds., *Metaphysical Grounding: Understanding the Structure of Reality*. Cambridge: Cambridge University Press, 122–38.
Schaffer, Jonathan. (2017). "Social Construction as Grounding; or: Fundamentality for Feminists, a Reply to Barnes and Mikkola." *Philosophical Studies* 174: 2449–65.
Schaffer, Jonathan. (2018). "Laws for Metaphysical Explanation." *Philosophical Issues* 27: 302–21.
Schaller, Susan. (1991). *A Man Without Words*. Berkeley: University of California Press.
Scharp, Kevin. (2013). *Replacing Truth*. Oxford: Oxford University Press.
Schiffer, Stephen. (1994). "A Paradox of Meaning." *Noûs* 28: 279–324.
Schiffer, Stephen. (1996). "Language-Created Language-Independent Entities." *Philosophical Topics* 24 (1): 149–67.
Schiffer, Stephen. (2003). *The Things We Mean*. Oxford: Oxford University Press.
Sękowski, Krzysztof, and Ethan Landes. (Forthcoming). "Conceptual Engineering Is Old News." *Philosophical Quarterly*.
Sellars, Wilfrid. (1958). "Counterfactuals, Dispositions, and the Causal Modalities." In Herbert Feigl, Michael Scriven, and Grover Maxwell, eds., *Minnesota Studies in the Philosophy of Science*, vol. 2: *Concepts, Theories and the Mind-Body Problem*. Minneapolis: University of Minnesota Press, 225–308.
Shalkowski, Scott. (2010). "IBE, GMR, and Metaphysical Projects." In Bob Hale and Aviv Hoffmann, eds., *Modality: Metaphysics, Logic, and Epistemology*. Oxford University Press, 167–87.
Shields, Matthew. (Forthcoming). "Alice Ambrose and the History of Analytic Metaphilosophy."
Sider, Theodore. (2011). *Writing the Book of the World*. Oxford: Oxford University Press.
Sider, Theodore. (2017). "Substantivity in Feminist Metaphysics." *Philosophical Studies* 174: 2467–78.
Simion, Mona, and Christoph Kelp. (2020). "Conceptual Innovation, Function First." *Noûs* 54 (4): 985–1002.
Sober, Elliott. (1993). "Mathematics and Indispensability." *Philosophical Review* 102 (1): 35–57.
Spencer, Quayshawn. (2019). "How to Be a Biological Racial Realist." In Joshua Glasgow, ed., *What Is Race? Four Philosophical Views*. New York: Oxford University Press, 73–110.
Steinberg, Alexander. (2013). "Pleonastic Possible Worlds." *Philosophical Studies* 164: 767–89.
Stevenson, Charles Leslie. (1937). "The Emotive Meaning of Ethical Terms." *Mind* 46 (181): 14–31.
Strawson, P. F. (1964). *Individuals*. London: Routledge.
Strawson, P. F., and H. P. Grice. (1956). "In Defense of a Dogma." *Philosophical Review* 65 (2): 141–58.
Tarski, Alfred. (1944). "The Semantic Conception of Truth and the Foundations of Semantics." *Philosophy and Phenomenological Research* 4 (3): 341–75.
Taverniers, Miriam. (2003). "Grammatical Metaphors in SFL: A Historiography of the Introduction and Initial Study of the Term." In Anne-Marie Vandenbergen,

Miriam Taverniers, and Louise Ravelli, eds., *Grammatical Metaphor: Views from Systemic Functional Linguistics*. Amsterdam: John Benjamins, 5–34.

Taverniers, Miriam. (2017). "Grammatical Metaphor." In Tom Bartlett and Gerard O'Grady, eds., *The Routledge Handbook of Systemic Functional Linguistics*. London: Routledge, 354–72.

Thomasson, Amie L. (1999). *Fiction and Metaphysics*. Cambridge: Cambridge University Press.

Thomasson, Amie L. (2002). "Phenomenology and the Development of Analytic Philosophy." *Southern Journal of Philosophy* 40 (1): 115–42.

Thomasson, Amie L. (2003a). "Foundations for a Social Ontology." *Protosociology* 18–19: 269–90.

Thomasson, Amie L. (2003b). "Realism and Human Kinds." *Philosophy and Phenomenological Research* 67 (3): 580–609.

Thomasson, Amie L. (2005). "Ingarden and the Ontology of Cultural Objects." In Arkadiusz Chrudzimski, ed., *Existence, Culture, and Persons: The Ontology of Roman Ingarden*. Frankfurt am Main: Ontos Verlag, 115–36.

Thomasson, Amie L. (2004). "The Ontology of Art." In Peter Kivy, ed., *The Blackwell Guide to Aesthetics*. Oxford: Blackwell, 78–92.

Thomasson, Amie L. (2005). "The Ontology of Art and Knowledge in Aesthetics." *Journal of Aesthetics and Art Criticism* 63 (3): 221–29.

Thomasson, Amie L. (2007a). *Ordinary Objects*. New York: Oxford University Press.

Thomasson, Amie L. (2007b). "Conceptual Analysis in Phenomenology and Ordinary Language Philosophy." In Michael Beaney, ed., *The Analytic Turn: Analysis in Early Analytic Philosophy and Phenomenology*. London: Routledge, 270–84.

Thomasson, Amie L. (2009). "Social Entities." In Robin le Poidevin, Simons Peter, McGonigal Andrew, and Ross P. Cameron, eds., *Routledge Companion to Metaphysics*. London: Routledge, 545–54.

Thomasson, Amie L. (2013). "Fictionalism versus Deflationism." *Mind* 122 (488): 1023–51.

Thomasson, Amie L. (2014). "Quizzical Ontology and Easy Ontology." *Journal of Philosophy* 91 (9–10): 502–28.

Thomasson, Amie L. (2015a). *Ontology Made Easy*. New York: Oxford University Press.

Thomasson, Amie L. (2015b). "What Can Philosophy Really Do?" *Philosopher's Magazine* 71 (4th Quarter): 17–23.

Thomasson, Amie L. (2016a). "The Ontology of Social Groups." *Synthese* 196: 4829–45.

Thomasson, Amie L. (2016b). "Metaphysical Disputes and Metalinguistic Negotiation." *Analytic Philosophy* 57 (4): 1–28.

Thomasson, Amie L. (2017a). "Metaphysics and Conceptual Negotiation." *Philosophical Issues* 27: 364–82.

Thomasson, Amie L. (2017b). "Husserl on Essences: A Reconstruction and Rehabilitation." *Grazer Philosophische Studien* 94: 436–59.

Thomasson, Amie L. (2017c). "What Can We Take Away from Easy Arguments?" *Australasian Philosophical Review* 1 (2): 153–62.

Thomasson, Amie L. (2019). "What Can Global Pragmatists Say About Ordinary Objects?" In J. Cumpa and B. Brewer, eds., *The Nature of Ordinary Objects* Cambridge: Cambridge University Press, 235–59.
Thomasson, Amie L. (2020a). *Norms and Necessity.* New York: Oxford University Press.
Thomasson, Amie L. (2020b). "A Pragmatic Method for Normative Conceptual Work." In Alexis Burgess, Herman Cappelen, and David Plunkett, eds., *Conceptual Engineering and Conceptual Ethics.* Oxford: Oxford University Press, 435–58.
Thomasson, Amie L. (2020c). "Truthmakers and Easy Ontology." In Karen Bennett and Dean W. Zimmerman, eds., *Oxford Studies in Metaphysics*, vol. 12. Oxford: Oxford University Press, 3–34.
Thomasson, Amie L. (2021a). "Philosophy as Conceptual Engineering." *The Philosopher* 109 (3): 7–14.
Thomasson, Amie L. (2021b). "Conceptual Engineering: When Do We Need It? How Can We Do It?," *Inquiry*, November 2021 (special issue on Conceptual Engineering), 1–26. https://doi.org/10.1080/0020174X.2021.2000118.
Thomasson, Amie L. (2022). "How Should We Think About Linguistic Function?" *Inquiry* 67 (3): 840–71. https://doi.org/10.1080/0020174X.2022.2074886.
Thomasson, Amie L. (2023a). "How It All Hangs Together." In Miguel Garcia-Godinez, ed., *Philosophers in Depth: Thomasson on Ontology.* London: Palgrave Macmillan.
Thomasson, Amie L. (2023b). "A Neo-Pragmatist Approach to Modality." In Joshua Gert, ed., *Neo-Pragmatism in Practice.* New York: Oxford University Press, 70–97.
Thomasson, Amie L. (Forthcoming). "Metaethics and the Functions of Moral Language."
Thompson, Geoff, Wendy Bowcher, Lise Fontaine, and David Schönthal, eds. (2019). *The Cambridge Handbook of Systemic Functional Linguistics.* Cambridge: Cambridge University Press.
Thompson, Naomi. (2019). "Questions and Answers: Explanation and the Structure of Reality." *Journal of the American Philosophical Association* 5 (1): 98–116.
Thompson, Naomi. (2023). "Realism, Deflationism and Metaphysical Explanation." In Miguel Garcia, ed., *Philosophers in Depth: Amie Thomasson on Ontology.* London: Palgrave Macmillan, 61–83.
Tirrell, Lynne. (2017). "Toxic Speech: Toward an Epidemiology of Discursive Harm." *Philosophical Topics* 45 (2): 139–61.
Twardowski, K. (1901). *Zasadnicze pojęcia dydaktyki i logiki.* Lviv: Nakładem Towarzystwa Pedagogicznego.
Unger, Peter. (1979). "Why There Are No People." *Midwest Studies in Philosophy* 4 (1): 177–222.
Van Inwagen, Peter. (1990). *Material Beings.* Ithaca: Cornell University Press.
Van Inwagen, Peter. (2009). *Metaphysics.* 3rd ed. Philadelphia: Westview Press.
Van Inwagen, Peter. (2020). "The Neo-Carnapians." *Synthese* 197: 7–32. https://doi.org/10.1007/s11229-016-1110-4.

Van Inwagen, Peter, and Meghan Sullivan. (2021). "Metaphysics." In Edward N. Zalta, ed., *Stanford Encyclopedia of Philosophy*. Winter 2021 ed. https://plato.stanford.edu/archives/win2021/entries/metaphysics/.

Vetter, Barbara. (2015). *Potentiality: From Dispositions to Modality*. Oxford: Oxford University Press.

Warren, Jared. (2016). "Sider on the Epistemology of Structure." *Philosophical Studies* 173 (9): 2417–35.

Warren, Jared. (2017). "Epistemology versus Non-Causal Realism." *Synthese* 194: 1643–62.

Warren, Mark. (2015). "Moral Inferentialism and the Frege-Geach Problem." *Philosophical Studies* 172: 2859–85.

Warren, Mark, and Amie Thomasson. (2023). "Prospects for a Quietist Moral Realism." In Paul Bloomfield and David Copp, eds., *The Oxford Handbook of Moral Realism*. Oxford: Oxford University Press, 526–53.

Williams, Michael. (2011). "Pragmatism, Minimalism, Expressivism." *International Journal of Philosophical Studies* 18 (3): 317–30.

Williamson, Timothy. (2007). *The Philosophy of Philosophy*. Oxford: Blackwell.

Wilsch, Tobias. (2016). "The Deductive-Nomological Account of Metaphysical Explanation." *Australasian Journal of Philosophy* 94 (1): 1–23.

Wilson, Jessica. (2014). "No Work for a Theory of Grounding." *Inquiry* 57 (5–6): 535–79.

Wisdom, John. (1937). "Philosophical Perplexity." *Proceedings of the Aristotelian Society* 37: 71–88.

Wittgenstein, Ludwig. (1953/2001). *Philosophical Investigations*. Trans. G. E. M. Anscombe. Oxford: Blackwell.

Wittgenstein, Ludwig. (1958). *The Blue and Brown Books*. Oxford: Blackwell.

Wright, Crispin, and Bob Hale. (2001). *The Reason's Proper Study: Essays Towards a Neo- Fregean Philosophy of Mathematics*. Oxford: Clarendon Press.

Wright, Cory, and Dingmar van Eck. (2018). "Ontic Explanation Is Either Ontic or Explanatory, but Not Both." *Ergo* 5: 997–1029.

Yablo, Stephen (2000). "A Priority and Existence." In Paul Boghossian and Christopher Peacocke, eds., *New Essays on the A Priori*. Oxford: Oxford University Press, 197–228.

Yablo, Stephen. (2005). "The Myth of the Seven." In Mark Eli Kalderon, ed., *Fictionalism in Metaphysics*. Oxford: Oxford University Press, 88–115.

Yablo, Stephen. (2009). "Must Existence Questions Have Answers?" In David Chalmers, David Manley, and Ryan Wasserman, eds., *Metametaphysics: New Essays on the Foundations of Ontology*. Oxford: Oxford University Press, 507–25.

Yalcin, Seth. (2011). "Nonfactualism About Epistemic Modality." In Andy Egan and Brian Weatherson, eds., *Epistemic Modality*. Oxford: Oxford University Press, 295–332.

Index

For the benefit of digital users, indexed terms that span two pages (e.g., 52–53) may, on occasion, appear on only one of those pages.

abstract objects, 37–38, 39–42, 156, 168–75, 198–99
Alexander's dictum, 23
Ambrose, Alice, 16–17, 17n.20, 109–11
analytic entailments, 35–38
  See also trivial inferences; easy inferences
analytic/synthetic distinction, 13, 198
Appiah, Anthony, 116, 210–12, 231
application conditions, 92–96, 117
arbitrariness, avoiding, 122, 130–31, 202, 203, 209, 213–21
Armstrong, David M., 32, 50–51, 60–61, 62–63, 65–66, 67–70
art, 224–25, 228–29
assertive content, 27–28, 30
Austin, J. L., 134
bad company problem, 35–36, 199n.48

Barnes, Elizabeth, 53, 80
Bennett, Karen, 4–5, 6–7, 8–9, 81, 84n.17, 86n.21, 86–87
Berkeley, George, 113–14, 223, 226
Blackburn, Simon, 68n.11, 69–70
Brandom, Robert, 137–38
bureaucracies, 137–38, 155–56, 157–58, 159, 165, 170–71, 193, 210–12

Cameron, Ross, 7, 62, 63–65
Canberra plan, 14n.14, 85n.19
Cappelen, Herman, 126, 132–33, 134
Carnap, Rudolf, 13, 94–95, 103, 107–8, 111–12, 115, 179–80n.20, 182–83, 216–17
catching cheaters, 62, 67–72
category mistakes, 165–66, 172–75, 190, 198–99, 200, 222

causal redundancy arguments, 23
chance, 43, 168–69, 176–77, 180–81, 186–87, 188–89
Chomsky, Noam, 139–40
concepts
  concepts, comparative, 182
  concepts, psychological understanding of, 127–30
  concepts, quantified, 182–83
  concepts versus language in conceptual engineering, 123–30
conceptual analysis, 7, 12, 13, 113–15, 125. *See also* reverse engineering
conceptual engineering, 112–18
  conceptual engineering, as task for philosophy, 18–19, 103–7, 112–23, 130–31, 198–201, 222–35
  conceptual engineering, constructive, 16n.19, 18–19, 108–13, 115–16, 117–21, 122, 226–27, 228
  conceptual engineering, history of, 107–12
  conceptual engineering, pragmatic approach to, 202–21
  conceptual engineering, psychological approach to, 125
  See also reverse engineering
conceptual interrelations, 74–75, 91, 92–94, 95–96, 97
confirmation of ontological content of a theory, 25–30
congruent language, 142–43n.14, 150–51, 154–55, 163, 168, 170, 173–74, 180–81, 184–85, 188–89
contrastive confirmation, 29–30
core properties, 138

critique, 208–9, 221

Dasgupta, Shamik, 43–44, 49n.1, 86, 86–87n.23
death, concept of, 116–17, 213–14, 218
disability, concept of, 229–30
division of labor view, 11–13
dormitive virtue explanations, 33–34

e-representation, 142–43n.14, 150–51
easy inferences, 35–39, 95, 169–71, 186, 194. *See also* trivial inferences
easy ontology, 34–39, 75
  See also easy inferences
Eggins, Suzanne, 144n.15, 146–47, 155, 178–79, 194n.42
Eklund, Matti, 218n.20
Eleatic arguments, 23, 32
eliminativism, 8–9, 168–72, 186–89, 196, 198–200, 209–10
entry rules, 95–96, 99, 163, 165n.6, 182, 186–87, 188, 194–95
epistemological mystery, problem of, 6–11, 19, 45–46, 52–53, 54–55, 63–65, 81, 88–89, 103, 121–23
events, 40–41, 45n.39, 56, 158, 165, 169, 170–71, 194
experimental philosophy, 119
explanatory power criterion, 8–9, 22–23, 24–25, 30–39, 41–43, 45–48, 166–67, 171–72
explication, 107–8, 115
expressivism, 16–17, 44–45, 58, 69–70, 142–43n.14, 175–76
  expressivism, global, 142–43n.14
  expressivism, local, 142–43n.14

fail-safe presuppositions, 27–28
feminist metaphysics, 53–54, 80–81, 82
feminist philosophy, 230
Field, Hartry, 198
Fine, Kit, 75, 77, 78–79, 90n.26
Firth, John Rupert, 85n.19, 140
fish, concept of, 55, 115, 216–17, 233–34
free will, 114–15, 223, 224–25, 226–27
Frege-Geach problem, 134n.3, 179–80n.20, 194–95n.43
Frege, Gottlob, 11, 35n.26, 105

fueling predictive success, 26–27, 40–42, 46
functional monism, 15, 17–18, 22n.5, 48, 52–53, 56–59, 60, 69–70, 71–72, 74, 84–85, 97–98, 100, 128, 200, 202–3
functional monist assumption. *See* functional monism
functions
  functions in early childhood language, 141–44
  functions, etiological (*see* functions, proper)
  functions, intended, 135–36, 137–38, 160–61, 208
  functions, material versus formal dimensions of, 206–9
  functions in mature language, 144–49
  functions, proper, 135–36, 160–61
  functions, role of in conceptual engineering, 200, 203–17, 220–21
  functions, system, 135–37, 160–61
  functions, versus uses, 134–35
fundamental structure, 49–50, 53–54, 57
fundamentality, 62–65, 66–67, 73–74, 76–78, 80–82, 97–98, 167, 168

gender, concepts of, 53, 54, 80–81, 111–12, 210–12, 233–34
genealogy, conceptual, 164–65, 204–5
Gert, Bernard, 116, 213–14, 218–19
Gert, Joshua, 16, 122n.21, 206n.7
grammatical form, 144–45, 205–7
grammatical metaphors, 137–38, 148–49, 151, 153–59, 165, 168, 170–73, 174, 193–94, 204, 207–8
  grammatical metaphors, functions of, 155–59, 167, 198–99, 211–12
  grammatical metaphors, interpersonal, 154–55, 170n.7, 180–84, 185, 191, 193, 194–97
  grammatical metaphors of modality (*see* grammatical metaphors, interpersonal)
grounding, 73–80, 82–83, 96
  grounding, epistemology of, 89–92, 97
  grounding, local relations of, 85–96
  grounding, not generalizable as a metaphysical project, 92–96, 97–99

INDEX

Halliday, Michael, 139–40, 141–42, 143–59, 170, 172–73, 175n.14, 177–78, 196–97
Haslanger, Sally, 39–40, 111–12, 212
Hawking, Stephen, 4, 104–5
Hawley, Katherine, 27
Heil, John, 62n.3, 65–66, 67–68
heuristic function, 141, 142–43
hierarchical picture of reality. *See* layered picture of reality
Hirsch, Eli, 51–52
human factors, 219–20
Hume, David, 223, 225, 226
Husserl, Edmund, 11–12, 94–95, 105, 117n.17, 140

ideational metafunction, 143–44, 145, 146, 149–51, 152–53, 159, 170, 185, 193, 194–95n.43
imaginative function, 141
inference to the best explanation arguments in metaphysics, 8–12, 32–33
instrumental function, 141
interactional function, 141
interpersonal metafunction, 129–30, 145, 146, 147–48, 149–50, 151–53, 167, 177, 185, 188, 193, 194
Isaac, Manuel Gustavo, 123–24, 127–28

joint-carving, 50–52, 53, 54–59, 99, 167
Joyce, James, 44–45

Kelp, Christoph, 203n.2
Kitcher, Philip, 25–26
Koslicki, Katherine, 73, 76n.6, 86–87, 95n.35
Koslow, Allison, 127
Kuhn, Thomas, 231

language, as abstract cultural artifact, 127, 129–30, 135–36
language development, 141–44, 177–78, 185, 205–6
layered picture of reality, 73–74, 76, 82–85, 97
Lewis, David, 5, 8, 50–51, 183–84, 186–87

Locke, John, 223, 225, 226
Locke, Theodore, 90–91, 92–93, 95n.36
Lowe, E. J., 3
Lwów-Warsaw School, 108

MacDonald, Margaret, 16–17
Machery, Edouard, 6–7, 119, 125, 127–28
Magidor, Ofra, 172–73
Malinowski, Bronisław, 16n.19, 140, 164n.3
marriage, 215, 219, 229–30, 233–34
matter, 113–14, 223
McX, 31–32, 33–34
mentalistic discourse, 196–97
metaethics, 4–5, 19n.25, 152–53, 176–77, 196
See also moral discourse
metafunctions, 145–49
See also ideational metafunction; interpersonal metafunction; textual metafunction
metalinguistic negotiation, 108, 109n.6, 109–10, 225–27
metaphysical explanation, 77, 85–87, 90–91, 92–93, 94n.29, 97–98, 99
metaphysical malady, 15, 48, 60, 163
"metaphysics", conceptual engineering of the term, 223–27
Midgley, Mary, 16–17, 111–12, 232–33
Mikkola, Mari, 53, 80
Millikan, Ruth, 135–36
mind, problems of. *See* mentalistic discourse
Misak, Cheryl, 16–17
modal epistemology, 6–7, 90–91, 190–93
modal properties, 181, 184, 186–90, 191
modal system, functions of, 151–53, 177–84
modality
modality, deontic, 175–76, 194–96
modality, flavors of, 175–76, 180–81, 204
modality, knowledge of (*see* modal epistemology)
mood system, 146, 147–48, 151, 165, 177–80, 193, 196–97
Moody-Adams, Michele, 230, 233, 234n.10

moral discourse, 44–45, 69–70, 152–53, 176–77, 179–80n.20, 194–96, 230
moral properties, 43–45, 70–71, 195–96

natural kind terms, 50–51, 57–59. *See also* joint-carving
natural properties, 50–51
neo-pragmatism, 16–17, 40–41, 132, 161, 164–65
neo-Quinean approach to metaphysics, 13–14, 20–23, 49
neo-Quinean approach to metaphysics, problems for, 24–30
nominalizations. *See* grammatical metaphors
nonsense, 11–12, 103, 111
See also pseudo-problems
normative discourse, 194–96
normative questions, as remaining for philosophy, 105–7, 118–19, 122, 227–28
Nozick, Robert, 6–7, 190–91
numbers, 27–28, 37–38, 39–42, 45n.39, 56, 75, 89, 94–96, 97–98, 113, 167, 169–72, 173–75, 198–99, 207–8, 209–10

obligations, 157–58, 159, 178–79, 180–81, 194–96
ontologese, 52
ontological commitment, 21, 31, 33, 61, 63–64, 66, 128–29
ontological dependence relations, 74–76, 88, 89, 96
See also grounding
ontological flexibility of language, 63–64, 81, 149
ontological questions, 13, 19n.24, 20–21, 22–23, 24, 26–27, 47, 60, 61, 121, 165–66, 169–70, 171, 223
ordinary language philosophy, 11–13, 16–17, 104, 114–15, 119, 224–25

paradoxes, 113–14, 173, 177, 223
Paul, L. A., 7–9, 25–26
pejoratives, 117, 229
permission, 58, 157–58, 159, 180, 194–95
person, concept of, 225, 226

personal micro-function, 141
pessimistic induction, 25–26
phenomenology, 12, 104, 114–15, 224–25
Philosophical Survey, 5–6
placement problems, 70–71, 84–85, 171–72, 173–74, 189–90
Platonism, 29n.16, 35–36, 95, 126
platypus, 188–89
pleonastic inferences. *See* easy inferences
Plunkett, David, 109–10, 219, 225–26
possible worlds, 5, 152, 161, 168–69, 176–77, 181, 183–84, 186–87, 191, 199–200, 209–10
Povich, Mark, 29n.16
presupposition failure, 45–46, 165–66, 171, 172–74, 190
Price, Huw, 14n.14, 16, 17–18, 20–21, 46n.40, 69–70, 138, 139, 142–43n.14, 150–51, 153n.24, 164–65, 172–73
privacy, 214–15
problem of missing value, 43–44
processes, 155, 158, 165
proliferation of metaphysical views, 5–6, 11, 19, 24, 103, 118, 120–21
properties, 33–42, 95–96, 153–54, 168–75
See also modal properties; moral properties; natural properties
protolanguage, 141–44, 205–6
pseudo-problems, 74, 83, 128, 171, 177, 194, 198–99, 200–1, 222
Psillos, Stathis, 26–27, 27n.14
psychologism, 11, 105
psychology, 104, 119–20, 230–31
See also concepts, psychological understanding of

Queloz, Matthieu, 113, 160–61, 204–8, 219–20
Quine, Willard Van Orman, 13–14, 20–21, 25, 31–32, 33, 34–35, 41–42, 46n.40, 61, 115–16, 128–29, 198, 199

race, 39–40, 111–12, 116, 210–13, 219
Ramsey, Frank, 16–17, 69–70, 71–72, 192n.39
Rayo, Agustin, 39–40

redundant inferences. *See* easy inferences; trivial inferences
regulatory function, 141
representational function, 142–44
See also ideational metafunction
representationalism, 69, 127–28
requirements, 44, 157–58, 159, 178–81, 194–96, 211–12
reverse engineering, 18–19, 112–13, 114–15, 121–22, 125, 163, 164–66, 193, 198–201, 203–9, 210–13, 228
Ritchie, Katherine, 211n.14
rivalry with the sciences, problem of, 4–5, 11, 18–19, 24, 54, 81, 104, 118–20
Ryle, Gilbert, 11–12, 16–17, 44–45, 58, 67–69, 113–14, 172–73, 176, 180, 192n.39

Saul, Jennifer, 231
Schaffer, Jonathan, 62n.3, 66–67, 75–77, 82–83, 85–87
scientism, 21–22, 30, 46, 49–50, 53
Sellars, Wilfrid, 69–70, 175–76, 192n.39, 196–97
Sider, Theodore, 7, 12–13, 24–25, 49–55, 56–58, 67–68, 167
Simion, Mona, 203n.2
site constraints, 217–19
skepticism about knowledge in metaphysics, 5–7, 10, 19, 118, 120–21, 130
Sober, Elliott, 29
speech act theory, 15n.16, 194–95n.43
states of affairs, 194
subject naturalism, 17–18, 139

subtraction of presuppositions, 27–28, 40
Sundell, Tim, 225–26
supervenience, 84n.18, 189–90
systemic functional linguistics, 17–18, 38–39, 133, 139–59, 161, 167, 170–71, 175, 177–79, 180–81, 185, 205–6

Taverniers, Miriam, 150n.20, 170n.7, 180–81
textual metafunction, 145, 146–47, 148
theoretic virtues, 8–10, 81
therapeutic conceptions of philosophy, 16n.19, 108–9, 114, 164–65
Thompson, Naomi, 73n.2, 73–74, 77, 86–87n.23, 88–89, 90–91, 94n.29
trivial inferences, 33, 34n.24, 34–39, 75, 94–95, 169–70, 182, 183, 184, 186, 194–95, 196
See also easy inferences
truthmaker maximalism, 68
See also truthmaker principle
truthmaker principle, 67–68, 70–71
truthmakers as constraint. *See* catching cheaters

usability, 219–20

vagueness, 220
van Inwagen, Peter, 3

Wisdom, John, 109, 111
Wittgenstein, Ludwig, 16–17, 40–41, 69, 108–9, 114, 140, 164–65

Yablo, Stephen, 27–28, 39–40

www.ingramcontent.com/pod-product-compliance
Ingram Content Group UK Ltd.
Pitfield, Milton Keynes, MK11 3LW, UK
UKHW022301160226
468114UK00005B/75